*The University of Minnesota Press
gratefully acknowledges
the support for its program
of the Andrew W. Mellon Foundation.
This book is one of those
in whose financing
the Foundation's grant
played a part.*

The
Collected
Letters
of
Sir Arthur Pinero

Edited by
J. P. Wearing

University of Minnesota Press
Minneapolis

Introduction and notes © copyright 1974 by the University of Minnesota.
Letters © copyright 1974 by Samuel French Limited — Trustees for the late
    Sir Arthur Wing Pinero.
All rights reserved. Printed in the
United States of America at Jones Press, Minneapolis.
Published in the United Kingdom and India by the
Oxford University Press, London and Delhi.

Library of Congress Catalog Card Number: 74-76742

    ISBN 0-8166-0717-6

For my mother

Acknowledgments

During the preparation of this edition, I have asked many people and institutions for assistance and almost without exception I have been treated most generously. My initial work on Pinero benefited greatly from the advice and encouragement of Professor C. J. L. Price of the University College of Swansea, Wales. To the following I am indebted, in varying degrees, for information, assistance, supplying microfilms and manuscripts, and much else: The American Academy of Arts and Letters, New York; Mr. C. V. Appleton; Mrs. Margaret Bannerman; Miss Esmé Beringer; Mr. A. J. Caraffi, Clerk of Birkbeck College, London; Birmingham Public Libraries; the University of Birmingham Library; the Bodleian Library, Oxford; Boston Public Library; the Central Library, Bradford; Dr. A. N. E. D. Schofield of the Department of Manuscripts, the British Museum; the British Theatre Museum; Mr. John Cadell; Mr. Christopher Calthrop; the University Library, Cambridge; the University of Chicago Library; Columbia University Library; Dr. L. W. Conolly; Dame Gladys Cooper; Cornell University Library; Sir Noël Coward; Mr. W. Darlington; Mr. W. J. Denning; Dr. Joseph W. Donohue, Jr.; Edinburgh Public Library; Edinburgh University Library; Mr. St. John Ervine; Miss Jane Fellows; Miss Julie Fitzgerald; Mrs. C. A. Kyrle Fletcher; the Folger Shakespeare Library, Washington, D.C.; the Folio Fine Art Society; Mr. Harold F. Dyer of Samuel French Ltd.; the Garrick Club; Miss Freda Gaye; Miss Rosand Gilder; Miss Ethel Griffies; the Walter Hampden Memorial Library, New York; Mr. Nicholas Hannen; Miss Phyllis Hartnoll; the Houghton Library, Harvard University; Sir Rupert Hart-Davis; the Historical Manuscripts Commission; Mr. Alfred Hitchcock; Hove Central Library; the Henry E. Huntington Library; Mr. Laurence Irving; Professor Dan H. Laurence; the Brotherton Collection, University of Leeds; the Victorian Studies Centre, University of Leicester; Liverpool Public Library; Miss Marie Löhr; the University of London Library; the Lord Chamberlain's Office, St. James's Palace, London; Dr. Robert F. Metzdorf; Mr. Raymond Mander and Mr. Joe Mitchenson; Miss Elizabeth Maude; Mr. John Maude; the Middlesex Hospital; Miss Phyllis Neilson-Terry; New York Public Library; Dr. Theodore Grieder, New York University Libraries; Miss Marie Ney; Mr. Stanley Noble; Professor Allardyce Nicoll; Mr. Brian Pinero-Terriss; Mr. Peter Potter, B.A.; Princeton University Library; University of Rochester Library; Mr. Milton Rosmer; Mr. George Rowell; the Royal Academy of Dramatic Art; Mrs. J. M. Patterson of the Royal Society of Literature; Miss Toni Block of the Shaw Society; Mrs. James N. Smith; the Society of Authors; the Society for Theatre Research; Dr. Russell Stephens; University College of Swansea Library; the University of Texas (at Austin) Library; Mr. Peter H. Turnbull; the Victoria and Albert Museum; the University of Virginia Library; Mr. Ronald Ward; Professor Stanley Weintraub; Miss Alison Wertheimer; Miss Gillian Wilce; Miss Marie Willis, B.A.; Yale University Library.

This edition was completed with the aid of an Izaac Walton Killam Memorial Post-Doctoral Fellowship held at the University of Alberta. Over the years I have also received generous financial assistance from my grandmother, Mrs. L. E. Hall, for which I am very grateful. I owe my deepest debt of gratitude to my mother who has, in her own special way, continuously encouraged and supported my work.

Permissions

Sir Arthur Pinero's letters included in this edition are used by permission of the Trustees of the Pinero Estate, Samuel French Ltd. (London), and by permission and courtesy of the following: Bochumer Antiquariat; the Bodleian Library, Oxford; Boston Public Library; the Trustees, the British Museum; the British Theatre Museum; the Brotherton Collection, University of Leeds; the University of Chicago Library; the University of Chicago Press; the *Daily Telegraph*; the Folger Shakespeare Library, Washington, D.C.; the Walter Hampden Memorial Library at The Players, New York; the Harvard College Library; Harvard University Press; Hutchinson Publishing Group Ltd.; the Lilly Library, Indiana University; the Henry W. and Albert A. Berg Collection, The New York Public Library, Astor, Lenox, and Tilden Foundations; the Manuscripts and Archives Division, The New York Public Library, Astor, Lenox, and Tilden Foundations; the Fales Library, New York University Libraries; the George C. Tyler Collection, Princeton University Library; Clement Scott and Pinero Papers, Rare Book Department, University of Rochester; the Royal Society of Literature of the United Kingdom; the Humanities Research Center Library, the University of Texas at Austin; the *Times*; the *Times Literary Supplement*; the Richard Harding Davis Collection, Clifton Waller Barrett Library, University of Virginia Library; the Beinecke Rare Book and Manuscript Library, the Osborn Collection, and the George Pierce Baker Papers, Yale University Library.

The specific location of a letter is given in the code attached to each letter; codes are described fully in the following two keys.

Contents

THE COLLECTED LETTERS
OF SIR ARTHUR PINERO

Introduction

Peregrine: Pray you let's see, sir. What is here?—"*Notandum,*
A rat had gnawn my spur leathers; notwithstanding,
I put on new and did go forth; but first
I threw three beans over the threshold. Item,
I went and bought two toothpicks, whereof one
I burst, immediately, in a discourse
With a Dutch merchant 'bout *ragion del stato.*
From him I went and paid a *moccenigo*
For piecing my silk stockings; by the way
I cheapened sprats, and at St. Mark's I urined."
Faith, these are politic notes!
   Sir Politic: Sir, I do slip
No action of my life, thus but I quote it.
                 (Ben Jonson, *Volpone*, IV, i, 135–147)

Fortunately the letters of Sir Arthur Pinero have much more significance than Sir Politic Would-Be's notebook. Sir Politic's life consisted of trivia and, while briefly amusing in the context of Jonson's play, it would deserve to be consigned to the oblivion of all "laundry-list" literature if, Heaven forbid, it were recorded fully. By contrast, the Pinero correspondence which does survive is remarkable for its small proportion of trivia. There are a few, unimportant domestic references, but generally his letters are a fascinating record of the life of a man who was one of the most important and influential playwrights of the English stage. And, also rather remarkably, his letters all more or less have as their focus the theatre in one or another of its aspects. Unlike Shaw's correspondence, which ranges over a multitude of interests, Pinero's is nearly all confined to the theatre. He was totally absorbed by his work as a dramatist and this led him to associate almost exclusively with others of like mind—dramatists, theatre managers, actors, actresses, critics. Whatever impinged upon the English stage at the close of the nineteenth century and the beginning of the twentieth was of paramount significance to Pinero. It is in this regard that his correspondence deserves to be read, for the light it throws both upon the state of the English theatre of the period and upon one of that theatre's leading practitioners.

What I have attempted in this edition of letters, all but a few of which are published here for the first time, is to select three hundred and thirty-seven from the nearly fourteen hundred extant that reflect the various phases of Pinero's life, his attitude toward his work, the contemporary theatre, fellow dramatists, associates, and friends. I have not tried to chronicle every word and thought contained in the letters I have located. Often letters of a particular date to various correspondents contain similar material, and little, if anything, would be served by such repetition. Instead, I have chosen letters that *illustrate* the various facets of Pinero's life and work, that representatively record his activities and opinions.

If he had followed family tradition, Arthur Wing Pinero would never have had anything to do with the stage. His family had emigrated from Oporto, Portugal, in the eighteenth century to settle prosperously enough in London, where, once thoroughly established, the name of Pinheiro was anglicized to Pinero. Both his father and grandfather were reasonably successful members of the legal profession, although Pinero's father became rather negligent in his business affairs as he approached middle age. Pinero, born on 24 May 1855, had an uneventful early childhood with nothing to distinguish him or point to his later career. His father's laxity obliged him to take some part in the senior Pinero's work at a fairly early age, and later he was also engaged in a solicitor's office in Lincoln's Inn Fields. A legal career seemed to be firmly mapped out for him. However, there was in London an institution that provided some opportunities in the realm of higher education—the Birkbeck Literary and Scientific Institution, now Birkbeck College in the University of London. One of Birkbeck's offerings was the elocution class in which Pinero enrolled, thereby initiating his active theatrical career. The class staged various pieces and recitals to which friends and relatives were cajoled into attending. The group even ventured to present a series of recitals and plays in towns as far afield as Edinburgh and Bristol, and, it appears, with moderate success. These activities were supplemented with frequent visits to the London theatre, which usually took in Irving's performances at the Lyceum and the Bancrofts' at the Prince of Wales's, as well as those of other stars. The fascination Pinero felt, shown in his letters to his aunt, Mrs. Eliza Schneider, grew into an irresistible lure and in May 1874 he decided to break with the legal profession and go on the stage.

Pinero's first engagement was as a "utility man" with R. H. Wyndham's Company at the Theatre Royal, Edinburgh, then one of the better English provincial theatres.[1] The position required him to act many small parts in the regular company's productions which were staged in rapid succession. Theatres (far more numerous in England than at present) were the chief source of mass entertainment, and consequently there was a steady demand for new productions. The modern notion of the "long run," or even a true repertory season, would have been inadequate to satisfy the role these theatres played in society, a role similar to that now fulfilled by television. So several plays would be presented weekly and only at Christmas time would a pantomime run for a month or possibly two. This local diet was supplemented at frequent intervals by visits from a "star" hawking a few of his or her popular successes around the provincial theatre circuit. "Stars" would play at the theatre for a week or so with the resident company usually as the supporting cast. As early as May 1858 E. A. Sothern had created the part of Lord Dundreary in Tom Taylor's *Our American Cousin*; this same role still provided his chief attraction in the 1870s, and he duly performed it on his visit to the Theatre Royal, Edinburgh, in September 1874 when Pinero was a member of the supporting cast. Henry Irving had a stock repertoire based on the "star" parts in *Hamlet*, *The Lady of Lyons*, *Richelieu*, *Louis XI*, *Charles I*, *The Bells*, and *The Lyons Mail*, and after his winter season at the Lyceum Theatre, London, he would draw on his repertoire for a provincial tour. Indeed, every major actor and actress toured at some time or another, and the resulting system not only brought the best of the London theatre to provincial audiences, but enabled actors in provincial companies to

---

1. For a fuller account of Pinero's life as an actor, see my "Pinero the Actor" and "Pinero's Professional Dramatic Roles, 1874–1884," *Theatre Notebook*, XXVI (1972), 133–144.

gain otherwise unobtainable experience with the leaders of their profession.

This was the situation Pinero found himself in, first at the Theatre Royal, Edinburgh, and, when that theatre burned down on 6 February 1875, at the Alexandra, Liverpool. His life was hectic, and he was left with little time to spend outside the theatre. But he was exposed to many plays and to several prominent actors—Sothern, Mathews, Mrs. John Wood—and became thoroughly schooled in the internal workings of the theatre and drama. A role in Wilkie Collins's *Miss Gwilt* (transferred from Liverpool to the Globe) gave Pinero his first view of the London stage from behind the footlights, and when that production closed he was able to take up an offer to join the Lyceum Company. So in just under two years Pinero had made considerable progress; he was back in the capital, if not as a leading actor, at least as a reasonably competent supporting artist.

Life at the Lyceum was less demanding; in place of frequent variations in the program, with its attendant frenzy of rehearsals, the Lyceum offered a more stable bill, with long runs and several revivals during a season. In 1879, for example, Pinero played Salarino in *The Merchant of Venice* for no less than 250 consecutive nights. Such an assignment was doubtless frustrating, but it did leave him with more leisure for what had become a fresh theatrical interest—playwriting. Indeed, Irving had encouraged Pinero in this direction, staging his third piece, a curtain raiser entitled *Two Can Play at That Game*, in 1878. His talent was fostered further when, in 1881, he transferred to the Haymarket Theatre which was under the direction of the Bancrofts. Not only did it have the same substantial runs as the Lyceum, but the Bancrofts' artistic policy was more congenial to Pinero's ideas on the theatre. Irving reserved the limelight for himself as star; the Bancrofts, from the beginning of their managerial career, had stressed ensemble work which in turn made for theatre where realism was better achieved, a keynote to Pinero's own later serious plays. The experience gave further impetus to the dramaturgical urge within him, to the extent that by the time he left the Haymarket in 1884 he had written sixteen plays. Pinero the actor was well on the way to being forgotten, while Pinero the playwright was emerging as a name to be reckoned with.

Writing plays absorbed Pinero fully, so much so that it is difficult to record his being involved in any other activity. During his formative years as a dramatist he wrote as many as four plays in a twelve-month period; three of his plays were produced in 1880, two in 1881, three in 1883, three in 1884, two in both 1885 and 1886. This flurry of creativity is also notable because the prevailing theatrical conditions often militated against the production of an unknown dramatist's work. Managers tended to require assured successes, and all too often that meant adaptations of proven French plays. It is of some significance, therefore, that of Pinero's early plays (those produced up to the end of 1885) only two were adaptations from the French; the remainder were "original dramas." On the other hand, this work hardly constituted a revolution in English drama. True, two pieces met with moderate success: *The Squire* (1881) and *The Ironmaster* (1884) played for 170 and 200 performances respectively, a creditable achievement for an up-and-coming playwright. But most of his early works have little to distinguish them from the veritable plethora of contemporary drama. Perhaps *The Squire* showed the most talent and its reputation was enhanced by a controversy which followed its production, in which Pinero was accused of plagiarizing from Thomas Hardy's *Far from the Madding Crowd.*

Pinero really came to the fore with *The Magistrate* (1885), part of his series of "Court farces" produced at the Court Theatre which also included *The Schoolmistress* (1886) and *Dandy Dick* (1887). All three plays achieved considerable success as well as developed more cohesive themes which managed a degree of mild ridicule of the Victorians' overconcern for their social reputations. Pinero's popularity extended further with the immensely successful—and sentimental—work *Sweet Lavender* (1888).

The close of the 1880s saw Pinero ready to make a significant contribution to the development of the theatre: he knew his craft thoroughly and was successful, mostly with light dramatic fare. His career turned the corner with *The Profligate* (1889), his first work to deal with social problems in a consistently serious manner. The fair success *The Profligate* met with prompted him to write other plays in a similar vein; the result was a more refined piece, *The Second Mrs. Tanqueray* (1893), which startled its first-night audience, ran for 225 performances, and firmly established its author as the foremost British dramatist of the era. Essentially these two plays, and seven subsequent ones written through to 1909 (*The Notorious Mrs. Ebbsmith, The Benefit of the Doubt, Iris, Letty, His House in Order, The Thunder-*

bolt, and *Mid-Channel*), depict the plight of women in a certain sector of Victorian society laboring under the moral demands made of them by that society. Whereas men were permitted a large degree of license, particularly in sexual matters (a situation sustained by the legislation then current), women were judged severely for similar behavior. Consequently women with "histories" were forced either to adopt extreme measures (such as suicide) or passively to suffer ostracism. Pinero handled the problem in a manner sympathetic to such women: he neither condemned nor condoned their dubious moral histories or behavior; rather he attacked the double standard of morality which discriminated between men and women. The underlying notion behind these plays is that men and women could best live harmoniously together in a situation where the wife was the true partner of the husband, where both judged and were judged equally, and where both saw the hearth and "household gods" as their central objective. In this Pinero was clearly not a social revolutionary or a reformer, but his genuine concern for the injustices perpetrated on women (usually through hypocrisy) was atypical of the English theatre until the production of *The Second Mrs. Tanqueray.*

Pinero's dramatic work in these middle years (1889–1909) was not limited solely to problem plays; his diversity of interest was revealed in eight other plays. Some pieces worked over earlier modes: *The Cabinet Minister, The Times,* and *The Amazons* were variations on the Court farce series, and *A Wife without a Smile* was another (disastrous) attempt at farce. In *Lady Bountiful* he tried to re-create the sentimentality of *Sweet Lavender,* although with far less success. However, he gained appreciative audiences with two comedies of manners, *The Princess and the Butterfly* and *The Gay Lord Quex,* which, with something of a different emphasis, echoed thematically the problem plays. Both *Trelawny of the "Wells"* and *The Beauty Stone* do not fit into any general category. *Trelawny* in light, rather sentimental fashion pays tribute to the contribution T. W. Robertson made to the English theatre in the 1860s, a contribution Pinero saw as of paramount importance to the development of drama. *The Beauty Stone,* for which he collaborated with J. W. C. Carr and Sir Arthur Sullivan, is simply a musical historical romance, which Pinero regarded purely as a welcome relief from his more serious responsibilities to the stage. This middle period culminated in 1909 by which time Pinero was the mogul of his profession, an achievement that received the customary

English form of recognition—a knighthood. He was only the second person to be knighted specifically for his work as a dramatist, W. S. Gilbert having preceded him to that estate two years previously.

It is the common notion that Pinero wrote little after 1909; in fact, his later years were almost as productive as his early career. However, the difference was that, quite naturally, younger men had succeeded him in catching the public eye, often as a result of the progress he himself had made in the 1880s and 1890s. But as late as 1922 a play from Pinero's pen was still a theatrical event and demanded attention. Actually he never ceased practicing his craft; his last piece, *Late of Mockford's*, which remains unperformed, is dated 1934, the year of his death.

About half of the sixteen plays of this period are reworkings of earlier successful formulas and they in due turn achieved moderate recognition—most notably *Preserving Mr. Panmure*, *The "Mind the Paint" Girl*, and *The Big Drum*. The remainder are of more significant interest because they reflect a playwright still pursuing his art with vigor and imagination. It would have been easy and natural for Pinero to rest on his considerable reputation. Instead in such plays as *Playgoers*, *Monica's Blue Boy*, *A Seat in the Park*, *The Enchanted Cottage*, and *Dr. Harmer's Holidays* he experimented with fresh ideas and techniques. *Playgoers* has in it all the elements of what is now generally referred to as the theatre of the absurd; *A Seat in the Park* is a modulation in a similar vein. For example, *Playgoers* superficially depicts the domestic troubles of a middle-class English couple, but the scene is portrayed in more abstract terms (characters are labeled simply "The Master," "The Mistress") and there is a strong sense of the absurdity of life in which people suffer anonymity and feel futile in the face of universal disorder and purposelessness. Other plays demonstrate Pinero's technical innovation; *Monica's Blue Boy* is a mime without words, *The Enchanted Cottage* employs fantasy "masque" effects, while *Dr. Harmer's Holidays* amounts to a film scenario. For a dramatist reputedly "over the hill" this corpus of late plays is no mean achievement.

Pinero's correspondence traces well the growth of his work and is especially valuable because he himself wrote little publicly on dramatic theory in general or on his own plays in particular. His views were reserved for those people whom he knew to be genuinely interested in his work. The letters reveal a dramatist who knew exactly what he wanted in the theatre and how he felt that ought to be realized on stage. His experience as an actor quite obviously prepared him for this attitude. Pinero, therefore, reports in his letters to various correspondents his plans for plays, their casting, production, and reception. He was totally involved in a play from its conception to the rise of the curtain on opening night because, unlike many dramatists of the period, he believed playwrights had absolute responsibility for their work. Dramatists earlier in the century, he felt, had too readily abdicated their rights and responsibilities to theatre managers and stage managers. The time had come to assert the dramatist's importance in the overall production of a piece, for only then could true *artistic* success be achieved. This was necessary because the theatre had fallen on parlous times, in which pure commercial success was the only gauge of a play's worth. Advances in the state of the art had been made by T. W. Robertson and the Bancrofts, who sought to combine social comedies and realistic presentation, but their example had been ignored. The weakness in the system was the dramatist who, for obvious reasons, yielded to the dictates of commercialism and further lowered his art by relinquishing control over the very processes which realized that art and brought it to the public. (Again Robertson had been an exception; the Bancrofts allowed him full directorial control over his plays, a practice far from common.) Pinero's achievement in asserting his authority over his own work is remarkable in the light of such circumstances. Even more remarkable is the fact that, having demanded the right to direct his plays and to influence strongly the choice of cast and effects, he gained a long series of popular successes in the commercial theatre. The importance of this attitude and its subsequent results would have been entirely different and much less significant if Pinero had retreated to what he termed "side-show" theatres, minority performances subsidized by a few well-meaning friends of the dramatist. To him that was just as much a debasement of the playwright's integrity as was the earlier practice. The commercial theatre, despite its inherent dangers, was the place where plays with artistic merit had always won "victories" over the public at large; to skulk in the theatrical back streets was to deny the very life-giving pulse of the medium. Moreover, the pragmatic solution to the problem was not to theorize and exhort in treatises or prefaces as other writers did, but to demand certain conditions of production and to refuse to allow a play to be staged under any others. Pinero once remarked that he would have sooner burned the manuscript of *The Sec-*

ond Mrs. Tanqueray than have the piece reach an audience under inimical, or spurious, conditions. Such was his integrity.

As a result, Pinero was often accused of being an autocrat and dictator in the theatre; even the slightest deviation from his dialogue by an actor would evoke a firm request to adhere strictly to the words. His stance also brought him into conflict with theatre managers, as the correspondence with Sir George Alexander illustrates. Alexander, too, had a very definite conception of his authority in his own theatre, the St. James's; so much so that there was a dramatic breed known as the "St. James's play," the sort of piece which would appeal to a society audience wishing to be pleasantly entertained. That same audience was of vital concern to Pinero since it frequently practiced the hypocrisy he attacked in such plays as *The Second Mrs. Tanqueray*. To reach *them*, and not favorably disposed friends, was his obvious objective. Thus it speaks large that Alexander gave Pinero a more or less free rein in production at the St. James's—one autocrat yielding to another. Pinero's letters to Alexander reveal a full discussion of each play destined for the St. James's stage and for the most part Pinero gained every concession he desired in terms of cast, staging, incidental effects, and so on. There must have been some occasional compromise during rehearsals, but never to the extent that a play was seriously impaired artistically. When firmer opposition did arise from Alexander, as it did during the production of *The Princess and the Butterfly*, Pinero informed Alexander (in the friendliest though firmest of terms) that he would not work at the St. James's until such time as he could have a free hand. The decision kept him out of that theatre for nine years. His attitude may appear willful, almost petty, but given the prevailing theatrical conditions and his artistic integrity anything less would have been a perversion of all he believed in.

The same directorial determination emerges in Pinero's negotiations with two American managers, Augustin Daly and R. M. Field. Here distance complicated matters further, but there is the same close attention to how a piece would be produced in America. Pinero's concern that his artistic conception be fully realized prevented him from allowing, for example, the production of *The Profligate* under what he considered poor conditions, even though he might well have profited financially. The series of letters to Alexander, Daly, and Field constitute, therefore, a detailed record of the problems of theatre production at

11

the close of the nineteenth century and how one (important) dramatist attempted to solve them within the limits of his principles.

Pinero's methods, ideas, and viewpoints interested his fellow workers in the theatre, but, although he was acquainted with many people, his reserve (and the limitations imposed on his leisure time by his intense activity) made him selective in his choice of intimate friends. Three above all emerge clearly in the correspondence—William Archer, Henry Arthur Jones, and Louis Evan Shipman.

His most profound friendship was with William Archer, a Scotsman who became one of the leading theatre critics of the period as well as a proponent of Ibsen's work in England. Probably Archer's own integrity and critical honesty were the chief characteristics that drew Pinero to him. The correspondence between the two men is frank, straightforward, and full of lengthy discussions about current theatrical ideas and problems, proposals for the development of the drama, and Pinero's own work and progress. Although a strong advocate of Pinero, Archer was unswervingly forthright in criticizing his plays and his criticisms were accepted in a spirit of thoughtful consideration. Pinero frequently defended his views and methods, but, on the other hand, Archer's opinions often had a marked influence. Their intimacy is thrown into true perspective when Pinero's letters to Archer are compared with those to Clement Scott, another theatre critic. Pinero merely gave Scott information on his current work, possible castings—in fact, theatre gossip—which he could utilize in his newspaper columns if he wished. The opportunity of exchanging views and criticisms was never presented. Pinero saw Scott only as a representative of the theatrical press, never anything more.

The same contrast appears in his associations with two fellow dramatists, H. A. Jones and G. B. Shaw. Jones, like Archer, was a complete intimate, a co-worker in the struggle to develop the English theatre. Although their respective careers might suggest that Jones and Pinero were arch-rivals, such was far from being the case. Both men earnestly desired the success of the other's work and were genuinely distressed if he failed to achieve it. Failure was a rebuff to the evolution of the theatre to which they were jointly dedicated. This preoccupation with a mutual ideal naturally led to the formation of a close relationship, such as did not exist with Shaw. Pinero and Shaw got to know one another fairly late in their respective careers; their work for the Society of Authors in the first decade of this century brought them together.

But the relationship, which it seems Shaw was more anxious to press than Pinero, was more nearly that of business associates. They shared professional interests and concerns but evidently without the same rapport as that which existed between Jones and Pinero. It is significant that Pinero would withhold information from Shaw which he would freely convey to Jones and Archer. His friendship with L. E. Shipman also began quite late, not until about 1910 in fact. However, it grew quickly and warmly and resembles closely that with Jones. But it has an added dimension since Shipman was an American and consequently the correspondence between them (mostly from opposite sides of the Atlantic) often refers to current world events—most notably, of course, the First World War, one of the few external matters that thoroughly penetrated Pinero's absorption with the theatre.

Actors and actresses figured largely in Pinero's life and again he had his intimates. Chief among them were Sir Henry Irving and the Boucicaults (Dion the younger and his wife, Irene Vanbrugh). Pinero maintained his friendship with Irving after leaving the Lyceum Company; as in the days when he was a solicitor's clerk, he attended most of Irving's performances, although now with an experienced eye. He was anxious too that Irving should achieve the highest degree of artistic success and to this end he often proffered thoughtful advice and criticism on his friend's productions. Usually, as is evident in this edition, his advice was directed to the small details of a particular scene which Irving acted, and his suggestions were almost invariably adopted. His appreciation of Irving's abilities was therefore genuine, lacking any of that falsity often found in theatrical circles. Naturally this portion of the correspondence also throws valuable light on Irving's work in general, all the more so because the reporter was an attentive member of Irving's audience. The Boucicaults acted in a large number of Pinero's plays; indeed, they first met each other during the production of *Trelawny of the "Wells."* Subsequently all three became good friends and in the two actors Pinero found willing and sympathetic interpreters of his work; in addition Boucicault was, through his association with the Duke of York's Theatre, responsible for helping to stage several of Pinero's plays. All in all, it was a mutually deep and significant relationship.

Many other incidentals to Pinero's life and work emerge in this correspondence, and I trust readers will find them valuable for the light they shed not only on Pinero but on the theatre of the period in general. In editing the letters I have tried to tamper with them as little as possible. Pinero's hand is not difficult to read and he dated most of his correspondence carefully. The few changes I have made do, I think, make for easier reading. Where Pinero is inconsistent in giving the title of a play, book, or article (he would underline it, place it in quotation marks, or both), I have followed modern practice. Titles of plays, books, newspapers, and similar volumes are italicized; titles of poems, articles, and shorter works within larger volumes are placed in quotation marks. I have, however, retained his spelling of such titles, as well as his inconsistent capitalizations. I have followed his spelling including any personal, consistent vagaries; only obvious errors have been silently corrected. (The use of *sic* has therefore been eliminated. Any misspellings which remain, such as proper names, are Pinero's.) Superscripts have been lowered to the line and are followed by a period; similarly I have always provided a period after "Mr." where Pinero was occasionally inconsistent. I have made no attempt to indicate variations or deletions made by Pinero since none of these has any importance. Consequently every letter here is published intact without omissions of substance; nor has there been a need to omit letters to preserve the good name of any person.

I have also preserved all forms of address, salutation, and valediction together with Pinero's punctuation, although I have run on the endings of each letter. All addresses are in London (which has been omitted), unless otherwise stated. The dates given are Pinero's, with any editorial conjecture placed in brackets. The names of recipients (recorded by Pinero at the end of some letters) and postscripts have been retained and follow on a separate line after his signature.

Letters previously published in periodicals and newspapers are so designated in the code attached to each letter, which also indicates the location of each letter. Where a letter has been published in a book, I have not given page references since in all instances they are easily found. I have not made any attempt to show inaccuracies in previously published letters, although discrepancies often do exist between these and the original. Wherever possible I have taken my transcriptions from original manuscripts or photocopies of them.

As a further aid, I have provided headnotes which I hope will help the reader to understand references in the letters, although I have generally omitted information on well-known figures outside the theatrical profession, who are tangential to the correspondence. I have provided the date of the first London production of a play, although occasionally, where necessary, I have given production dates elsewhere. Actors and actresses are notoriously coy about the question of age; it is therefore difficult in many cases to give absolutely accurate birth and death dates. I trust readers will bear with me if they discover that such information does not tally exactly with their own.

I'm sure several dusty attics containing caches of Pinero letters still remain to be cleared out, and I should be glad to learn the location of any material not included here.

A Brief Chronology
of Pinero's Life and Works

1855 Born 24 May, at 21 Dalby Terrace, Islington, London.

1870 Enrolls in the elocution class, Birkbeck Scientific and Literary Institution.

1874 4 May: Concludes agreement to join R. H. Wyndham's Company at the Theatre Royal, Edinburgh.

1875 6 February: Theatre Royal, Edinburgh, burns down; Pinero joins Edward Saker's Company at the Alexandra, Liverpool.

1876 15 April: Plays Mr. Darch in Wilkie Collins's *Miss Gwilt* at the Globe, London.
September: Joins the Lyceum Company and goes on Irving's provincial tour.

1877 6 October: Pinero's first play, *£200 a Year*, produced at the Globe.

1878 22 April: *La Comète, or Two Hearts*, Theatre Royal, Croydon.
20 May: *Two Can Play at That Game*, Lyceum.

1879 20 September: *Daisy's Escape*, Lyceum.

1880 5 June: *Hester's Mystery*, Folly.
18 September: *Bygones*, Lyceum.
5 November: *The Money Spinner*, Prince of Wales's, Manchester (produced St. James's, 8 January 1881).

1881 27 July: *Imprudence*, Folly.
August: Joins the Bancrofts at the Haymarket.
29 December: *The Squire*, St. James's; subsequent plagiarism controversy.

1882 1 November: *Girls and Boys*, Toole's.

1883 24 March: *The Rector*, Court.
19 April: Marries Myra Emily Holme (née Moore).

30 July: *The Rocket*, Prince of Wales's, Manchester (produced Gaiety, 10 December 1883).

24 November: *Lords and Commons*, Haymarket.

1884 12 January: *Low Water*, Globe.

17 April: *The Iron-Master*, St. James's.

19 July: Retires as an actor, playing Sir Anthony Absolute in *The Rivals*.

19 September: *In Chancery*, Lyceum, Edinburgh (produced Gaiety, 24 December 1884).

1885 21 March: *The Magistrate*, Court; first of the "Court farces."

20 July: Takes part in farewell performance of the Bancrofts.

31 October: *Mayfair*, St. James's.

1886 27 March: *The Schoolmistress*, Court.

23 October: *The Hobby-Horse*, St. James's.

1887 27 January: *Dandy Dick*, Court.

Elected to Garrick Club.

1888 Friendship with William Archer begins.

21 March: *Sweet Lavender*, Terry's; his most successful play, running for 684 performances.

28 September: *The Weaker Sex*, Theatre Royal, Manchester (revised version produced Court, 16 March 1889).

1889 Vice-presidential member of Birkbeck Council.

24 April: *The Profligate*, Garrick.

1890 23 April: *The Cabinet Minister*, Court.

1891 7 March: *Lady Bountiful*, Garrick.

24 October: *The Times*, Terry's.

1893 Appointed honorary examiner in elocution at Birkbeck.

7 March: *The Amazons*, Court; last of the "Court farces."

27 May: *The Second Mrs. Tanqueray*, St. James's, establishes Pinero as leading English dramatist. Accused by Clement Scott of plagiarizing from Paul Lindau's play, *Der Schatten*.

1895 13 March: *The Notorious Mrs. Ebbsmith*, Garrick.

19 July: Presents address to Irving on his knighthood, Lyceum Theatre.

16 October: *The Benefit of the Doubt*, Comedy.

1897 29 March: *The Princess and the Butterfly*, St. James's.

Temporary rift in association with George Alexander; lasts until 1905.

1898 20 January: *Trelawny of the "Wells,"* Court.

17

28 May: *The Beauty Stone*, Savoy.

1899   8 April: *The Gay Lord Quex*, Globe.

1901   21 September: *Iris*, Garrick.

1903   24 February: Gives lecture, "Robert Louis Stevenson as a Dramatist," to the Philosophical Institution, Edinburgh.
8 October: *Letty*, Duke of York's.

1904   Involved in Archer's schemes for a national theatre.
12 October: *A Wife without a Smile*, Wyndham's.

1906   Chairman of the Executive Committee for the Ellen Terry Jubilee Celebrations.
1 February: *His House in Order*, St. James's.

1908   9 May: *The Thunderbolt*, St. James's.

1909   Gives evidence to Parliamentary Committee on Theatrical Censorship.
June: Knighted.
Chairman of the Dramatic Sub-Committee of the Society of Authors.
First president of the Dramatists' Club.
2 September: *Mid-Channel*, St. James's.

1910   Fellow of the Royal Society of Literature, and member of the society's Academic Committee.

1911   19 January: *Preserving Mr. Panmure*, Comedy.

1912   17 February: *The "Mind the Paint" Girl*, Duke of York's.
14 October: *The Widow of Wasdale Head*, Duke of York's.

1913   Member of the Council of the Royal Society of Literature.
31 March: *Playgoers*, St. James's.

1914   Chairman of the First Battalion (United Arts Rifles) Central London Regiment.

1915   1 September: *The Big Drum*, St. James's.

1917   15 January: *Mr. Livermore's Dream*, Coliseum.

1918   14 February: *The Freaks*, New.
8 April: *Monica's Blue Boy*, New.

1919   30 June: Lady Pinero dies.
14 November: *Quick Work*, Stamford Theatre, Stamford, Connecticut.

1921   January: Chairman of the General Committee of "Warrior's Day."

1922   21 February: *A Seat in the Park*, Winter Garden.
1 March: *The Enchanted Cottage*, Duke of York's.

1924 *Dr. Harmer's Holidays* written; performed 16 March 1931, Shubert-Belasco Theatre, Washington, D.C.

1928 14 May: *A Private Room*, Little.

1930 *Child Man* published; unperformed.

1932 20 May: *A Cold June*, Duchess.

1934 *Late of Mockford's* written; unperformed.

23 November: Dies.

Keys to Description and Location of Correspondence

KEY TO DESCRIPTION OF CORRESPONDENCE

A   Holograph letter.
B   Letter in another hand, signed by Pinero.
C   Copy of a letter, made independently of either correspondent.
G   Telegram.
P   Letter previously published elsewhere.
T   Typed letter, signed by Pinero.

These symbols may be modified by one or more of the following:
c   Transcription from carbon copy of the original.
e   Extract or incomplete letter.
p   Transcription from a published source.
x   Transcription from a photocopy of the original.
u   Unsigned by Pinero.

Where Pinero's signature is included in a letter it is printed thus, Arthur W. Pinero. Unverified signatures are printed in capitals.

KEY TO LOCATION OF CORRESPONDENCE

1. The Bodleian Library, Oxford.
2. Boston Public Library.
3. The British Museum: (i) Add. MS. 45294. (ii) Add. MS. 45982. I. (iii) Add. MS. 49337. (iv) Add. MS. 50547. (v) Add. MS. 52586. (vi) Add. MS. 56779.

4. The Henry Irving Archive, the British Theatre Museum.
5. The Miscellaneous MSS. Collection, Special Collections, University of Chicago Library.
6. The Folger Shakespeare Library, Washington, D.C.
7. The Walter Hampden Memorial Library at The Players, New York.
8. Harvard University: (i) Houghton Library. (ii) Theatre Collection.
9. The Lilly Library, Indiana University.
10. The Brotherton Collection, University of Leeds.
11. New York Public Library, Astor, Lenox, and Tilden Foundations: (i) Berg Collection. (ii) De Coursey Fales Collection, Manuscripts and Archives Division. (iii) Lucile Watson Collection, Manuscripts and Archives Division.
12. The Fales Library, New York University Libraries.
13. George C. Tyler Collection, Princeton University Library.
14. The Royal Society of Literature of the United Kingdom.
15. The University of Rochester: (i) Pinero Papers, Rare Book Department. (ii) Clement Scott Papers, Rare Book Department.
16. The Humanities Research Center, the University of Texas at Austin.
17. The Richard Harding Davis Collection, Clifton Waller Barrett Library, University of Virginia Library.
18. J. P. Wearing.
19. Yale University Library: (i) Beinecke Rare Book and Manuscript Library. (ii) Osborn Collection. (iii) George Pierce Baker Papers.
20. Charles Archer, *William Archer: Life, Work and Friendships.* London, 1931.
21. Marie and Squire Bancroft, *The Bancrofts: Recollections of Sixty Years.* London, 1901.
22. Mrs. Patrick Campbell, *My Life and Some Letters.* London, 1922.
23. *The Daily News.*
24. *The Daily Telegraph.*
25. Wilbur Dwight Dunkel, *Sir Arthur Pinero: A Critical Biography with Letters.* Chicago: University of Chicago Press, 1941.
26. *The Era.*

27. Hamilton Fyfe, *Sir Arthur Pinero's Plays and Players*. London, 1930.
28. Doris Arthur Jones, *The Life and Letters of Henry Arthur Jones*. London, 1930.
29. _____, *What a Life!* London: Jarrolds, 1932.
30. Wisner Payne Kinne, *George Pierce Baker and the American Theatre*. Cambridge, Mass.: Harvard University Press, 1954.
31. Hermann Heinrich Küther, *Arthur Wing Pinero und sein Verhältnis zu Henrik Ibsen*. Münster, 1937.
32. A. E. W. Mason, *Sir George Alexander & the St. James's Theatre*. London, 1935.
33. Louis Evan Shipman, *The True Adventures of a Play*. London, 1914.
34. *The Star.*
35. *The Theatre.*
36. Marjorie Thompson, "William Archer: Dramatic Critic 1856–1924," *Theatre Notebook*, XI (1956–1957), 6–11.
37. *The Times.*
38. *The Times Literary Supplement.*
39. Irene Vanbrugh, *To Tell My Story*. London: Hutchinson [1948].
40. J. P. Wearing, "Pinero's Letters in the Brotherton Collection of the University of Leeds," *Theatre Notebook*, XXIV (1969–1970), 74–79.
41. _____, "Pinero the Actor," *Theatre Notebook*, XXVI (1972), 133–139.

LETTERS

Letters

1. TO MRS. ELIZA SCHNEIDER

[A/16] 69A Great Queen St., / WC.   April 20th. 1873.
[The sequence of letters 1–30 deals with Pinero's experiences with the London theatre and as an actor in the English provinces. (For a detailed account of Pinero's acting career see my articles, "Pinero the Actor" and "Pinero's Professional Dramatic Roles, 1874–1884," *Theatre Notebook*, XXVI, 1972, 133–144.) Mrs. Schneider was Pinero's aunt, although nothing further is known about her or Lilly and Crissy, his cousins. The program Pinero mentions was for one of the performances staged by the elocution class of the Birkbeck Scientific and Literary Institution (now Birkbeck College in the University of London), where Pinero was a student from 1870 to 1874, during which time he was appointed as reader to the elocution class. *The Fate of Eugene Aram* by W. G. Wills (1828–1891) was first produced at the Lyceum on 19 April 1873 with Henry Irving (1838–1905; knighted 1895), the famous actor-manager of the Lyceum from 1878 to 1901.]

My dear Mrs. Schneider.

Ma has informed me that on Monday last while warming your feet at your fire—you put your foot in it. I trust that no unpleasant consequences ensued.

I take the liberty of enclosing a programme for Friday next, on which occasion I solicit your kind patronage. Ma desires me to say that she will expect you & offsprings to tea.

Mind you come early.

Tell those two evil disposed young ladies not to detain you by their taking too long a time to dress. I don't take nearly so long to dress myself, and I am *quite* as nice looking.

Bye the by, I have not yet seen Mr. M. Reed, of whom I have heard you speak, and after weighing everything carefully in my mind I have come to the conclusion that no such person exists. Unless he is very shortly produced I shall write to some of the papers on the subject.

I shall also write on note paper (humourous joke)

These remarks also apply to Mr. & Mrs. Tom.

I went last night to see *The Fate of Eugene Aram.* It is a very fine play—rather melancholy & ghastly. I waited from 5.30 at the doors, & even then only sat in the 3rd. row.

Mention me respectfully to Miss Lilly (who I trust is well) also to Miss Crissy. Both of these ladies are ever in my mind, a circumstance which cannot fail (when they hear it) to make their hearts beat with pleasure.

This pen is abominable.

It is also steel

(humourous joke)

I trust you are quite / I remain / Yours to command / Mr. Pinero. P.S. *Well.* I have left this word out in the course of my note. Please rectify the omission.

2. TO MRS. ELIZA SCHNEIDER

[A/16] New Music Hall / Oxford St. / Ilfracombe.   1 Octr. 1873.
[Pinero and a group of students from Birkbeck gave a series of "recitals" and plays in Ilfracombe and Bristol in October 1873, and in Edinburgh, Leith, Liverpool, and Greenwich in February and March 1874. *Richelieu* (Covent Garden, 7 March 1839) by Edward Robert Bulwer Lytton (1831–1891) was revived at the Lyceum on 27 September 1873 with Irving and Isabel Emilie Bateman (1854–1934) in the leading roles.]

My dear Mrs. Schneider.

My dear Lil.

My dear Cris.

Having long meditated offering you a token of my regard, I have pleasure in enclosing a ticket for our entertainment which took place last night in the presence of a small but appreciative audience.

We suffered in consequence of the evening being fine. Everybody went on the promenade. Therefore, although we certainly have cleared *something* it is not sufficient to warrant our staying longer in this most detestible place of enjoyment. We therefore leave precipitately. Notwithstanding this you will be pleased to hear we are enjoying ourselves, apropos of which I will ask you a conundrum.

"Why are we like the lady whose remains were found in the Thames!

Because we are cut up, but are in excellent spirits. I saw *Richlieu* on Saturday evening. It is the finest perfce. Irving has given.

[drawing of a house]

You see that though our "Recitals" did not pay very much, I can draw a good house.

We are now off to Bristol. Any letters addressed to "Post Office Bristol" will reach me, if I am alive. / Accept me fondest love. / Yours affectionately / Arthur.

My face before last night.
[drawing of Pinero's face—happy]
Since last night.
[drawing of Pinero's face—long, drawn out]

3. TO MRS. ELIZA SCHNEIDER

[A/16; Pe/41] 69A Great Queen Street.   17th. Octr. 1873.
[Sir Squire Bancroft Bancroft (Butterfield; 1841–1926; knighted 1897) married Marie Effie Wilton (1839–1921) in 1867. They opened the Prince of Wales's in 1865, establishing their reputation with productions of plays by Thomas William Robertson (1829–1871). Later, from 1880 to 1885, they managed the Haymarket, after which they retired. They revived Robertson's *School* (Prince of Wales's, 16 January 1869) at the Prince of Wales's on 20 September 1873, with Charles F. Coghlan (1838 or 1842–1899) taking the role of Lord Beaufoy. Much of Coghlan's subsequent career was spent in the United States where he died. The Philharmonic Theatre, Islington, was also known as the Islington Empire (see Diana Howard, *London Theatres and Music Halls 1850–1950*, London, 1970, pp. 121–123).]

My dear Mrs. Eliza Schneider.

I am in receipt of your daughters communication of this date for which I am obliged.

I write at the instance of my mother.

She has been rather unsettled by Emma going home unexpectedly and Aunts Harriet & Carry &c &c. coming to London, but she trusts by strict attention to business, to merit a continuance of the patronage hitherto bestowed on her.

She strikes only on the box!

If our plans are not frustrated in any way we will, with your permission, or without it, it don't matter which, pay you a visit on Wednesday next.

Last night Ma & I went to the Prince of Wales's to see *School*—words fail to describe it. Coghlan will send you away delirious. Tell your youngest daughter (C. H.) that I have not yet been to the Philharmonic. Tell your Eldest daughter (L) that a piece of music—I should say a song, is on its way, which I trust will be in the right *key*. She will find this out directly she *locks* at it. (Joke). The song is in z.

This joke is very crisp—so crisp that I must now break off—for I am going up to Pethericks to celebrate his sisters birthday. Today she reaches man's estate (qy).

Accept the sentiments of my tenderest regards, & convey the like to Cris & Lil, & the remaining members of your world renowned troupe. / Dear Mrs. Eliza Schneider / Your affectionate / Arthur.
P.S. When you ask for Glenfields Starch see that you get it.

4. TO MRS. ELIZA SCHNEIDER

[A/16] Lincoln's Inn Fields.   6th. Novr. 1873.
[Wates was mayor of Gravesend from 1872 to 1873; he was not re-elected in the November municipal elections. Emily Soldene (1840–1912) was a music-hall performer and the leading lady of the Light Opera and Opera Bouffe Company at the Philharmonic, Islington. She played the role of Mdlle Lange in a version of *La Fille de Madame Angot* by Henry Brougham Farnie (d. 1889), produced at the Gaiety on 10 November 1873 (see letter 5). *Griselda; or, the Patient Wife* by

Mary Elizabeth Braddon (1837–1915) was produced at the Princess's on 13 November 1873. *The Wandering Heir* by Charles Reade (1814–1884) was produced at the Queen's on 15 November 1873 with Mrs. John Wood (née Matilda Charlotte Vining; 1831–1915) in the lead. Later Mrs. Wood was famous as manageress of the Court. "Desmarets" is a role in *Plot and Passion* (Olympic, 17 October 1853) by Tom Taylor (1817–1880), dramatist, editor of *Punch*, and professor of English at London University.]

My dear Aunt Schneider

I write you on the assumption that you were not burnt yesterday.
News.

I this morning recd. a telegram announcing that Mayor Wates yesterday assaulted the legendary bucket. For which crime he was taken up.

I am staying at home tonight like a good boy. On Monday evening I went to the Opera Comique with a friend. Next week I shall see Soldane (Long Emily) in Mdlle Lange—*Griselda* at the Princesses, and *The Wandering Heir* at the Queens.

Willy has gone another edition this evening, having been out of print for some time.

I have been much engaged with an elaborate preparation for next Wednesdays "Desmarets" for whom I shall have to sacrifice my moustache!

By the bye—are you or any of your illustrious family coming to the Institution to see *Plot & Passion.* I wont recommend it, as I hav'nt any idea whether it will be amusing or not—in addition to which I do not like to cry my wares too loudly. Still, if you care abt. coming to the Institution on Wednesday next, there will [be] a knife & fork ready waiting your arrival (on the stage in the farce). So please write & let us know.

If you do not let us know, please to let the sky snow, for I would sooner have cold weather than these damp.

I trust Lil & Cris arrived home safely on Sunday.

I enclose a slight token of my regard. Let it be treasured. I shall have the pleasure of hereafter presenting a larger sample.

I hope Aunt Sourmerlud is better. Give her my love.

Au revoir.

Accept my esteem & affection—same to Lil & Cris—and Co. / In haste. / Yours / A. W. Pinero.
Mrs. Schneider.

5. TO MRS. ELIZA SCHNEIDER

[A/16] Great Queen Street, / WC.   Last day of Novr. 1873.
[Julia Mathews (1842–1876) played in an adaptation of *La Fille de Madame Angot* by Henry James Byron (1834–1884), which was produced at the Philharmonic on 4 October 1873. Byron, an actor and author of over 140 plays, was also, for a short time, co-lessee of the Prince of Wales's with Marie Wilton (Lady Bancroft). For details of the many versions of *Madame Angot* see W. Davenport Adams, *A Dictionary of the Drama*, I (London, 1904), 515.]

My dear Auntie,
      What has become of you and the young ladies? We have been expecting you evening after evening, & *I* have stayed at home with the hope of passing a few hours in your society. Your behavior is cruel!
      I have been to no end of places since last we met. You *must* see Sol-dene at the Gaiety. There is no comparison betw. Julia Matthews & her. She is immeasurably superior. There now!
      I cannot write any more now as Fanny has one of her young ladies here—Miss Judy Carnion[?]—and writing in company is rude, you know.
      I trust Mrs. Sourmerlud is improving.
      Give my love to Lillums, Crissums, & the little ones.

      Accept my dooty. / Dr. Auntie. / Your affectc. Nephew / Arthur W. Pinero.
Mrs. Schneider.

6. TO MRS. ELIZA SCHNEIDER

[A/16; Pe/41] 55 Lincoln's Inn Fields, / WC.   6 May 1874.
[Robert Henry Wyndham (1814–1894) was a Scottish actor-manager, who successively managed the Adelphi, Queen, and Theatre Royal theatres in Edinburgh. *The Bells* by Leopold David Lewis (1828–1890)

was originally produced at the Lyceum on 25 November 1871 with Irving as Mathias, one of his most famous roles.]

My weekly letter.

My dear Aunt.
[drawing of Pinero in Highland dress with bagpipes]
Here you see represented your humble servant as he will appear in a very short time.

You will be pleased to know that on the 4th. inst I concluded an engagement with the Lessee of the Theatre Royal Edinburgh where I "open" on the 22nd. of next month.
From that time my diet will be restricted exclusively to the native porridge of "the land of my adoption."
As the Theatre Royal Edinburgh is considered next to a London Theatre in position, I should not consider myself altogether unfortunate.

Ma, Fanny & I went to see the *Bells* on Saturday evg last. They were paralized.
I am in hopes you will be home in time to see it.
Fanny went up on Monday to see the poor lonely Lilly.
I have not much time so pardon my brevity. / I send my love to Chrissy Arthur & yourself. / Affectionately / Arthur MacPinero.
P.S. Eee noo, an I seupose you will not muckle like ganing awa' fra' Hastings.

7. TO MRS. ELIZA SCHNEIDER

[A/16] 55 Lincoln's Inn Fields, / WC.   1 June 1874.
[Miss Bateman's benefit, held at the Lyceum on 30 May 1874, featured Hamilton Aidé's play *Philip* (Lyceum, 7 February 1874) with Irving playing Philip.]

My dear Aunt.
Your kind invitation reached me per the lips of Mange No. 1.

The duration of my visit will depend upon when I leave business. (I may be able *only* to run up & retn. directly, but I hope not.)

I went with Tolman to the Lyceum (to Miss Bateman's benefit) on Saturday Evening last. When Irving made his entrance (finding he wore the same clothes as on the production of the piece) we quietly said, loud enough to be heard all over the house "What! those clothes not worn out yet?" The effect was electrical—Irving seemed overcome by his feelings for a moment.

I trust Chris is none the worse for her walk on Saturday. Give her all the sentiments of my ardent attachment also to Lilly, though the conduct of the latter at the corner of the Kings Rd, Grays Inn Road, will never cease to leave its sting upon my memory. / Accept my dear Aunt, my tenderest embraces. / Ever Yours / Arthur W. Pinero. Mrs. Schneider.

P.S. I have just been madly ducking my head. Oh! you should see me! ! [drawing of Pinero, in bow tie, with hair sticking out]

8. TO MRS. ELIZA SCHNEIDER

[A/16] Temperance Hotel, / 21 Leith Street, / Edinburgh.

18th. June 1874.

[Pinero's debut as a professional actor at the Theatre Royal, Edinburgh, was made on 22 June 1874. Wybert Reeve (1831–1906), actor, manager, and playwright, was particularly noted for his playing of Count Fosco in *The Woman in White* by William Wilkie Collins (1824–1889). Collins's work was published as a novel in 1860 and dramatized at the Olympic on 9 October 1871. Joseph Kline Emmett (1841–1891), an American actor and former variety artist, made his debut as an actor in 1868 in the title role of *Fritz, Our Cousin German* by the American actor-dramatist Charles Gayler (1820–1892). When Emmett moved to London he played the same role in a version of *Fritz* revised by Andrew Halliday (1831–1877), which opened at the Adelphi on 30 November 1872. Ellen Lancaster Wallis (1856–1940), actress and author, became notable later when she opened the newly built Shaftesbury Theatre in 1888, an enterprise which proved a failure (see Raymond Mander and Joe Mitchenson, *The Lost Theatres of London*,

London, 1968, pp. 492–501). J. B. Howard (1841–1895) was an actor and manager of a group of theatres in Edinburgh and Glasgow in association with R. H. Wyndham. *Sisterly Service* (Strand, 9 February 1860) was written by J. P. Wooler (1824–1868). Pattie Laverne (d. 1916), a soprano opera singer, was particularly successful in the role of Clairette in a version of *La Fille de Madame Angot*. Selina Dolaro (1849–1889) was an actress, singer, and author of the play *In the Fashion* (Ladbroke Hall, 28 December 1887).]

My dear Aunt.
     I am located very comfortably as above.
     We open on Monday night with the *Woman in White* Count Fosco, Mr. Wybert Reeve, who is the *"star"* for a week. After that comes J. K. Emmett in *Fritz* and *The Swiss Boy* and then Miss Wallis & J. B. Howard. I can't say at present whether I play in the *Woman in White* on Monday night or not, for Mr. Reeve did not turn up in Edinburgh to-day, but I play a part called "Victor" in *Sisterly Service*— a comedietta which will be played a few nights after the opening of the Season. I shall know more tomorrow.
     The place is really magnificent—it surpasses all my expectations. The people are a very polite well behaved lot—except the policemen who are either fearfully stupid or confoundedly cautious.
     I am going to the Theatre Royal tonight to hear Patti Laverne in *Madame Angot*. Saturday is her last night here, & then on Monday Selina Dolaro arrives with anr. *Madame Angot* at the Princesses Theatre.
     Have the photos been fetched? Be sure you tell Ma to send them down for me to look at.
     I look forward to a letter from you. / Fondest love to yourself Chrissy & Lilly. / Affectionately Yours / Arthur W. Pinero.
Mrs. Schneider.
P.S. I will send you a longer Budget soon.

9. TO MRS. ELIZA SCHNEIDER

[A/16] 20 Alva Place, / London Road, / Edinburgh.   8 July 1874.
[Stephen is a role in *The Hunchback* (Covent Garden, 5 April 1832), the most successful play written by James Sheridan Knowles (1784–

1862), actor, dramatist, and friend of Hazlitt, Coleridge, and Lamb. In a letter to Mrs. Schneider, dated 23 June 1874, Pinero wrote of Emmett's "transgressing": "I hope his wife will accompany him. I hear that when she is near him he is a gentleman, but when away from her influence he is too frequently disguised in liquor! ! ! ! !" *Fazio* (Surrey, 22 December 1816) was written by Rev. Henry Hart "Dean" Milman (1791–1868), sometime Dean of St. Paul's and Professor of Poetry at Oxford. *The Lady of Lyons* by Bulwer Lytton was first produced at Covent Garden on 15 February 1838. *Rob Roy* was one of several adaptations of Scott's novel (published in 1817); Allardyce Nicoll (*A History of English Drama 1660–1900*, vol. VI, Cambridge, 1959, pp. 432–433) lists twelve such works.]

My own Aunt!

I will now proceed to answer your conundrums.

My lodgings are cheaper, but *not* nastier—in fact it is a small paradise here—I shall be glad to see you when passing.

How do I pass my time in the day?—*I* don't pass the time, *it* passes *me*—(humorous joke) I may however state that Garside and I take very long walks, attend rehearsals, & make properties.

I am alone (during the run of *Fritz*) at about 11 p.m.—I rise at 8.30 a.m.—I do nothing *after* the performances are concluded save going to bed, so there now.

I commence with Stephen on Monday next. Stephen is a pretty good little part.

As regards Emmett, he has *not* yet "transgressed"—see my letter of admonition to the ubiquitous Chris.

As regards your question as to how the Stock acts, I am afraid you have been "transgressing," for I can't call to mind where stock, which stock, who stock, or why stock. Do you mean the policeman's collar, if so its pretty well thank you, & very often asks after you.

The paper & review *did* arrive safely—accept tears of gratitude.

Next week I play, in additn. to Steve—the part of "Piero" in *Fazio* and "Major Desmoulins" (better known as the "3rd Officer") in the *Lady of Lyons*—the latter a very mangy part but with a nice dress. Next week the shapes, tights &c will come into use.

I shall hear shortly whether I get on for the winter season or not. If I do I fancy I shall take a little better business—but of course

I must not be in a hurry "a contented mind is a continual feast."
(What a saving in dinners to a satisfied person)

The winter season opens with a grand production of *Rob Roy*.

I can't call to mind any more news, or any more questns. to
answer so adieu. / Dear Aunt / Your loving Nephew / Arthur
W. Pinero.

Aunt.

P.S. I fancy Billy Wright is coming to spend a week with me!

In case I shd. have omitted to answer any of your questns. "When
its a-jar" is the only &c &c.

10. TO MRS. ELIZA SCHNEIDER

[A/16; Pe/41] 20 Alva Place, / London Road, / Edinburgh.

2nd. August 1874.

[H. J. Byron's two plays *Orpheus and Eurydice* and *War to the Knife*
were first produced in 1863 and 1865 respectively. *Black Ey'd Susan* by
Douglas William Jerrold (1803–1857) was first produced at the Surrey
on 8 June 1829. Jerrold, actor, manager, and dramatist, was successively
the resident dramatist at the Coburg and Surrey theatres, manager of
the Strand in 1836, and associated with the founding of *Punch* in 1841.
Mrs. R. H. Wyndham was born Rose Saker, sister of Edward Saker
(1831–1883), the manager of the Alexandra, Liverpool. She married
Wyndham in 1846 and died in 1923.]

My dear Aunt.

The Season terminated last night and with it (for the present)
my labors.

During the last week I have played "Radamanthus" (the Lord
Chancellor in H-ll) in the burlesque of *Orpheus & Eurydice*—
"Harcourt" in *War to the Knife* and (last night) "Captain Crosstree"
in *Black Ey'd Susan*. The two last are capital parts—Captain Crosstree
especially.

Taking a retrospective view of my doings for the last six weeks
you will be glad to hear that I am *very satisfied*. I have been put
forward very much by the management, &, the other day, Mrs.
Wyndham (the manageress of *next season*) sent me a message that

"she was very pleased with me & that it would be my own fault if I did not get on"—so far so good.

I shall doubtless have to do the gentleman for the intermediate period—for nothing has turned up sufficiently enticing for me to undertake. It is on the "tapis" that something may present itself, however, during the ensuing week.

Referring to your letters I find a question as to whether I find "any unpleasantness from envy or jealousy in any of my fellow actors"—I must admit that such feelings do make themselves apparant but if you can look at it as a mere matter of business, it is of no consequence.

Still a question to answer, as to what J. B. Howard is like. He is an awful duffer as an actor, but a very gentlemanly fellow privately.

I return the photos. I think them first class. You must be careful, however, how you take them off—taking care to damp the back before doing so. The idea is taken, by *Figaro* from the French. It leads one to form a fair estimate of what a Photographers *profits* must be.

Have you seen Fanny's new Photo? You know I suppose, they are off to Yarmouth.

I have received all the papers you have sent. I have not had time however to read them, but have tied them up in a bundle & shall commence to peruse with avidity next week.

I don't think I have any more news to tell you today. Don't forget to write to me. / Accept my fondest love. / Dear Aunty / Your affectionate Nephew / Arthur.
Mrs. Schneider.

I wish you would pop in & see me.

11. TO MRS. ELIZA SCHNEIDER

[A/16; Pe/41] 20 Alva Place, / London Road, / Edinburgh.

13th. Augt. 1874.

[*The Sphinx* was an adaptation and translation of Octave Feuillet's (1821–1890) original work performed at the Théâtre français, Paris, on 23 March 1873. Mdlle Beatrice (Marie Beatrice Binda; 1839–1878) was an Italian actress and manageress who first appeared in England in 1864 at the Haymarket. From 1865 she toured extensively in the

English provinces, and in 1870 formed her own company which toured with a repertoire consisting mainly of French translations.]

My dear Aunt.

I have almost exhausted all my news in my letter to Lilly, so you must (on this occasion only) pardon my brevity.

The *Sphinx* was produced here last night by Mdlle Beatrice & her really splendid Company—Doubtless you will see it when it is played in London.

It is intensely interesting from beginning to end & well acted throughout. It has however, in common with most French pieces, rather an unhealthy tone about it and you leave the theatre, after seeing it, with a nasty taste in your mouth. The death of the woman, at the end, is distressingly horrible. Nevertheless it is a wonderful piece & shd. be seen without fail.

Mdlle Beatrice is one of the few women who wear handsome dresses (*really* handsome dresses) on the English stage. It is worth a visit to see her costumes alone (especially to a woman.) Her first appearance is in a sort of a kind of a salmon colored silk dress trimmed with steel—

I have got through my newspapers, and have, today, attacked the *Sunday Times* you have so kindly sent.

I *do* think the Review mangy.

I also think it rather mangy not having a rise of screw next season to begin with. It however arose as follows. They engaged their company the *second* week I was here, when I had only played a groom & a policeman, so that they didn't know whether I was worth anything or not. Very likely I shall get a rise in the middle of the Season.

Next season I shall get an engagement specifically for walking Gents. At present I am merely in my *novitiate*. / Lots of love & kisses from / Your affectionate Nephew / Arthur.

12. TO MRS. ELIZA SCHNEIDER

[A/16; Pe/41] 20 Alva Place, / London Road, / Edinburgh.

6th Septr. 1874.

[Edward Askew Sothern (1826–1881) was renowned for his creation of Lord Dundreary in Taylor's *Our American Cousin* (Laura Keene's

Theatre, New York, 12 May 1858; Haymarket, 11 November 1861). His other famous creation was the title role in T. W. Robertson's *David Garrick* (Prince of Wales's, Birmingham, April 1864; Haymarket, 30 April 1864). (For another account of Pinero's encounters with Sothern see his article, "Mathews and Sothern," *Era Almanack and Annual*, 1884, pp. 86–88.) *A Regular Fix* (Olympic, 11 October 1860) was written by John Maddison Morton (1811–1891), whose most famous farce is *Box and Cox* (Lyceum, 1 November 1847). John Clayton (John Alfred Clayton Calthrop; 1845–1888) acted many roles and with fellow actor Arthur Cecil (Blunt; 1843–1896) became manager of the Court Theatre. Both men played leading roles in Pinero's early "Court farces," *The Magistrate* (21 March 1885), *The Schoolmistress* (27 March 1886), and *Dandy Dick* (27 January 1887). Lytton Edward Sothern (1856–1887) often played "juvenile business" but was inevitably overshadowed by his father in what was a short career. Minnie Walton (d. 1879) was an American actress who, having made her debut in California in 1868, first appeared in London in *Our American Cousin* at the Haymarket on 10 October 1874. *King René's Daughter* (Strand, 11 December 1849) was written by Sir Theodore Martin (1816–1909), parliamentary solicitor, author, and husband of the actress Helen Saville Faucit (1817–1898). She took a leading part in Macready's Shakespearean revivals, although she ceased to act regularly after her marriage in 1851.]

Good people,

As I am very tired, I hit upon the device of concentrating my news into one sheet for the blessed three.

My news is few.

Sothern departed last night after a very successful week. He finished up by playing the *Regular Fix*—I played Charles Surplus. *He does not play "Hugh de Brass" so well as Clayton.* He played Dundreary & David Garrick during the week. I was in hopes that he would have done something fresh, as I have seen him so often in these two parts.

He is a jolly fellow to have anything to do with. I had to enter with him in the *American Cousin* so he and I had sundry chats every evening at the wing. He never speaks of a man as a man, but always as a *fellah*. His hair is very grey now—quite silvery.

His son Lytton is a very nice young man, but very diminutive.

Sothern appears at the Haymarket in October I believe. He has
brought with him from America a young lady called Minnie Walton
who will appear with him. I think he has brought her because she is a
flame of his sons—but I pity Little Lytton if he marries her. She
is not much good as an actress, and she is less good as a young person.

I have played some very good parts in farces during the week.

Tomorrow night I only play two small parts, one in *Romeo &
Juliet*—tother in a farce—but on Wednesday and Thursday I play
le Beau in *As you like it* which is very good, *what there is of it*.

I also have a very long part to study in *King Rene's Daughter* (Sir
Geoffery of Orange)—*a leading part*. (enter me very nervous again) / I
have no more news just now. / Fondest love and heaps of kisses. /
Arthur.

P.S. Notwithstanding that I don't like his De Brass, I think Sothern's
Dundreary & Garrick splendid. I enjoyed them all the more as I
had never seen him act till last Monday night.

Dont let such spelling as this occur again.

13. TO MRS. ELIZA SCHNEIDER

[A/16; Pe/41] 20 Alva Place, / London Road / Edinburgh.

20th Septr. 1874.

[Mrs. Mary Frances Scott-Siddons (1843–1896), the granddaughter of
Sarah Siddons, was noted for her interpretation of Shakespearean
heroines.]

Dearest Trio.

Receive and be thankful for a short effusion from a person
exhausted with a fortnights harassing labor at the "Legitimate"

I took an affectionate farewell of Mrs. Scott Siddons last night,
inwardly rejoicing that she was going at last. She is bound for the
hot place—don't be alarmed—I mean she is about to start on a tour
through India.

During her stay here she has played 7 pieces. I played in all
of these, in addition to the farce.

Mrs. John Wood commences on Monday. I don't think I shall
play all the week—so that will be a rest.

"Le Beau" I played as a young fop.

"Snake" in the *School for Scandal*, I played with a very sallow complexion, red eyebrows and very weak looking eyes. After playing this part I went and bowed approvingly to myself several times in the green room, and went home.

I received a *Hornet* from *some one* last week. As his criticism were marked in ink, I suppose it was from Irving. I am sure I'm very much obliged to him.

I had a letter yesterday from Chrissy's Lewis.

Tell me if you like this Tria junta in Uno style of letter writing.

Of course you know Ma has taken a house at Stoke Newington. By the bye I don't know where S.N. is.

You didn't tell me what you thought of Mdlle Beatrices gowns. / With a little bit of love and a kiss or two. / Believe me / Yours obediently / Arthur W. Pinero.

14. TO MRS. ELIZA SCHNEIDER

[A/16] 20 Alva Place, / London Road, / Edinburgh.

Octr. 18th. 1874.

[Pinero played Frederick Noble in *The Game of Speculation* (Lyceum, 2 October 1851) by "Slingsby Lawrence" (George Henry Lewes; 1817–1878). *Used Up* by Dion Boucicault the elder (1820–1890) and Charles James Mathews (1803–1878) was first produced at the Haymarket on 6 February 1844. Boucicault, an actor-dramatist, is best known for his Irish dramas, *The Colleen Bawn* (1860), *Arrah-na-Pogue* (1865), and *The Shaughraun* (1875). Mathews was more famous as an actor than as a dramatist and made a significant contribution to theatre history in his joint-management of the Olympic in 1836 with Madame Vestris (née Lucia Elizabeth Bartolozzi; 1797–1856). (See Leo Waitzkin, *The Witch of Wych Street: A Study of the Theatrical Reforms of Madame Vestris*, Cambridge, Mass., 1933, and William A. Armstrong, "Madame Vestris: A Centenary Appreciation," *Theatre Notebook*, XI, 1956–1957, 11–18.) An account of Mathews's acting in *Used Up* appears in George Henry Lewes, *On Actors and the Art of Acting* (London, 1875), pp. 67–68. Ada Cavendish (Mrs. Frank Marshall; 1847–1895) began her career at the Royalty and Haymarket theatres. She played Mercy Merrick in

Collins's *The New Magdalen* (Olympic, 19 May 1873) and the title role in Collins's *Miss Gwilt* (Globe, 15 April 1876), when Pinero played Mr. Darch.]

My dearest Aunt.

I am very sorry indeed to [hear] that Chrissy has the whooping korf. How juvenile it must make her feel!

During the week I have been playing very good parts in the *Game of Speculation* and *Used Up* with young Charley. He is a delightful young fellow, brimming over with the funniest anecdotes you ever heard. The worst of him is that he is too lazy to rehearse and we have to jog along at night in the best way we can.

I shall only play two nights next week. There is however an Opera Company in the town and this will occupy my time.

Ada Cavendish is the next "star"—She plays *The New Magdalen* (in which I shall figure as a Surgeon who leaves Grace for dead) and one or two Shakespearian plays. / With fond embraces & lots of kisses to Chrissy and yourself / Dear Aunt / Your professional Nephw. / Arthur.

Upon re-reading news from home, I find *Samuel* has also got the W. Cough—What a day you are having!

15. TO MRS. ELIZA SCHNEIDER

[A/16] 20 Alva Place, / London Road, / Edinburgh.

Novr. 5th. 1874.

[Nelson Wheatcroft (1852–1897) played juvenile roles in Swansea before moving to Bristol and then to London (in 1880). He joined Daniel Frohman's stock company at the New York Lyceum in 1884, and later founded and directed the Empire School of Acting in New York. *Hamlet* was revived at the Lyceum on 31 October 1874. Henry Talbot (1833–1894) was a tragedian and architect, who had made his debut as Macbeth at Drury Lane on 13 October 1866.]

My dearest Aunt.

[drawing of skull & cross-bones over a coffin]

The scarlet fever is very prevalent here just now. A lady friend of mine has lost 2 little girls through it, this week. I merely mention this to you because I don't [know] whether you & your family have had it, and I have known it conveyed by *a letter*. I have only to add that I have just left the house where it has been raging.

Miss Cavendish has been playing *the New Mag* (as I think I told you) and *As you like it*—Tomorrow she plays *Much Ado about Nothing* (I play Borachio) and on Saturday *Mr. Macbeth* (I figure as "Rosse" again).

By the bye, Wheatcroft (I think you remember him) is at Bristol Theatre Royal. I saw a bill of his last week by which I find he has been playing *Rosse* in *Macbeth*—so we are treading the same ground. Of course he play'd much better parts at Swansea, because there it is a 4th. rate theatre—*anybody* can play good business *there*.

Hamlet appears to be a glorious success at the "Lyceum"—I have read nearly all the papers upon the subject—I do hope I shall have an opportunity of seeing it.

On Monday next the Italian Opera comes for 9 nights—during which time I shall have nothing to do here—so I am going for 6 nights to a place called Arbroath (58 miles from here) to play leading business.

After the Opera is over, Mr. Talbot comes with Shakespears tragedies—with him I play "Lorenzo" in *The Merchant of Venice*— "Montano" in *Othello* &c&c.

I hope both Chrissy & the Tragedian are better—give them my fondest love & the same to Nelly Lilly & yourself. / Dear Aunt / Your affece. Nephew / Arthur W. Pinero.
Of course I look for *your* opinion of *Hamlet*.

16. TO MRS. ELIZA SCHNEIDER

[A/16; Pe/41] 20 Alva Place, / London Road, / Edinburgh.

Novr. 22nd. 1874.

[John Clarke (1829–1879) was a member of the original cast of T. W. Robertson's *Ours* (Prince of Wales's, 15 September 1866). In 1873 he married Teresa Elizabeth Furtado (1845–1877). Sir John Hare (Fairs; 1844–1921; knighted 1907) was an actor-manager, who first appeared on stage at the Prince of Wales's under the Bancrofts and later managed the Court, St. James's, and Garrick, the first two theatres in association with W. H. Kendal (William Hunter Grimston; 1843–1917). Kendal acted a great deal in the English provinces and later married Madge (Margaret) Robertson (1849–1935) before joining Hare. He also included several of Pinero's plays in his repertory when touring America.]

My dear Aunt.

You must excuse my apparent neglect of you, which however *is* apparent and not real. The fact is, that all Mr. Talbot's business is fresh study for me, and directly I returned from Arbroath I had to set to work like a Briton.

Arbroath is a miserably cold town in the north, composed partly of fishing and partly of flax mills. Despite many inconveniences in the way of board & lodging I enjoyed myself very much & returned better for the trip.

Mr. Talbot has been playing *Merchant of Venice* (I play'd Lorenzo) *Richard III* (Catesby) and *Othello* (Montano).

Catesby, in the *acting* edition of *Richd III*, has about 25 entrances. It is the most difficult (though a bad) part I have ever played. We pull'd it off last night, and I never was so nervous in all my life.

Tomorrow week John Clarke and Miss Furtado open for 6 nights with T. W. Robertson's comedy of *Ours*—I play Hare's part "Prince Perovsky" which is a great come up for me as it is a leading part.

I am sorry I did not tell you what sort of a woman Miss Cavendish is, but I do so now. She is simply a delightful creature, and everybody in the theatre was sorry when she left. There is not a sensation of pride about her.

As regards the *Hornet*, I grieve to say that between many stools I have fallen to the ground. When I first came to the city of Edinburgh I used to have *three* copies per week which of course were two many. One from Wright, one from Tolman, and one from yourself. Lately however Tolman & Wright have found out that they both send & have discontinued it under the impression that each forwards me a copy. This is rather mixed up I am afraid, but be this as it may— this week I have *had none at all*. Agony! !

I will write long budgets to all members of your family when I get Prince Perovsky off my mind. / With heaps of love to yourself &

Nelly, Lilly, Chris and the infant Samuel. / Dear Aunt / Your affecte.
Nephew / Arthur.
Macbeth again tomorrow night

17. TO MRS. ELIZA SCHNEIDER

[A/16] 20 Alva Place, / London Road, / Edinburgh.

Jany. 16th 1875.

[The pantomime at the Theatre Royal, Edinburgh, was *Jack and the Beanstalk* in which Pinero played Count Tiptopa. *The Day after the Wedding; or, A Wife's First Lesson* by Marie Thérèse Kemble (Mrs. Charles Kemble; 1773–1838) was first produced at Covent Garden on 18 May 1808. Irving's quotation appeared in the *Era Almanack and Annual* (1875), p. 44. The pantomime at the Globe was *Blue Beard* by H. B. Farnie. The Alhambra was noted for its comic operas and ballets (see Mander and Mitchenson, *Lost Theatres of London*, pp. 15–50).]

My dear Aunt.

The monotony of the pantomime precludes my having any startling news to communicate. It is getting rather tiresome—the only enjoyable thing about it is the laughter of the little children in the front of the house. I play in the farce now (*The Day after the Wedding*).

The "business" is really tremendous, and we turn away money nightly.

I am very sorry to hear some distressing accounts of the state of Irving's health. It would appear also that he himself has some misgivings on the subject, for in the collectn. of mottoes and autographs in the *Era almanac*, he writes:

"I fear me I may fade away from thee"

Charles I

Henry Irving

Perhaps however you may have seen the *Almanac*.

I dare say you have seen many of the Christmas Entertainments already, but if you have not been to the Globe by all means go. I believe it is the best affair in London.

I suppose you heard that Ma & Fanny went to the *Alhambra*!
What my family will come to next I do not know.

Fondest vibrations of the human heart for Lilly Chris and yourself.

I owe you heaps of thanks for the papers I receive. I must pay
for them in kisses when I see you. / Dear Aunty, always / Your
affectionate Nephew / Arthur.

Mrs. Schneider.

18. TO MRS. ELIZA SCHNEIDER

[A/16] 8 Gill Street, / Pembroke Place, / Liverpool.

24th. Feby. 1875.

[The Theatre Royal, Edinburgh, burned down on 6 February 1875, and
Pinero secured a position at the Alexandra, Liverpool, with Edward
Saker, the Wyndhams' brother-in-law. *London Assurance* was written
by Dion Boucicault the elder, and Mathews had created the role of
Dazzle in the original production at Covent Garden on 4 March 1841.
Mathews's *The Liar* was first produced at the Olympic on 9 March
1867.]

My dear Aunt.

Here I am, safe and sound, and in pretty comfortable apartments.
It is frightfully cold and I can hardly write.

This, as you doubtless know, is a very fine town in fact *London
the 2nd.* I have not seen much of it yet however, and must reserve a
more detailed account.

I went into the theatre last night for a little while. London does
not possess a handsomer. It is a kind of cross between the Opera
Comique and the Haymarket. The pit is one of those which does not
extend under the boxes. The landings and vestibule are very much
like those of the London Gaiety.

We open March 1st. not with the *School for S[candal]* as I
expected—but with Charles Matthews in *London Assurance* and *The
Liar* in which latter I play Pompillion the french valet. I will send
you an opening bill.

I expect to be in London on the 14th. March. Keep a look out! /

With fondest love to yourself and all / Dear Auntie / Your affectionate
Nephew / Arthur
Mrs. Schneider
Newspaper to hand. thanks!

19. TO MRS. ELIZA SCHNEIDER

[A/16] 8 Gill Street, / Pembroke Place, / Liverpool.   April 4th. 1875.
[Pinero played the Honorable Chomondley Chawkins in *Round the
Globe; or, A Well-won Wager*, a version of Jules Verne's (1828–1905)
Le Tour du Monde by John Francis McArdle, first produced at the
Alexandra, Liverpool, on 29 March 1875. Carl August Nicholas Rosa
(Rose; 1843–1889) was a German opera impressario who began his
opera company in 1875 with the aim of popularizing opera sung in
English. "Colonel" Hezekiah Linthicum Bateman (1813–22 March
1875) was an American actor-manager who moved to London in 1865
and managed the Lyceum from 1871 to 1875. He was the father of four
actresses: Kate Josephine (Mrs. Crowe; 1843–1917); Ellen Douglas
(1844–1936); Virginia (Mrs. Edward Compton; 1853–1940); and Isabel
Emilie. Bateman's wife was Sidney Frances (1825–1881), manageress
and dramatist, who managed the Lyceum from 1875 to 1878 and Sadler's Wells beginning in 1879.]

My dearest Aunt.

Have been so tired with the bustle and confusion at the theatre
or I would have written before. After the piece was produced (and
very successfully so) and we were congratulating each other on three
weeks rest, Mr. Saker was served with a notice of an application
for an injunction to restrain us playing it, at the instance of the
Princess's people, who bought the "right" of the French authors. Mr.
Saker was thereupon compelled to leave town—his part was taken
by another person, and I took this person's part as well as my own
two characters. In addition to this we had to rehearse & study
alterations & additions in case it should be necessary to change certain
scenes, & in fact we all got generally muddled.

In the end however Mr. Saker settled the matter by paying a
royalty to the London folks, and our *Round the Globe* revolves as
usual.

On the 19th instant Mr. Carl Rosa's Company comes for a week, during which time we are going some where but where I know not.

The Liverpool season ends May 22nd.

What a sad thing about Bateman's death! I only met him on the Saturday previous in the Strand. It is all nonsense to say he was looking in his usual health. I saw a great change in him. He looked white, and thin, and worn out. He was the only really legitimate London manager.

I hear from Ma that you have got into your new place. I hope you are comfortably settled. / Accept, dear Aunty, my fondest love, and give the like to Lilly, Chrissums, and the smaller editions. / Your very affectionate Nephew / Arthur.

20. TO MRS. ELIZA SCHNEIDER

[A/16] 73 Joy Street, / Belfast.   June 22nd 1875.
[*The Two Orphans* by John Oxenford (1812–1877) was first produced at the Olympic on 14 September 1874. Oxenford, as well as being a dramatist, was drama critic of the *Times* beginning in 1850. *The Chevalier of the Moulin Rouge; or, The Days of Terror* (Theatre Royal, Acton, 1 August 1859) was written by Colin Henry Hazlewood (1823–1875).]

My dear Aunt.

Many thanks for the *Sunday Times*, received this morning. Thanks also for the suggestion implied by the line round the matrimonial advertisement. I will think about it.

The *orphans* was (or were) produced last night, to a very good and enthusiastic house. The piece is I think a great success. I will send you a Bill the next time I write. (I have forgotten to ask for any.) The cast is very good, though I dare say you will recognize no names. The *Chevalier* went very well and got his "call" after his fencing act.

The future arrangements are not known, as the proprietor of the company lives at Bolton in England. Whether we go anywhere else with it I cannot yet say, and indeed may not be able to, till the last moment.

Belfast is a very fine city, the only drawback being the poor manner it is paved. The police are dressed like our Riflemen, and are

a fine handsome body of men. There are a lot of them, & they are
needed. In the time of the riots here, the people shot each other down
like dogs. / With dearest love to you—and to Lil and to Chris, and
to Nell. / Your affectionate Nephew / Arthur.

21. TO MRS. ELIZA SCHNEIDER

[A/16] 74 Gladstone Road, / Edge Hill, / Liverpool.

July 13th. 1875.

[Pinero played in *The Two Orphans* at the Royal Amphitheatre, Liverpool, from 31 July 1875 to 14 August 1875. *Our Boys* by H. J. Byron
was first produced at the Vaudeville on 16 January 1875. *Rank and
Fame* by Leonard Rae and F. Stainforth was produced at the Standard
on 29 March 1875. *Giroflé Giroflá*, a comic opera by Clement O'Neil
and Campbell Clarke, was produced at the Philharmonic, Islington, on
3 October 1874. *La Perichole* (Princess's, 27 June 1870) was an adaptation by Frank Desprez (1852–1916) of the opera by Offenbach.]

My dear Aunt.

It is not often I have to say I have been ill, but ill I have been,
and indeed am not up to much now.

I left Belfast on Wednesday night last, and arrived here on
Thursday mid-day, after a very jolly passage. These apartments are
very comfortable—indeed almost orientally luxurious. I have gone up
in the social scale, and have two rooms.

I open at the Alexandra on the 16th. August, but prior to that
I shall very likely participate in a revival of those *Orphans* in this town.
Till then I am very much at liberty. I have had an offer to go to
Glasgow, but no more long journeys for me yet awhile.

I am amusing myself by seeing the sights. Last week I saw *Our
Boys* at the Alexr. It was played by a splendid company. Everyone
good. I also saw *Rank & Fame* at the Theatre Royal, played by the
London Standard Company (Geo Hamilton, leading man). An alarm
of fire did not improve the enjoyment of this entertainment.

Last night I saw Mrs. John Wood's company at the Amphitheatre
play the *School for Scandal* & tonight I shall see *Girofle Girofla* at
the Alexr. Tomorrow I may give Dolaro as *La Perichole* a look in,

at the Prince of Wales'. You see there is no lack of amusement. In additn. to those I have mentd. there are four other theatres.

Write and tell me all your news. / With fondest & best love to Lil, Chris, and yourself. (I hope you are strong again) My dear Aunt / Your affecte. Nephew / Arthur.

22. TO MRS. ELIZA SCHNEIDER

[A/16] 74 Gladstone Road, / Edge Hill, / Liverpool.

July 26th. 1875.

[Ira David Sankey (1840–1908), an American evangelist and an effective singer, visited England from 1873 to August 1875 with another evangelist, Dwight Lyman Moody (1837–1899). (Thomas) Barry Sullivan (1821–1891) was an Irish actor who toured extensively in Britain, Ireland, the United States, and Australia. George Rignold (1838–1912), an actor-manager, acted in Bath and Bristol before making his London debut in 1870 at the Queen's. He played Lord Clancarty in Tom Taylor's *Lady Clancarty* (Olympic, 9 March 1874), which was revived at the Queen's on 17 July 1875.]

My dear Aunt.

An absence of any news has prevented me writing ere this.

On Saturday next, I open for thirteen nights at the Amphitheatre here in the *Two Orphans* finishing just in time to run through to Glasgow where I am engaged for four weeks commencing 16th. August at the Gaiety Theatre. This will be my first engagement for "Juvenile Lead." At the expiration of this, I return to Liverpool just in time to commence the winter season here.

In company with a friend I have been visiting nightly all the obscure places of "recreation" in Liverpool. I needn't tell you that attractions of the most peculiar character have presented themselves. At one place *Young Sankey, the Negro Revivalist* appeared with great success. He sang all M & S's hymns to an accompaniment of the bones, tambourine &c. I came away feeling much improved in my religious tendencies.

Barry Sullivan is playing here (previous to the departure for America) for 3 nights. I have first written him for an order. He is the god of the Liverpool folks. I have never seen him, but, from what I

hear, he is a fearful man. / With fondest love to you, dear Aunt, and the chickabiddies, / Your affectionate Nephew / Arthur.
P.S. It has just struck me that you will notice an alteration in my arrangements since I last wrote you. I told you then I was to play at the Alexandra on the 16th. So I was to have done, but the explanation is *more coin*.

Tell me what you think of George Rignold as "Clancarty"? ! ! !

23. TO MRS. ELIZA SCHNEIDER

[A/16] Mr. Whiteside's, / 122 Renfrew St, / Glasgow.

Augt. 17th. 1875.

[Dion Boucicault the elder claimed *Faust and Marguerite* (Princess's, 19 April 1854) as his (see *Era*, 2 June 1861), although T. W. Robertson also laid some claim to it (see Adams, *Dictionary of the Drama*, pp. 502–503). E. H. Brooke (Edwin James Macdonald Brook; 1843–1884), actor and dramatist, was associated with the Lyceum (1876–1877) and the Adelphi (1879–1883). Tom Mead (1819–1889), an actor-manager, played at various London theatres, managed the Elephant and Castle for a short period, and then moved to the Lyceum under Mrs. S. F. Bateman and Irving. Rose Leclercq (ca. 1845–1899), a specialist in the grand style of comic acting, later acted in Pinero's *The Amazons* (Court, 7 March 1893) and *The Princess and the Butterfly* (St. James's, 29 March 1897). *Macbeth* was revived at the Lyceum on 25 September 1875.]

My dear Aunt.

I opened here last night as "Valentine" in a revival of *Faust & Marguerite*.

Faust.	E. H. Brooke
Mephisto.	T. Mead.
Marguerite.	Rose Leclercq.

(the latter, a charming woman). The Gaiety here is a beautiful little place & nearly new. It embraces almost all the patronage of the Glasgow folks. The "Royal" here is a fine theatre, but like a wilderness in size. Hare and his company are there at present. They liked the acting of himself & Company in the provinces but the piece does not take the people by storm.

Mr. Mead goes back to the Lyceum for the First Witch. Mr. Irving is resting.

I wear fair hair in Valentine to match the Marguerite. Standing in the entrance last night with Miss Leclercq, she remarked "Well, I'm sure I have a pretty brother" said I (always on the look out for an opportunity) "It is only a weak attempt, Miss Leclercq, to be worthy of such a sister"—she replied "Thanks very much for the compliment, but I'm out of sorts this evening, in looks and in temper; my face is spotty and I feel wicked." This struck me as being very original. / With fondest love to Lilly, Chris, and yourself. / My dear Aunt / Your very affecte. Nephew / Arthur.

24. TO MRS. ELIZA SCHNEIDER

[A/16] 122 Renfrew St. / Glasgow.   Sept. 9th. 1875.
[Louise Willes (d. 1889) was an American actress who played mainly in the English provinces. Matthew Locke (1630–1677) composed the music for Davenant's production of *Macbeth* in 1664, although Locke's authorship has been questioned.]

My dearest Aunt.

I leave here on Sunday night for Liverpool, where I open on the 20th. instant. I shall be very glad to settle down after so much knocking about from place to place.

We are playing *As you like it* this week, with Miss Willes, a clever actress, (though not known in town) as Rosalind. I am playing "Silvius" and "Le Beau."

I dare say you are looking forward to *Macbeth* on the 18th.—I have two friends playing in it. I am sorry however they are going to omit Locke's music, which is always such a feature, and relieves the gloom of the play.

I have found Glasgow, though a fine city, very wet and very dull. By the aid of a Library, however, I have attacked Thackeray, and have got through the time much better than I expected.

Give my fondest love to Lilly, Chrissy and Nelly, not forgetting the youngster. I hear such bad accounts of Harry, from home, that I

am afraid to enquire after him. / With best love to you, my dear
Aunt, / Your affecte. Nephew / Arthur.

25. TO MRS. ELIZA SCHNEIDER

[A/16] 69 Dorothy St, / Edge Hill, / Liverpool.   Octr. 15th. 1875.
[Pinero played Arbaces in Lord Byron's (1788–1824) *Sardanapalus*
(Drury Lane, 10 June 1834). John Lawrence Toole (1832–1906), an
actor-manager, was a popular "low" comedian. In 1879 he took over the
Folly, reconstructed it, and reopened it in 1882 as Toole's (see Mander
and Mitchenson, *Lost Theatres of London*, pp. 530–550, and Pinero,
"J. L. Toole: A Great Comic Actor: The Natural Man," *Times*, 12
March 1932, pp. 13–14). Charles Calvert (1828–1879) was an actor-manager associated mainly with the theatre in Manchester, although he had
produced *Sardanapalus* at the Alexandra, Liverpool. The reference
here is presumably to one of Calvert's sons, Louis or William, who
might have taken a minor role.]

My dearest Aunt.

Ma tells me in her letter that you are not well. I hope you have
not another serious illness like the old affair. Please ask one of the
commercials to write me about you, if you are not well enough to do
so yourself.

I have little to tell you on my part. We finish with *Sardanapalus*
on Saturday, and Toole opens with us on Monday next. He is followed
by Sothern.

Did you see my friend the *Hornet*'s opinion of me? That however
is nothing to the remarks of a Liverpool satirical paper called the
Wasp, which said "as for Messieurs Calvert and Pinero, we should
like to pin-a-row of such actors up to a post to show the public to
what a level mediocrity can sink." ! ! !

The weather here is very miserable and uncertain. I hope it is
better with you. / With fondest love, my dear Aunt, to you & all. /
Believe me / Your affectionate Nephew / Arthur

26. TO MRS. ELIZA SCHNEIDER

[A/16] 69 Dorothy St, / Edge Hill, / Liverpool.   Octr. 30th. 1875.
[Pinero played Mr. Smith in T. W. Robertson's *David Garrick* and
Fripperifop in *Sinbad the Sailor*, which ran from 27 December 1875 to
4 March 1876 at the Alexandra, Liverpool. Linda (Ethelinda) Dietz (d.
1920) was an American actress who came to England in 1873 and was
Sothern's leading lady in 1875. She later played the Baronne de Prefont
in Pinero's *The Ironmaster* (St. James's, 17 April 1884) and Louison in
Mayfair (St. James's, 31 October 1885).]

My dearest Aunt.

    I hope this letter will find you in better health than when you
last wrote me. I have been very unwell myself & in fact am not up
to much now, but I know my small ailments are nothing to your
illnesses. The weather here is sloppy & bleak, & everyone has a cold.

    Mr. Sothern is playing with us now, and is doing some very great
business. Last evening the orchestra had to play upon the stage to
make room for the stall folks. We are doing *Garrick* now. I am playing
"Mr. Smith" the vulgar tradesman. After Sothern leaves, the Opera
comes, during which the company goes to the Rotunda, another
(smaller) theatre in Liverpool. Our pantomime, which has been many
months in preparation, is *Sinbad*.

    Miss Linda Dietz accompanies Mr. S, and is a charming young
lady. Sothern has aged a good deal since I last saw him, and his hair
is like silver.

    I hope, dear Aunt, when I hear from you next it will be that you
are much better. / With fondest love to all, / Your very affece.
Nephew, / Arthur.

27. TO MRS. ELIZA SCHNEIDER

[A/16; Pe/41] 69 Dorothy St, / Edge Hill, / Liverpool.
Novr. 16th. 1875.
[Pinero took an unknown role in Wilkie Collins's own adaptation of
his novel *Armadale* (1866)—entitled *Miss Gwilt* (Alexandra, Liverpool,
9 December 1875)—and later played Mr. Darch when the play transferred to the Globe Theatre, London, on 15 April 1876.]

My dearest Aunt.

I return the two portraits of Chrissy with many thanks for the inspection. They have been shown about a good deal, and any amount of flattering opinions have been expressed regarding her. Tell her to take heart—she may yet get a husband.

By the enclosed bill, you will see we are still at the Rotunda. As this theatre is, as it were, situated in the "East End" of Liverpool, our advent has created some excitement and the houses have [been] crammed to excess nightly. On Saturday the people broke the barricades down 20 minutes before the time of opening. After the place was full there still remained a crowd outside, and to quiet them, an undertaking was given to repeat the bill the following (this week). The fun of it was, that it was a pouring wet night and the multitude that did get in simply sat and *steamed*. It looked, from the stage, like a thick fog. The people were like potatoes—boiling in their jackets.

The Italian Opera has not done so well at the Alexr. this visit as on former occasions. They attempt to cram bad band and a weak chorus down the people['s] throats, but they won't have it.

We are having rain every day, and the aspect of the place is most depressing. I don't like a Liverpool winter at all. / I hope all is well. / With fondest love / Your affecte. Nephew /Arthur.
P.S. The cast of *Armadale* went up last night. There are but few parts in it, and those not good. I am not in it.

Be sure to let me know when Lilly is married.

28. TO MRS. ELIZA SCHNEIDER

[A/16] [Liverpool]   Decr. 24. 1875.
My dear Aunt,

I just scribble you a line to wish you a merry Xmas. I have not had a moments time for a very long period.

I was rehearsing all last night, and am now going out to commence again. I do not expect to return till the small hours tomorrow morng.

With my dearest love to Lill, Chris (Merchants) and the whole bilin' not forgetting yourself / I am, my dear Aunt / Your very pantomimic Nephew / Arthur.
Have you heard from any one at home, that I have had an offer from Mrs. Bateman for the Lyceum?

54

29. TO MRS. ELIZA SCHNEIDER

[A/16] 69 Dorothy St, / Edge Hill, / Liverpool.   Feby. 27th 1876.
[Robert Brough (1857–1906) was an actor-manager who, after gaining experience in Liverpool and Dublin, and touring with D'Oyly Carte, moved to Australia and managed the Bijou, Melbourne (with Dion Boucicault the younger) from 1886 to 1889. Robert Charles Lyons (1853–1892) was an actor with a career almost identical to Pinero's as an actor. Lyons made his debut at the Theatre Royal, Edinburgh, in 1869, joined the Alexandra, Liverpool, in 1875, and moved to the Lyceum after playing in *Miss Gwilt* at the Globe. Leonard Boyne (1849–1920) was an Irish actor who made his debut at the Theatre Royal, Liverpool, in 1869 before joining the St. James's in 1874. He later played Allingham in Pinero's *The Benefit of the Doubt* (Comedy, 16 October 1895).]

My dearest Aunty.

I am very glad you have thought of me at last. I should, in any event, have written you today, but had I not received yours of yesterday, this would not have been such a *genteel* letter as it is.

Although it is a long time since you have heard from me, you have not lost much "news." The pantomime has been (& indeed is still) dragging along its weary length. We manage to endure it however, by playing whist during our waits in the Dressing Room, and a few practical and other jokes on the Stage.

That wonderful man Charles Matthews comes to us on Monday (tomorrow) week, for six nights, after which we have a dose of "legitimate." I am very glad to begin work again.

Tomorrow night, for the benefit of the Clown, two members of our Company (Messrs. Brough & Lyons) and I, do enact *Clown, Harlequin* & *Pantaloon* respectively. What do you think of this?

Oh by the bye, I know you delight in little bits of chitchat. Let me tell you that Leonard Boyne is "spoons" on Ada Cavendish! After he had left the theatre, his dresser found some verses in his handwriting (I have verified it, by comparing it with a letter of his in my possession)—addressed to "Ada," and of the most languishing description. Of course all the fellows in the theatre have read the verses which are constantly quoted by some of us.

Well, goodbye, for the present. Give my dearest love to everyone and (although I dont know whether you quite deserve it) the same, with some kisses to yourself. / My dearest Aunt / Your affectionate Nephew / Arthur.

30. TO MRS. ELIZA SCHNEIDER

[A/16; Pe/41] Alexandra Theatre, / Liverpool.   Octr. 4th. 1876.
[Pinero spent from September to December 1876 on Irving's provincial tour, having joined the Lyceum Company when *Miss Gwilt* closed at the Globe on 4 July 1876. Irving visited Manchester, Birmingham, Liverpool, Newcastle, Edinburgh, Dundee, Glasgow, Belfast, and Dublin. Pinero stayed with Irving until 1881. *Charles I*, by W. G. Wills, was first produced at the Lyceum on 28 September 1872. On this tour Irving played the title roles in *Hamlet* and *Charles I* and Mathias in *The Bells*. Georgiana Pauncefort (1825–1895) joined the Lyceum in 1871; her roles in these three plays were, respectively, Gertrude, Lady Eleanor Davys, and Catherine. Claire Pauncefort, an actress, died in 1924. Mrs. Swinbourne was the wife of Thomas Swinbourne (1823–1895), who joined the Lyceum in 1874 and took the roles of the Ghost and Cromwell. Katherine Mackenzie Compton (1853–1928) was the daughter of Henry Compton (1805–1877) and the wife of the actor-dramatist Richard Claude Carton (Critchett; 1853–1928). She later acted in Pinero's *Imprudence* (Folly, 27 July 1881) and *Low Water* (Globe, 12 January 1884). John Archer (1835–1921) began his acting career in the provinces, notably in Edinburgh, before joining the Lyceum Company.]

My dearest Aunt.

Many thanks for your letter, in which you scold me less than I expected, and perhaps deserve. But you can form no idea how unsettled this travelling from place to place makes one feel. No sooner do we get into a place, than we begin to prepare to get out of it, and the few hours rest that I get, are generally devoted to putting my feet on the hob and pulling away at a soothing pipe.

The weather that we have encountered is simply awful. We were not a day in Manchester without rain. In Birmingham (a much pleasanter place however) we were cooked up with a muggy heat, and here it is again wet and miserably cold. Added to these little pleasantries, comes the fact that we have never been free from rehearsals. We have only played three pieces—*Hamlet Charles* and *Bells*, but, of course, we have to rehearse, for the fresh people, wherever we go.

Looking on the brighter side, we are a very jolly company—both ladies and gentlemen. The former are in stronger force than you imagine. There are Mrs. Pauncefort, and her daughter, whom she takes as a companion (a very nice girl—soft!) Mrs. Swinbourne, Mrs. Charman (wife of the acting manager) and Mrs. Carton (a daughter of Mr. Compton, the comedian.) The names of the gentlemen I think you know.

In Manchester and Birmingham, I shared apartments with Bob Lyons, but finding that our tastes and habits do not assimilate, we have dissolved partnership. I am lodging now at the old place in Gill Street, and share my sitting room with Mr. Archer. After we leave here however, I join Mr. and Mrs. Carton, who are very nice quiet people, and I look forward to this, as a very happy arrangement.

The people have flocked to see *Hamlet* in great force wherever we have been. We played it 10 times in Manchester, and 8 in Birmingham, and it has every appearance of success here. The papers mangled the whole lot of us dreadfully in our first town, were very good to us in Birmingham, and rather cold and indifferent here. There is always a certain amount of jealousy of a London Company in these provincial towns. It however does not affect the business one jot.

The Batemans are very, *very* nice people, and Irving himself is the pleasantest man imaginable.

It does seem very odd playing in the old theatre again: I can hardly make it out sometimes.

I have got Mrs. Pauncefort (and her daughter) into my old apartments at Edge Hill. She is very comfortable there, but they will amuse her with anecdotes of *my* former "manners & customs." They even tell her what I used to have for my meals, and advise her to do likewise.

Please tell Lilly and Chris to do everything to conciliate their respective men, as from what I hear, good males are becoming scarcer and scarcer.

Give my dearest love to them, and to everyone in the house, and with kisses for yourself. / dear Aunt. / Your affectionate Nephew / Arthur.

P.S. Do you happen to remember my address, when I was in *Belfast?* I am however ashamed to think that perhaps I didn't write to you from there.

It was some number in "Joy Street."

31. TO MISS ALMA MURRAY

[Ax/15(i)] Oldberry House, / Harmer Street, / Gravesend.

Sept: 21st. 1879.

[Alma Murray (Mrs. Alfred Forman; 1855–1945) played Daisy in Pinero's *Daisy's Escape* (Lyceum, 20 September 1879) and also Ruby in *Bygones* (Lyceum, 18 September 1880). She later played Raina in Shaw's *Arms and the Man* (Avenue, 21 April 1894).]

My dear Miss Murray.

I cannot by any act of mine repay you for the interest you have shewn and the trouble you have taken in and about my little piece, but I can, at least, acknowledge my appreciation of your charming performance of Daisy. I am sure you have rendered me a great service.

If I ever have another opportunity I think I shall be selfish enough to ask you to again assist me. / Most truly yours, / Arthur W. Pinero.

32. TO THE EDITOR, THE *DAILY NEWS*

[Pp/26; P/23] Haymarket Theatre.   December 31st. 1881.

[Letters 32 to 37 deal with the controversy surrounding the production of Pinero's *The Squire* (St. James's, 29 December 1881), which he was accused of plagiarizing from Thomas Hardy's (1840–1928) *Far from the Madding Crowd* (1874).

Hardy's *The Trumpet Major* was published in 1880. Pinero's *Hester's Mystery* was produced at the Folly Theatre on 5 June 1880. His "village love story" was *Girls and Boys a Nursery Tale & A Village Love Story* (Toole's, 1 November 1882) which was originally entitled *A Village Love Story*. This letter was published in the *Era*, XLIV, no. 2259 (7 January 1882), 10, where this sequence is conveniently collected.]

Sir,—

Will you permit me to give my most emphatic denial to the statement that my play *The Squire* is founded upon, or was in any way suggested by, Mr. Thomas Hardy's novel called *Far from the Madding Crowd*? My play originated, long before I had opened a book of Mr. Hardy's, in a memorandum which I have now before me, in my notebook. This is the memorandum:—"The notion of a young couple secretly married—the girl about to become a mother, finding that a former wife is in existence. The heroine amongst those who respect and love her. The fury of a rejected lover, who believes her to be a guilty woman. Two men face to face at night time. Qy.—Kill the first wife?" When the opportunity came to me to follow this idea, I beat about for a locality for my dramatic action. In attempting to illustrate rustic life I followed a plan which I had pursued some time previously in my little play called *Hester's Mystery*, produced at the Folly Theatre, and which plan I had continued in a three-act play, a village love story never yet performed. In *Hester's Mystery* my principal character was a woman-farmer, my scene a farm. *The Squire* is simply the result of the encouragement I received at this time. I thought it was worth while still to try and get the scent of the hay over the footlights, and this induced me to again fix the action of a play in a rural district. Gunnion is an elaboration of Joel in *Hester's Mystery*, and Joel owed his existence to some rambles in Kentish lanes. But it was not till long after *Hester's Mystery* had been produced, and when the notion of *The Squire* was thoroughly in my head, and after I had hinted the scheme to Mr. Hare, that I read Mr. Hardy's charming books *Far from the Madding Crowd* and *The Trumpet Major*. Those readers of *Far from the Madding Crowd* who witness my play will have no difficulty, I venture to think, in perceiving that my motive, characterisation, and dialogue differ wholly from Mr. Hardy's; I merely put my horse's head to the open country and take the same hedges and ditches with him, though perhaps my hack is a very sorry one and lacks the blood and muscle of my neighbour's animal. / I am, Sir, your obedient servant, / ARTHUR W. PINERO.

33. TO THE EDITOR, THE *DAILY NEWS*

[Pp/26; P/23] Haymarket Theatre.   January 3d. 1882.
[In letters dated 1 January 1882 Hardy and Joseph William Comyns

Carr (1849–1916), a dramatist and manager, stated that *The Squire* and *Far from the Madding Crowd* were in fact very similar and suggested that Pinero based his play on Carr's *The Mistress of the Farm*, submitted to Hare and Kendal in the spring of 1880 and subsequently rejected by them on 11 November 1880. (See a discussion of the adaptations of *Far from the Madding Crowd* in Richard Little Purdy, *Thomas Hardy: A Bibliographical Study*, London, 1954, pp. 28–30.) However, this acrimony did not survive long; Carr managed the Comedy Theatre from 1893 to 1896, where he produced Pinero's *The Benefit of the Doubt*. They later collaborated on *The Beauty Stone* (Savoy, 28 May 1898) with Sullivan.

Edouard Pailleron (1834–1899), a French dramatist, was best known for *Le Monde Où L'on S'ennuie* (Français, Paris, 25 April 1881). *La Petite Pluie* (Français, 4 December 1875) had been produced at the Gaiety in the summer of 1877. Letters from "An Occasional Playgoer" appeared in the *Daily News* on 3, 5, and 10 January 1882, maintaining that *Daisy's Escape* and *La Petite Pluie* could have been entitled "Julie's or Celestine's Escape." Letter 33 was published in the *Era* and the *Daily News*, 4 January 1882, p. 6.]

Sir,—

I take this, my first opportunity, to deny, with every indignant feeling, the wanton accusations made by Mr. Hardy and Mr. Carr. Not until the afternoon of Saturday last, the 31st December, did I hear of the existence of this adaptation by Mr. Carr of Mr. Hardy's novel, and at this moment I am entirely ignorant of the nature of that or of any other adaptation of the story. Moreover, let me state here emphatically that my play originated from no suggestion made to me at any time by Mr. Hare or Mr. Kendal, but was solely the result of my own plan and purpose. I do not notice Mr. Hardy's letter at any length, because its gross inaccuracies are clearly attributable to the circumstance that Mr. Hardy remains at Wimborne, in Dorset, depending for his information upon Mr. John Comyns Carr. Mr. Carr is the author of a rejected play, and shares with all authors of rejected plays the bitterness of ill-success. He is evidently an angry gentleman as well as a disappointed one, and for that reason I desire to answer him most temperately. Let me give Mr. Carr my solemn assurance that I have never borrowed a suggestion nor an idea from any work in which he has had a hand. Let me further assure him, with equal solemnity, that I do not intend ever to do so. I notice in your issue of to-day that an anonymous writer charges me with adapting *Daisy's Escape* from *La Petite Pluie* of M. Pailleron. I have never read *La Petite Pluie*—have never seen it acted, have never had it described to me. I know absolutely nothing about it. Why on earth doesn't "An Occasional Playgoer" attach his name to his letter? I wonder whether I know him! / Your obedient servant, / ARTHUR W. PINERO.

34. TO THE EDITOR, THE *DAILY NEWS*

[Pp/26; P/23] Haymarket Theatre.   January 4th, 1882.
[Pinero's letter was published in the *Daily News* on 5 January 1882, p. 6, as a reply to Carr's letter (4 January 1882, p. 6; both reprinted in the *Era*). Carr maintained that "the following facts are clearly established:— (1) That if Mr. Hare is to be believed, when the original scheme of the play was first communicated to him it can have borne no sort of resemblance to Mr. Hardy's story; (2) that when the play was afterwards completed and read to the company this resemblance had become so marked that both Mr. Hare and Mr. Kendal were struck with surprise; and (3) that between these two dates Mr. Pinero, by his own confession, had read *Far from the Madding Crowd*."

Madge Kendal was a sister of T. W. Robertson and a much better actress than her husband was an actor. She played many leading roles and was made a Dame Commander of the British Empire in 1926.]

Sir,—

Will you allow me to trespass upon your space once more to notice Mr. J. Comyns Carr's letter of January 2d? The statement in Mr. Hare's communication to Mr. Carr, made on the morning after the production of *The Squire*, is, I fancy, a confusion by Mr. Hare of two occasions—that of the detailing of my scheme to him a long time ago, before I had read the book, and the occasion of my reading the completed play to Mr. and Mrs. Kendal and Mr. Hare at Birmingham not long since. At Birmingham, I think, only Mrs. Kendal asked me if I had read Mr. Hardy's book, and my reply was "Yes; but not till long after I had conceived and constructed my play." Let me inform

61

Mr. Carr, in answer to his Fact No. 1, that when I originally imparted my plan to Mr. Hare my story, locality, and situations were as they now are. As to Fact No. 3, I read Mr. Hardy's two novels, with many others of various authors, for no earthly reason but that if one reads only good fiction one must arrive at books written by Thomas Hardy. Mr. Carr thinks my original notion, contained in my memorandum, tallies with the story of the novel. Not at all. My central idea—a loving couple believing themselves to be man and wife, the woman in the desperate condition of my Kate Verity, sundered through no absolute fault on either side, and turning from each other voluntarily, from a strict sense of duty—is like nothing in Mr. Hardy's book. Mr. Carr kindly makes me a present of my dialogue, but adds that if I had borrowed Mr. Hardy's my play would have been a better one. And yet Mr. Carr is in despair about his play! Why surely, if I am in possession of Mr. Hardy's plot, and Mr. Carr has Mr. Hardy's beautiful dialogue, as far as dramatic attraction goes we must be quits. One word more. If Mr. Carr's play ever had in it the "chances of success" it is a better play now than it has ever been. Artistically it is entitled to all the credit due to priority of invention. Commercially, the authors have drawn a considerable amount of preliminary attention to it, and, in these days of "millions turned away nightly" theatrical enterprise, the statement at the head of their playbills—"The origin of *The Squire*"—is quite warrantable. For myself I have no warmer wish than that Mr. Carr's play should see the light; its production (as it stood before the performance of my piece) will be my best defence. / I am, Sir, your obedient servant, / ARTHUR W. PINERO.

35. TO THE EDITOR, THE *DAILY NEWS*

[Pp/23] Haymarket Theatre.   Jan 5 1882.
[Pinero's letter was published 6 January 1882, p. 2.]

Sir,—

"An Occasional Playgoer," who for some reason still conceals his identity, professes to give your readers the story of my little comedy, *Daisy's Escape*. Those readers of the *Daily News* who witnessed what "An Occasional Playgoer" calls my "one-act comedietta" will have no difficulty in perceiving two facts—firstly, that your

correspondent gives a version of my one-act comedy which is positively
an untrue one; secondly, as shown by the care with which he misstates
the points of my comedietta, that he well knows what he is doing.
I have an idea that "An Occasional, &c.," is himself a literary person,
connected with a London newspaper. I wonder? / Your obedient
servant, / ARTHUR W. PINERO.

36. TO THE EDITOR, THE *DAILY NEWS*

[Pp/26; P/23] Haymarket Theatre   January 7th, 1882.
[Pinero's letter was published in the *Era*, XLIV, no. 2261 (21 January
1882), 3, and the *Daily News*, 9 January 1882, p. 2.]

Sir,—

"An Occasional Playgoer" (whose name, I think, I could spell
"to a T") will pardon me if I ignore him for the moment, to ask your
readers what essential resemblance exists between M. Pailleron's
story and my boarding-school Daisy, with her bread-and-butter
philosophy, who, sick with a disappointed love for a handsome lad,
and weary of the rule of a gouty guardian, runs away with a cad—to
encounter, through an accident, her old lover, who proves to have been
faithful to her throughout, and who is just in time, by reviving the
bygone romance and by conjuring up memories of the scent of the old
roses in the garden where they used to play at lovers, to rescue her
from a life of "repentance at leisure." What resemblance in essentials,
I ask, is there between all this and *Petite Pluie*, with its unhappy wife
and her lover, who are manoeuvred out of danger by the typical
wise widow of the French stage? True, my play has an elopement and
so has M. Pailleron's; but the notion of an elopement belongs as
little to him as to me. Of this, however, "An Occasional Playgoer"
(unless his intimacy with stage literature begins with the production
of *Petite Pluie* in 1875) is fully aware. This, then, is my final
communication to you, Sir, on the subject of *Daisy's Escape*, a side
issue brought forward to prejudice a main question. I leave "An
Occasional Playgoer" to pursue for ever his ingenious method
of criticism, and I congratulate him on the existence of that "large
question of anonymous writing" behind which he is so snugly
ensconced. In the meantime, what has become of Mr. Thomas Hardy

and his friend and adapter Mr. John Comyns Carr? When last I heard
from them, neither of these gentlemen had seen my play *The Squire*.
But I am informed that since the writing of Mr. Carr's most recent
letter both he and Mr. Hardy, in company with a solicitor who is well
known and much fancied for his genial manner, have visited the St.
James's Theatre. But nothing has come of it. Now, I have been very
angry over this question—few, I think, can blame me—but I am sorry,
because although I know Mr. Hardy and his friend to be a couple
of sadly mistaken gentlemen, yet I cannot believe that they would, in
cold blood, do a thing deliberately unfair. So I should like to know
whether to the minds of Mr. Hardy and Mr. Carr my play of *The
Squire* proved quite so much like *Far from the Madding Crowd* as they
had been led to believe. / I am, Sir, your obedient servant, / ARTHUR
W. PINERO.

37. TO THE EDITOR, THE *DAILY NEWS*

[Pp/26; P/23] Haymarket Theatre   January 10th, 1882.
[Carr's letter appeared in the *Daily News* on 10 January 1882, p. 2,
Pinero's on 11 January, p. 2. Both are printed in the *Era*, 21 January
1882, p. 3.]

Sir,—

A thousand apologies to Mr. John Comyns Carr—I have sent him
to the St. James's Theatre on a wrong date. Of course, Mr. Hardy and
he, accompanied by "the legal adviser of Messrs Hare and Kendal,"
witnessed my very successful play after the writing of Mr. Carr's letter
dated 2d inst. I should have avoided this stupid mistake by remem-
bering that Mr. Carr had in that letter said unkind things about my
dialogue. But, really, who can wonder at this slip of memory on my
part? In what condition of mind must I be in after this lengthy
squabble? What misgivings must I not have as to whether even my very
name belongs to me? What doubts must not have arisen within me
as to whether I am or am not even an adapted son?

But Mr. Hardy's Best Friend has missed the point of my last
letter, which was —How is it that nothing very formidable has come of
the visit of Mr. Hardy, Mr. Carr, and a "real live" solicitor to the
St. James's Theatre? Is it because the resemblance between my work

and that of Messrs. Hardy and Carr didn't turn out to be quite so striking as they had been led to believe? Or is it because the "legal adviser of Messrs. Hare and Kendal" (who, to put it mildly, was "singularly unfortunate" in being detected in such company on such an occasion), discovering the awkwardness of having to run with the Hare and to hunt with Messrs. Carr and Hardy, thought it advisable that the matter should be allowed to drop?

And now, at the eleventh hour, it appears in print that Mr. John Comyns Carr is "a very humble representative" of his craft. Whether this declaration comes as a surprise, I don't know; perhaps the public mind, searching for Mr. Carr's achievements as a dramatist, may have anticipated the avowal. But Mr. Carr has all through this controversy been too scrupulous in concealing from your readers the fact of his industry as an aspiring playwright. We have learnt that his play was declined by the management of the St. James's, but we have not been told by Mr. Carr how many other managers and people of position on the stage have read it, said nice things about it (Mr. Carr is an "Art Critic"), and—rejected it. It is, however, necessary that we should know this is in order to estimate the value of a play from which, according to Mr. Hardy and his friend and adapter Mr. Carr, I have been able to derive a useful lesson in dramatic construction.

I am sorry that Mr. John Comyns Carr takes exception to the tone of my letters; but what on earth does Mr. Carr expect from me in answer to his charges?—and such charges! The compliments of the season, and so on? That Mr. Carr may be better able to appreciate the moderation of my replies, let him to-morrow call a man a thief at the street corner—the result, if not amusing, will be instructive.

Permit me a last word—it shall not come from my mouth, but from that of *The Rambler*. I present it to Mr. Carr as the moral of the whole story:—"Among the innumerable practices by which interest or envy have taught those who live upon literary fame to disturb each other at their airy banquets, one of the most common is the charge of plagiarism. When the excellence of a new composition can no longer be contested, and malice is compelled to give way to the unanimity of applause, there is yet this one expedient to be tried, by which the author may be degraded, though his work be reverenced; and the excellence which we cannot obscure may be set at such a distance as

not to overpower our faintest lustre." / I am, Sir, your obedient
servant, / ARTHUR W. PINERO.

38. TO THE EDITOR, THE *TIMES*

[Pp/37] Haymarket Theatre   March 7 1882.
[Pinero's letter was published 13 March 1882, p. 5. In the *Times* for 6
March 1882, p. 6, Herman Charles Merivale (1839–1906) had advised
novelists to produce a dramatized version of their work to prevent
plagiarism; only in this way could they "save themselves from being
Pinerized." *The Cynic*, originally entitled *The Modern Faust* (Theatre
Royal, Manchester, 19 November 1881), was produced at the Globe on
14 January 1882.]

Sir,

In *The Times* of yesterday Mr. Herman C. Merivale, a dramatic
author, under the pretence of treating the question of novelists and
their rights, insults me, a dramatic author, by attempting to cast a slur
upon my honesty. I doubt whether the brilliancy of the pun which
Mr. Merivale makes upon my name will quite atone, in the eyes of
the readers of *The Times*, for the utter absence from Mr. Merivale's
letter of any indication of the writer's good breeding. Mr. Merivale
should be careful to keep a schoolboy at his elbow to prompt him
in the observance of those very elementary rules of politeness which
are intuitive to men of culture and refinement.

With regard to the larger question of novelists, will you permit
me to say, Sir, that when the protecting arm of the law is thrown
around the novelist it will be a good day for the dramatist? Now-a-days,
on the production of a successful play, the writer of any novel dealing
with the same theme, however common the theme, and permeated
with the same atmosphere, however general the atmosphere, may start
up and claim the sole title to a common subject, and charge the
playwright with theft. The cause of the accuser is, of course, supported
by the rivals of the successful dramatist, and the sale of the novel
is advanced 50 per cent. But when the penalty of this shall be that
the novel-writer shall go into a court of law and prove his charge, then,
and not till then, shall we have a little less of the plagiarisms of the
playwrights. Why, I ask plainly, if these novelists are such clever

original writers, do they not give us clever original plays? Why, even
The Cynic, Mr. Merivale's play, a dramatization of his own novel
Faucit of Baliol, runs only about 50 nights to very poor houses at the
Globe Theatre! / I am, Sir, your obedient servant, / ARTHUR W.
PINERO.

39. TO R. M. FIELD

[Ax/11(i)] 9 Store Street, / Bedford Square, / WC.   4th. May 1883.
[Pinero built up a substantial association with the Boston Museum
Theatre as well as with the major American market centered in New
York (see letters 41, 43, 44, 47). In these earlier years Pinero carried
out all the negotiations to produce his plays directly with the manager
concerned. Richard Montgomery Field (1832–1902) was manager of the
Boston Museum Theatre from 1864 to 1898, having previously worked
as a typesetter with the *Boston Post*. Pinero's *The Rector* was produced
at the Court on 24 March 1883.]

My dear Mr. Field.
    I have seen my friend Mr. Carton—the holder of the English
Right of my three act play. He objects to its production in America
taking place before it is played here and though of course I am free in
the matter still, as Mr. Carton is a very old friend of mine, I am
anxious not to upset him in his calculations.
    What arrangement shall we come to, therefore? Do you care to
commission me to write you a play, you paying me a sum now and a
per centage on the receipts? Or what do you propose? Of course
I could promise you nothing before October or November, or
thereabouts.
    People here—some of them Americans, tell me *The Rector* is just
the play for the Boston Museum. Will you make some enquiries about
the piece?
    I shall be glad to hear from you. / Faithfully yours / Arthur
W. Pinero.
R. M. Field Esq.

40. TO H. A. JONES

[Ax/10] 10 Marlborough Crescent, / Bedford Park, / Chiswick.

9th. Augt. 1883.

[Henry Arthur Jones (1851–1929), a dramatist, was a lifelong friend of Pinero's (see my article, "Pinero's Letters in the Brotherton Collection of the University of Leeds," *Theatre Notebook*, XXIV, 1969–1970, 74–79). Beginning 30 December 1878 Pinero had played Rosencrantz at the Lyceum for well over 100 performances. Pinero's "Farcical Comedy" was *The Rocket* (Prince of Wales's, Liverpool, 30 July 1883; Gaiety, London, 10 December 1883). Jones's *The Silver King* was produced at the Princess's on 16 November 1882 and ran for 289 performances.]

My dear Jones.

It is very kind, indeed, of you to have troubled so much over the Cornwall business. When we go we shall be guided by your letter. I say *when* we go for I am a little upset by my Doctor who says the trip ought to be deferred to a colder month—Cornwall is relaxing, says he—try a bracing air in the north—it is absolutely necessary that the Brain (!) should have &c &c &c. The moment a man has written a Farcical Comedy, or played Rosencrantz to Irving's Hamlet, his Doctor begins to talk about Brain Tissues and Nerve Centres—whereas *you* know very well, my dear Jones, that a play of the substance of

(advt.) *The Rocket*

calls for little mental strain, while the construction of a work like

The Silver King

demands none whatever.

———————

Very seriously however, I am much obliged for your letter—we *shall* go to Cornwall, are looking forward to it a great deal, and your hints will be of considerable service. / With Best Regards, / Faithfully yours, / Arthur W. Pinero.

Henry A. Jones Esq.

41. TO ARTHUR WALLACK

[Ax/8(ii)] 10 Marlborough Crescent, / Bedford Park, / Chiswick.

28th. Nov. 1883.

[Pinero, anxious to develop the New York market for his works, approached two of the leading New York managers, Arthur J. Wallack (1849–1940) and John Augustin Daly (1839–1899), to explore further possibilities (see letters 43, 44, 47). *Lords and Commons* was produced at the Haymarket on 24 November 1883 and at Daly's, New York, on 15 November 1884. Joseph Brooks (1849–1916) was a well-known American manager who was for a time associated with James Dickson, particularly in the production of melodramas. Effie Ellsler (née Euphemia Murray; 1823–1918) was an American actress. George Osmond Tearle (1852–1901), an actor-manager, did much of his apprentice work in the English provinces before joining Wallack's Theatre as leading man in September 1880. In 1888 he organized his own Shakespearean touring company. William Terriss (William Charles James Lewin; 1847–1897) acted with the Bancrofts at Drury Lane and with Irving at the Lyceum. He was murdered while entering the Adelphi. Rose Coghlan (1850–1932) was an actress who, after an early career in Britain, moved to America and was the leading lady at Wallack's in the 1880s. She played Millicent Boycott in *The Money Spinner* (Wallack's, 21 January 1882; originally produced at the Prince of Wales's, Manchester, 5 November 1880, and St. James's, 8 January 1881).]

Dear Mr. Wallack.

Will you, if you can, make yourself acquainted with the nature of my play *Lords and Commons* just produced at the Haymarket Theatre, and I think—though time alone can prove this—a thoroughly substantial success?

I have an existing arrangement with Messrs. Brooks and Dickson relating to Miss Ellsler starring in this play, but I think we shall by mutual arrangement, for causes with which I need not trouble you, cancel this agreement.

The play contains a good leading part, suitable for Tearle or Terriss—and a woman's part adapted to Miss Coghlan or any strong emotional actress. I fancy the play has in it an element especially likely to gain the favor of the American public. / With regards, believe me, / Faithfully yours, / Arthur W. Pinero.
Arthur Wallack Esq.

42. TO THE EDITOR, THE *THEATRE*
[CLEMENT SCOTT]

[Pep/35]   [13 January 1884]
[Clement Scott (1842–1904) was drama critic of the *Illustrated London
News* and the *Daily Telegraph,* and, from 1880 to 1891, editor of the
Theatre. Pinero sent him many items of theatrical news as well as other
occasional contributions. His letter was published in the *Theatre,* n.s.
III (February 1884), 87–88.]

I am anxious that the "first-night" play-going public—at whose
hands I have from time to time received so much generous encouragement—should know that they are not indebted wholly to me
for the trial of their patience to which they were subjected last night.
Low Water has been produced at the Globe Theatre in direct
opposition to my wishes—in spite of my most earnest protests. The
control of the play unfortunately passed out of my hands a long time
ago, and all my endeavours to prevent its performance, under conditions which I knew would result in the complete obscuring of the
meaning of my work, were of no avail. I shall venture on some occasion
to present *Low Water* to the public in a manner which shall give form
and expression to my ideas. In the meantime I hope the play may be
speedily forgotten. / I am, Sir, faithfully yours, / ARTHUR PINERO.

43. TO AUGUSTIN DALY

[Ax/6] 10 Marlborough Crescent, / Bedford Park, / Chiswick.
                                                   14th. Jany. 1884.
[Daly began his managing career in 1869 (Fifth Avenue Theatre, New
York) and opened his own theatre, Daly's, in 1879 with John Drew
(1853–1927) and Ada Rehan (1860–1916) as the leading members of his
company. He opened Daly's Theatre in London in 1893 (see Mander
and Mitchenson, *Lost Theatres of London,* pp. 51–57). *Girls and Boys*
was produced at Daly's on 5–12 December 1883 and *Lords and Commons* on 15–24 November 1884. Leander Richardson (1856–1918) was
a dramatist and a journalist for the *New York Times.* The Standard
Theatre, New York, burned down on 14 December 1883, was rebuilt,
and then reopened on 23 December 1884. William Lewis Telbin (1846–
1931) came from an English family of scene-painters. After working at

the Theatre Royal, Manchester, he did sets and costumes for several London theatres. Mrs. Bernard Beere (née Whitehead; 1856–1915), an actress, played the title role in Herman Merivale's adaptation of *Fédora* (Vaudeville, Paris, 12 December 1882; Haymarket, 5 May 1883) by Victorien Sardou (1831–1908), the prolific French dramatist, best known for his play *Madame Sans-Gêne* (Vaudeville, Paris, 27 October 1893). Mrs. Beere acted Mrs. Devenish in *Lords and Commons* and went on to play, among many other roles, Mrs. Arbuthnot in Oscar Wilde's (1854–1900) *A Woman of No Importance* (Haymarket, 19 April 1893).]

A. Daly, Esq.
Daly's Theatre.
New York.
My dear Sir.

On the 6th. of last month Mr. Leander Richardson wrote me that you had produced *Girls and Boys*, at the same time forwarding me some press cuttings. Since then I have heard nothing further from Mr. Richardson. Will you be kind enough to forward direct to me an account of the business done—informing me, if you will, whether Mr. Richardson has collected my fees. I am at a loss to account for his silence. I had never much faith in *Girls and Boys* but I hope sincerely you have not suffered from its production.

I have not yet settled *Lords and Commons* (my Haymarket comedy now running successfully) in America. Messrs. Brooks & Dickson bought the refusal of it and paid fees in advance, but on the burning of the Standard Theatre I bought back my right in the play. Mr. Wallack has cabled me an offer but we have as yet come to no definite arrangement. Do you care to do anything in this direction? I want eight per cent on the gross receipts, with an advance, say of £150. I will send out Mr. Telbin's models &c. *Lords and Commons* is a strong play and I think well suited to your theatre and company. It contains a strong woman's part—Miss Rehan I should think would make much of it. Mrs. Beere, the English Fédora, is doing it here.

Be good enough to let me hear from you as soon as possible on both the points of my letter. With regard to *Lords and Commons* perhaps you will feel inclined to cable? At any rate I will, if I can, keep the matter open till you have had time to answer. My cable

address is Pinero / Bedford Park / Chiswick / London. / With best
wishes for this year, / I am / Faithfully yours, / Arthur W. Pinero.

44. TO AUGUSTIN DALY

[Ax/6] 10 Marlborough Crescent, / Bedford Park, / Chiswick.

8th February [1884].

My dear Sir.

I am in receipt of your statement of the week of *Girls and Boys*
for which accept my best thanks. Since writing you I have heard from
Mr. Richardson with a remittance for my share of the amount which
you appear to have paid him last July.

With nothing to say against Mr. Richardson or any other agent—
indeed I would prefer to deal directly with the New York Manager,
and in this spirit I forward you (by this mail) a book of *Lords and
Commons*. Having done this any words of mine expressing confidence
in you and your establishment are unnecessary.

The book I send you is merely a printed copy of my original
Manuscript, and not the prompt book which, of course, contains such
cuts, alterations and general improvements as long and careful
rehearsal under my own direction have produced. The accompanying
copy will however give you a sufficient notion of the play to guide your
judgement—*please return it to me when you have read it*. If you decide
to do the play I will then send out a prompt Book &c. &c.

I have just disposed of the Australian right to Messrs Rignold
and Allison—they pay me for the models of the three scenes, £15, and I
should have to ask you, or any other New York Manager, to do the
same. I have already conveyed my terms to you. To these I would add a
stipulation that the play be produced in the early and best part of
the next season.

If you see no objection, I think it would be better if you cabled
me Yes or No after reading the play, to enable me at once to arrest
or forward other negociations which may be pending. Pinero / Bedford
Park. / Chiswick. / London. / will reach me. / Very sincerely yours,
/ Arthur W. Pinero.
Augustin Daly, Esq.

45. TO WILLIAM TERRISS

[Ax/6] 10 Marlborough Crescent, / Bedford Park, / Chiswick.

16th. June 1884.

[*7-20-8* was the original title of Augustin Daly's *Casting the Boomerang* (Daly's, New York, 24 February 1883; Toole's, 19 July 1884), on which Terriss had asked Pinero's opinion regarding its suitability for a London audience (see, in this connection, letter 46).]

My dear Terriss.

I have read *7-20-8* carefully and have run my pencil through certainly not more than half a dozen lines which I think would be risky for a London audience. Nothing more is wanted—the play is very bright, full of character, and, for a farcical piece, most *human*. The first act is perhaps a little too long, but in my opinion the dropping of the curtain in the middle of it is dangerous and altogether inexpedient.

The characters being American; the action of the play taking place on American soil; and the performance being by American artists; I consider it quite unnecessary to disturb the local characteristics of the piece which are quite understandable and which I think will be found amusing by an English audience.

I return you the manuscript with this note. / Faithfully yours, / Arthur W. Pinero.
William Terriss Esq.

46. TO AUGUSTIN DALY

[Ax/6] 10 Marlborough Crescent, / Bedford Park, / Chiswick.

5th. Octr. 1884.

[Daly brought his company to Toole's Theatre for a six-week season, beginning 19 July 1884. For this venture William Terriss had acted as Daly's London representative. Daly arrived back in New York on 15 September, and on the same day his company opened a two-week run at the Chestnut Street Opera House, Philadelphia. Daly's regular New York season began on 7 October 1884.]

My dear Mr. Daly.

The music of *Lords and Commons* was poorly done at the Haymarket where there is an indifferent orchestra and a conductor to match. I have already sent you the words and music of the song, and on the other side of this I jot down a note or two of the *sort* of music required throughout the piece. You and your conductor will be able to settle the whole thing in ten minutes.

Glad to read of your arrival—the re-appearance of your company in Philadelphia—your speech, &c. &c. Accept my very best wishes for a successful season. Are you going to do *Lords and Commons before* the election business is over? You said not. / Faithfully yours, / Arthur W. Pinero.

Augustin Daly, Esq.

 Act I.
 1. Something Bright and pronounced to open.
 2. Harp Music and Song to follow.
 3. Serious and pathetic—expressive of a Farewell to Home, for Countess's business and end of act.
 Act II.
 4. Bright and lively to open.
 5. The melody of the Song, played in orchestra, to end Act.
 Act III.
 6. Bright—to open.
 7. Any tuneful and expressive waltz—but not one that will be recognized as new, because of the words in the play.
 8. Repeat of waltz.
 Act IV.
 9. Bright—to open.
 10. Harp and song, outside, to end.

I haven't my M.S. at hand at this moment, & have trusted to my memory. I dont think I have left out any ideas. / P.

47. TO AUGUSTIN DALY

[Ax/6] 10 Marlborough Crescent, / Bedford Park, / Chiswick.

20th. Octr. 1884.

[Apart from negotiations to stage Pinero's plays in America, Daly also wrote to him with other suggestions, as is reflected in this letter. Daly proposed that Pinero adapt some foreign plays in which he, Daly, had an interest and which he might stage in America and/or England.

Nothing concrete ever came of this proposal, although it was actively entertained by both men for some time (see also letters 52 and 57 in which Pinero mentions two of Daly's own works which Pinero tried to help place with London theatres).

Pinero's *In Chancery* was produced at the Lyceum, Edinburgh, on 19 September 1884, the Gaiety, London, on 24 December 1884, and the Madison Square, New York, on 8 June 1885. Edward O'Connor Terry (1844–1912), an actor-manager, played Montague Jolliffe in the London production. In 1887 Terry opened his own theatre, Terry's (see Mander and Mitchenson, *Lost Theatres of London*, pp. 506–517), where several of Pinero's plays were staged, most notably *Sweet Lavender* (21 March 1888), which ran for 684 performances.

Pinero's "comedy of modern English manners" was *The Weaker Sex*, which was never produced at the St. James's for the reasons Pinero gives in letter 68. It was eventually staged at the Theatre Royal, Manchester, on 28 September 1888, with a revised version appearing at the Court on 16 March 1889. Pinero married Myra Emily Moore (d. 1919) on 19 April 1883. She was formerly an actress under the name of Myra Holme, and for a time was a member of the Lyceum Company.]

My dear Mr. Daly.

Your kind letter reached me this afternoon. I answered your cable about the music of *Lords and Commons*. The music of the song I sent you with the M.S. Don't forget to return me the printed book of the play when you have quite done with it.

In Chancery.

I have not settled this for America yet as I am waiting the conclusion of Mr. Terry's arrangements. In any event I am afraid the play would be quite useless to you. It plays only two hours and affords no opportunity but to the low comedian. The piece is a great success in our provinces and we shall do it in London about Christmas. If Terry does not take it to America I had better I think dispose of it to a travelling American star. What do you think of your Mr. Nat Godwin whose name has been mentioned to me? Is he a good actor and a responsible man?

German plays.

Thank you for your kind offer. Will you entrust me with literal translations of such of these plays as you yourself believe in? I have no knowledge of the German language, but in any case it would be upon the spirit and not upon the letter of the original that I should found my labor. I agree with you that what is wanted is an equal proportion of comedy to serious interest. If you send me the plays I will let you know very quickly which, if any, of them appeal to my method—and should I see my way clear I would write you a letter embracing the terms of our agreement. Have you a Right in plays (a right of legal protection) for America and England? I suppose this is impossible. Your offer of 5% of your gross American receipts is very fair, but do you not think that an *equal* division of English results is less so? However, the days are early for this discussion.

I am very interested and anxious about your production of *Lords and Commons*. Pray heaven it may not be too substantial for these flimsy times! Don't spare the knife where you think it can be used without sacrifice of sense and effect.
If this reaches you before the production, send me a short cable after the performance with the result of the first night. At my expense, of course.

I have just finished an original three act comedy of modern English manners—I think a good play. It is written for the St. James's and is approved of, *but* (between ourselves) there is a little hitch. The part (a fine one) intended for Mrs. Kendal is that of a woman of 35 or thereabouts with a grown up daughter. You guess the difficulty? Oh, vanity of woman! I will let you know the result of things, as the play, which, at present, I believe in, might turn out to suit you. / Mrs. Pinero joins me in every good wish and very kindest regards. / Faithfully yours, / Arthur W. Pinero.

48. TO S. B. BANCROFT

[Ax/11(ii); Pe/21; Pe/27] 10 Marlborough Crescent, / Bedford Park, / Chiswick.   29th. Octr. 1884.
[The Bancrofts announced their retirement from management for the end of their 1884–1885 season by sending letters to those close friends and associates who would obviously be interested in such news. (See also letters 54 and 55.)]

My dear Bancroft.

I write a few words, immediately, upon receipt of your letter—words written upon impulse, and full of real emotion at the news you break to me in such a kind and friendly manner.

It is my opinion, expressed here as it is elsewhere, that the present advanced condition of the English stage; throwing as it does a clear natural light upon the manners of life and people, where a few years ago there was nothing but mouthing and tinsel; is due to the crusade begun by Mrs. Bancroft and yourself in your "little Prince of Wales's Theatre." When the history of the stage and its progress is adequately and faithfully written Mrs. Bancroft's name and your own must be recorded with honour and gratitude.

I am greatly shocked at the news your letter gives me and hope by-and-by to be better able to express my feelings. Apart from the general importance of the announcement you make, I have private interests which resolve themselves into a few words—the hope that nothing, no change in the Haymarket Theatre or out of it, will ever rob me of two of the best friends I have ever had or can ever hope to have.

My wife begs that I will couple her name with mine in sending the very warmest wishes for the happiness of Mrs. Bancroft & yourself. / Yours ever sincerely / Arthur W. Pinero.

49. TO AUGUSTIN DALY

[Ax/6] 10 Marlborough Crescent, / Bedford Park, / Chiswick.

9th. Decr. 1884.

[Arthur Elwood (1850–1903), an actor, was helped by Daly when he had been left financially stranded in New York. Elwood had played Capt. Jesmond Ryle in Pinero's *The Rector* and later played Lövborg in Henrik Johan Ibsen's (1828–1906) *Hedda Gabler* (Vaudeville, 20 April 1891). Sir Charles Henry Hawtrey (1858–1923; knighted 1922) was an actor, manager, and dramatist, especially noted for light comedy. His *The Private Secretary* opened at the Prince's on 29 March 1884 and transferred to the Globe on 19 May 1884; it ran for 785 performances. It played for 200 performances at the Madison Square, New York, where it opened on 29 September 1884. Both W. J. Hill (1834–1888) and William Sydney Penley (1852–1912) acted in *The Private Secretary* at the Globe. Penley went on to play Lord Fancourt

Babberley in Walter Brandon Thomas's (1856–1914) *Charley's Aunt* (Royalty, 21 December 1892) which ran for 1466 performances; in 1900 he managed the Novelty Theatre under the name of the Great Queen Street Theatre. Nothing came of the notion of a play for the Bancrofts at the Haymarket.]

My dear Mr. Daly.

I am very much obliged to you for your kind note of the 28th. Novr. As you suggest I will delay our "squaring up" until the next transaction occurs between us—an occasion, I trust, not far hence and full of profit and credit to both of us. I have made a note of my indebtedness to you—£28.18., fees overpaid on *Lords and Commons*, and £5 advanced to my friend Elwood.

You know, of course, of the success of *The Private Secretary* in London, a success which report says is repeated at the Madison Square theatre. I know little of the merits of this play—having seen only an act of it. It was a failure when first produced here; "they say" it has been built into an entertaining piece by time and the players. Now *The Private Secretary* will not run for ever, and I have already had a hint from the Management of the Globe Theatre that it would be glad of something suitable from me. I put it to you, is there anything amongst your German plays which could be made to assume the shape of a successor to *The P____S*, and if so will you let me try my luck with it on the terms set out in your letter of Octr. 9th? Carry in your mind, if you will, the peculiarities of fat Mr. Hill and little Mr. Penley—to suit them, with parts in strong contrast, is made a point at the Globe.

Bancroft too wants a play for the Haymarket—has spoken to me on the subject. This must be a good bright comedy with a part for Mrs. Bancroft, a rattling widow or something of that kind. / With kind regards / Sincerely Yours, / Arthur W. Pinero.

50. TO AUGUSTIN DALY

[Ax/6] 10 Marlborough Crescent, / Bedford Park, / Chiswick.

24th. March 1885.

[In letters 50, 52, and 53, Pinero negotiates the various matters concerning the production of *The Magistrate* in New York. The play was staged at Daly's on 7 October 1885 under Pinero's personal supervision and he made a curtain speech on the opening night. The actors and actresses mentioned were all members of Daly's regular company.]

My dear Mr. Daly.

My new comedy *The Magistrate* produced last Saturday is an enormous success. I send you a few notices—unfortunately I cannot send the best (*The Times* &c) for I have not got them in duplicate. But you will be able to judge of the play from the few I do send.

I am much pressed by the American folks here but consider myself bound to make you the first offer. May I ask you to cable me in reply?

I propose—if you see your way clear—that you make the piece your opening play next season, that you give me the same per centage as on *Lords & Commons*, advancing fees £150 (less my debt to you) and that you pay the fares of a man to explain the action of the play—movement &c not discernible on paper. In this case I think I can get John Clayton to come over to you, by way of a holiday. Don't think I want to send you a *Stage Manager*! But the action is intricate and I fear beyond description in a prompt book.

There are parts for Miss Rehan (Mrs. John Wood's part), Miss [Virginia] Dreher, [James] Lewis, [Charles] Fisher, &c. &c. &c. / Please cable. / Hastily Yrs. / Arthur W. Pinero.

51. TO MOY THOMAS

[Ax/5] 10 Marlborough Crescent, / Bedford Park, / Chiswick.

2nd. April 1885.
[W. Moy Thomas (1829–1910) was drama critic of the *Daily News*. Pinero's "new departure" was *The Magistrate*.]

My dear Sir.

Mr. John Clayton—whom I was with to-day—thinks you might care to acquaint the readers of your theatrical column with the nature of the public response to our "new departure" (if it be one) at the Court Theatre.

Will you therefore allow me to tell you that the present demand for seats is quite unprecedented in the history of that house—and that

during even this, passion, week (one of the worst in the theatrical season) the theatre is nightly crammed to its utmost capacity. / I am, my dear Sir, / Very truly yours, / Arthur W. Pinero.
Moy Thomas Esq.

52. TO AUGUSTIN DALY

[Ax/6] 10 Marlborough Crescent, / Bedford Park, / Chiswick.

7th. April 1885.

[Cis Farringdon was eventually played by an "imported" English actor, Edward Hamilton Bell (d. 1929?). Daly's version of Von Moser's *The Sabine Women* was *A Night Off* (Daly's, New York, 4 March 1885; Strand, 27 May 1886).]

My dear Mr. Daly.

I was very glad to receive your second cablegram expressing your willingness to take *The Magistrate*. I think you have a good thing—I know that (I speak from a commercial point of view and therefore may be forgiven for saying it) you have the comedy success of our season. I was compelled to wire you as I did because I have been driven half mad with offers from the States, including some of a most liberal kind which—were I to tell you them—would not make you less appreciative of the right of producing the play.

To state our position clearly, for our guidance in the future—you agree to open your next season with *The Magistrate* and to pay me seven per cent upon your gross receipts. You make an advance upon these fees of £150 (less my debt to you) and you agree to defray the expences of someone to illustrate to you my notions of the movement of the piece. As the play is produced here under my sole direction and is animated with the life and character I have instilled into it, I think it of vital moment that the same spirit should be infused into the New York production. As I said in my last, I hope you will not misunderstand me in this—if I produced one of your plays here I should consider it of the first moment to realize your original intentions.

I have told you that the play gives opportunity for Mr. Lewis, Mr. Fisher, Miss Dreher, and Miss Rehan—to these I think we may add Mr. Gilbert, Mr. Leclercq and, perhaps, Mr. Drew. The small parts—admirably done here—require great finish, and the character of the Boy, upon the proper presentation of which the success of the play in a great measure depends requires special consideration. When you read the piece you will see that "Cis Farringdon" must be quite a boy—pleasant in appearance and fresh and ingenuous in manner. He must *look* but 14 and *act* like a young man of 20. If you cannot put your hand upon this commodity in your country I think it will be worth your while to get me to send you out a young actor from here.

You shall have a prompt book as soon as I can get one prepared. I will, in due course, send also small models of the scenes. These are very simple—three interiors.

Although I have stipulated that you open your season with *The Magistrate* I look to you to advise me on this subject—I want the play done, of course, at the most favorable moment. As I have said, I think we have a good thing and one that will repay us for previous disappointments. In the event of a New York success, which I am sanguine enough to anticipate, I shall depend on you to make *The Magistrate* a substantial concern in your "provinces."

Excuse my long letter. Mrs. Pinero joins me in kindest regards to you / Faithfully yours, / Arthur W. Pinero.
Augustin Daly Esq.
P.S. I have not succeeded in settling *The Sabine Women*. I am very pleased to read of the conspicuous success your version has met with. Here, I am handicapped by the terms which I am obliged to ask—the managers pull long faces. Mr. Hawtrey (of *Private Secretary* repute) has however asked me to keep the play for him. Ought I to read yr. version? Would yr. play do for our theatres? Let me know yr. views.

The Big Bell I have not yet had time to read—will do so shortly. / AWP.

53. TO AUGUSTIN DALY

[Ax/6] 10 Marlborough Crescent, / Bedford Park, / Chiswick.

23rd. May 1885.
[As well as managing Daly's visit to Toole's in 1884, William Terriss arranged his visit to the Strand in 1886.]

My dear **Daly**.

I have sent you, by registered Book post, the prompt book of *The Magistrate*. It is written in a rather slovenly manner, but one is in the hands of the prompter of the theatre; and I thought there was hardly time to have it re-copied. It is however, so far as it goes, quite correct. If I come out to you I shall be able to explain anything that is not quite clear.

In about a week's time I will send you the models and some photographs of characters and situations. The cast *I* have had in my mind is

Posket . . . . Mr. Lewis.
Lukyn . . . . Mr. Fisher.
Agatha . . . . Miss Rehan.
Isidore . . . . Mr. Gilbert.
Blond . . . . Mr. Leclercq.

All the smaller parts are most important & have well repaid the actors here. The character of Vale—played as an ultra languid and feeble young officer—is very effective in London. Would your Mr. Drew care to do it? The proper performance of *Cis* is of vital moment. If you have no one by you who looks about 15 and yet has the experience of a thorough actor I can send you such a person in *Mr. Edward H. Bell* who was originally selected for the part in London but was prevented from playing it through another engagement. You would find Mr. Bell a serviceable actor *all round* if you would care to try him. Charlotte is a capital part, in the action. I am much obliged to you for your remittance of £119.7.0. which represents the advanced fees of *The Magistrate* £150 less my debt to you of $166.97. Your draft came to hand to-day. / With Kindest regards from Mrs. Pinero and myself. / Faithfully Yours, / Arthur W. Pinero.
P.S. I was only too pleased to be asked to send your message on to Terriss. I hope you have settled the arrangements for your next visit quite satisfactorily.

They are going to do my *In Chancery* at the Madison Square Theatre. My anticipations are not very sanguine. It is a sketchy little piece written to suit the manner of a particular star [Terry], without whom, I fear, the thing will crumble. If this happens please don't be nervous with regard to *The Magistrate*, which you will find comes well together on the stage. / P.

54. TO S. B. BANCROFT

[Ax/11(ii)] 10 Marlborough Crescent, / Bedford Park, / Chiswick.
4th. July 1885.
[Pinero played the role of Adolphus Spanker in *London Assurance* as part of the Bancrofts' farewell performance at the Haymarket on 20 July 1885.]

My dear Bancroft
I will do the little bit of "Spanker" on the 20th. with great pleasure.
On the 22nd. also make any use of me you please: you will perhaps let me know beforehand to what toast you wish me to speak. / Yours ever / Arthur W. Pinero.

55. TO S. B. BANCROFT

[Ax/11(ii)] 10 Marlborough Crescent, / Bedford Park, / Chiswick.
21st. July 1885.

My dear Bancroft.
Mrs. Pinero joins me in thanking you warmly for your kindness in enabling us to be present at the Farewell of last night. We shall never forget the occasion nor the scene: it is not, I think, possible for any theatrical event of like importance and impressiveness to again occur in our lifetime, and the slightest detail will hold a well-guarded place in our memories.
We send our best wishes for a very pleasant Holiday for Mrs. Bancroft and yourself—a happy rest, not too protracted! / Sincerely yours, / Arthur W. Pinero.
S. B. Bancroft, Esq.

56. TO R. M. FIELD

[Ax/11(i)] 64 St. John's Wood Road, / NW.   6th. Novr. 1885.
[As became usual practice, Field reported to Pinero on the reception of his current play at the Boston Museum; here *The Magistrate*.]

My dear Mr. Field.

A line in great haste to tell you how pleased I am at the news contained in yours of Octr. 20th. It gives me great satisfaction to think that *The Magistrate* may help to reward you for the pains bestowed upon other and less successful plays of mine.

I am naturally a little disappointed at the short run you are able to give *The Magistrate* but I hope you will contrive to revive it. I think you told me you are managing the piece through the New England States? I hope this is so.

I respond gladly to your wish that we may together be connected with many great successes. Yes—I received yr. kind telegram and have been going day after day to acknowledge it.

Please notice that I have just tumbled into my new house. Can I plead a better excuse for my remissness. / With best regards, believe me / Faithfully yours, / Arthur W. Pinero.

P.S. Please thank your Company on my behalf for the great service they have rendered me. I wish I could have seen them act the piece. / P.

57. TO AUGUSTIN DALY

[Ax/6] 64 St. John's Wood Road, / NW.   8th. Novr. 1885.
[Daly had sent Pinero a copy of a play, *The Test Arrow*, to evaluate its suitability for staging at the St. James's as part of the "American proposition." The latter was a suggestion that Daly's Company and the St. James's Company should exchange theatres for a short season, but the idea fell through.

Charles Eyre Pascoe (1842–1912) was a theatre historian, most notably as editor of *The Dramatic List: A Record of the Performances of Living Actors and Actresses of the British Stage*, 2 eds. (London, 1879 and 1880).]

My dear Daly.

I have received your letter, addressed to the St. James's, enclosing draft for £291.3.6. fees on The Magistrate for New York and Boston up to Octr. 24th. I am delighted with the returns—for my own sake and for the sake of those who have worked so well and heartily for me in America.

Since writing you I have found *The Test Arrow*. I have lent it to Hare to look through, as a matter affecting the American proposition. I have an appointment with Hare & Kendal next Wednesday night on this subject and will write you on Thursday, again. Things have been so mixed at the St. James's during the past week that I have not been able to get at the St. James's people earlier on other business than *Mayfair*. The new play has had a most severe reception at the hands of the Press, and the public is rubbing its eyes in wonder at Mrs. Kendal playing a woman who is not absolutely circumspect. Mrs. Kendal, as you know perhaps, occupies a peculiar position with us as a personification of all the virtues. However, last night there was not a seat to be had in the theatre, so at least we are being tried fairly. It now depends on whether or not the play is too "unpleasant" for the audiences.

Mrs. Pinero desires me to thank you for your kind promise respecting the photographs. They will have great interest for us. Mrs. P. has written to Mrs. Daly to-night. / With our kindest regards. / Sincerely Yours, / Arthur W. Pinero.
P.S. Mr. Pascoe has written me for particulars of your company. I have answered his letter with especial reference to your performances of old English comedy.

58. TO AUGUSTIN DALY

[Ax/6] 64 St. John's Wood Road, / NW.   1st. April 1886.
[*The Schoolmistress*, in fact, was staged at the Standard, New York, on 7 December 1886, and not by Daly. Rose Norreys (1864–1946) acted in all three early "Court farces" (*The Magistrate, The Schoolmistress,* and *Dandy Dick*) as well as *Sweet Lavender*. Daly's play *Nancy and Co.* was produced at Daly's, New York, on 24 February 1886 and the Strand on 7 July 1886. *Larks,* by J. Wilton Jones (1854–1897), was produced at the Pavilion, Southport, on 22 February 1886 and the Grand, Islington, on 29 March 1886.]

My dear Daly.

I duly received your Cablegram asking me to hold *The Schoolmistress* for you and I sent you an answer All Right. Up to the present the play is a greater go than *The Magistrate*—that is, our houses have as yet beaten those of the early days of *The Magistrate*. Unfortunately Mrs. Wood met with a slight accident last night and cannot play this evening (with every seat sold and Royalty coming) but I hope she will be right tomorrow and that the unfortunate affair will not check our booking. Miss Norreys ("Peggy") has made *the* hit of the piece, however.

As regard naming any guarantee, my dear Daly, (which you ask me to do) I don't think that is necessary in the present instance. I will simply keep the play for you—you will see it for yourself when you are over here and if you think it too light for your theatre then we can arrange between us to do it at another theatre in New York. All I shall expect of you is that if you don't produce it at your house you will help me in getting it out at another. I have an offer from the Madison Square theatre which I shall, of course decline—I mention this because it would be a good house for it if you consider yours unsuitable, and we might fix it up there by-and-by. I need not say however that I should prefer *you* to do it.

You will, I am sure, see from what I have written that my object is to work strictly in harmony with you and your ideas for our joint advantage and profit.

―――――――――――

I have not yet, I think, acknowledged your letters of Feby. 20, March 2 and March 16 which I do now with many thanks for the remittances enclosed in each. Accept my hearty congratulations on your success with *Nancy & Co*. I am glad to be able to tell you that *Larks* (the wretched play of which I sent you an account) is being done this week (six nights only) at the Grand Theatre Islington. This is a third rate outlying theatre, where *the* Playgoers do not visit, and no press notices have appeared. But this means, of course, that the play has been *done* here. Nobody being the wiser for the event it is the most satisfactory end to the affair we could have looked for. / Kindest regards to Mrs. Daly & yourself from both of us / Sincerely Yours / Arthur W. Pinero.

59. TO AUGUSTIN DALY

[Ax/6] 64 St. John's Wood Road, / NW.   20th. Sepr. 1886.

[As with other new pieces, Pinero and Daly discussed the possibility of staging *The Hobby-Horse* (St. James's, 23 October 1886) at Daly's New York theatre—this is the "piece" mentioned here (see also letters 61 and 62). There was some delay in negotiations because Hare was uncertain whether he could visit America and whether he would want to produce *The Hobby-Horse* there. (He did, eventually, but not until 4 January 1897 at the Knickerbocker.) Another complication was a request from Daly to alter the play to suit his company; Pinero refused saying, "Not that yr. proposition is in the slightest degree unreasonable—but I cannot tinker a play—never could—never shall be able to. All the pieces I write are the result of long consideration and when they are done, they are done, and I can't look at them again" ([Ax/6], 1 February 1887).

W. Harford, a scene-painter, was also responsible for other sets for Pinero, especially for *Iris*. Herbert Waring (Rutty; 1857–1932) appeared in many of Pinero's plays and also took the role of Torvald Helmer in Ibsen's *A Doll's House* (Novelty, 7 June 1889). Otis Skinner (1858–1942), a leading American actor, was with Daly in the 1880s.]

My dear Daly.

Mr. Harford, the scene painter, says I must be mistaken in asking for the colours of Act III as the model of that act is in colour. Act II was not coloured and of that act I now send a sketch of the treatment. The colouring of Act III represents yellow silk stuff on the walls while the window frames and architraves are oak. In thinking you have the colours of Act III cable me the word "colour" and I will repair the omission.

I commence rehearsing the piece the day after tomorrow at Liverpool—we produce Oct. 23rd. Kendal, who has been acting doleful parts lately, will play "Pinching" and Mr. Waring (whose position in the St. James's Compy. bears some analogy to Mr. Skinner's in yours) will do the Curate. We are having great difficulty in casting the part of "Tom Clark"—he is not in the St. James's Compy. and I don't see him in yours. The part wants a very bright handsome young fellow of about 21.

Send me a little memorandum of terms for this play—something on half a sheet of note paper to keep in my safe. Can you afford a little increase in the per centage for this play? I know your expenses are heavy—will you give me an increased per centage where the business rises above a certain amount, so that I may benefit in case we get a good success?

You shall have the book at the earliest possible date. Can you help me to a title? At present we have got as far as "Philanthropy." This of course is the *meaning* of the play, but it is an uninteresting title. / Yrs / A. W. Pinero.

60. TO H. A. JONES

[Ax/10; Pe/40] 64 St. John's Wood Road, / NW.   24th. Oct. 1886. [Jones congratulated Pinero on the production of *The Hobby-Horse*, staged the previous evening at the St. James's. Pinero's new "job" was to be *Dandy Dick*.]

My dear Jones.

A few words to thank you and Mrs. Jones for your kind thought of me yesterday. The play is out, thank goodness, and this morning I am a frivolous light-hearted creature. What the work is worth, commercially, the Box Office alone can show—last night the better parts of the house applauded, the gallery boo-hood—in the same style, the *Observer* notices us appreciatively, and a paper called *Reyno[ld]s* says the piece is *Rot*. However, the dear thing is a favourite child of mine—though perhaps like many favourite children it may die young.

You are hard at it, my dear Jones, I know—you always are. Good luck attend you. I start on a job at once and think of going to the Isle of Wight—but I hope to be present on your first "first night," though a fellow feeling makes other people's first nights almost as uncomfortable as my own.

My wife joins me in all kind messages to Mrs. Jones. Believe me / Ever yours sincerely / Arthur W. Pinero.
Henry Ar: Jones Esq.

61. TO AUGUSTIN DALY

[Ax/6] 64 St. John's Wood Road, / NW.   29th. Octr. 1886.
[The "Court play" was *Dandy Dick*.]

My dear Daly.

I yesterday sent you the prompt book of *The Hobby-Horse* and notified you by cable that I had done so. The piece is very much talked about and from a literary standpoint does everything I intended it to do. What hold it will obtain on the general public it is impossible for me to say—up to the present we are doing excellently. I have just had a letter from Hare in which he says—

"House to-night nearly £200, good booking and piece going very well"

£200, I may tell you is very nearly the maximum at the St. James's.

Mrs. Kendal has disappointed me very much in "Diana Jermyn." On the first night she was alternately tragic and broadly comic. The part simply wants acting with a high comedy earnestness from start to finish. I should think that Miss Rehan's spirit of unconscious drollery is just what is needed: she should be admirable. "Pinching" is a very amusing character and if Drew would play it it would be more effective with you than with us. Lewis is just suited, I think, in "Jermyn," as is Skinner in "Brice." But I do not see anything like "Tom Clark" in your company. He must be a lad—half boy, half man, about 20—full of spirits and impulsiveness. Perhaps you see your way out of the difficulty.

I am now going to start on the Court play—goodness knows what I'm going to write.

What about *The Schoolmistress*—I read somewhere that she had started in Toronto. Is this so? / Our kindest regards, / Yrs ever / Arthur W. Pinero.

62. TO AUGUSTIN DALY

[Ax/6] 64 St. John's Wood Road, / NW.   22nd. Decr. 1886.
[*The Schoolmistress* was produced at the Standard, New York, on 7 December 1886 with Rosina Vokes (Mrs. Cecil Clay; 1855–1894) as Peggy Hesslerigge.]

My dear Daly.

Thank you very much for delaying the production of *The Hobby-Horse* till I can come out. I think the play needs my personal direction—as your own plays need yours—to give it the exact tone. Whether the piece as a piece, and played correctly, is at all calculated to please your public is a question quite beyond me. If you think it is *not* I beg of you to be quite candid and tell me so. We always act quite openly with each other and I am willing to defer to your judgment. For the present all I can say is that I will come over to help at rehearsals if you think the piece is likely to repay us all for the trouble and expense. If, on the other hand, your faith is weak pray save me the long journey & yourself the responsibility of producing the play. I take it that it is to the interest of us both that we only play pretty sure cards. I have none of the small vanities of an author, I hope and think.

I am about to start on the last act of the Court piece and I hope to get it out by the end of January at latest. I can't tell you whether it will do—you shall know all about it later on.

What is *The Schoolmistress* doing? I received a New York paper this morning by which it appears that Miss Vokes has played "Peggy" in New York after all. The piece is a weak fragile thing but, as an entertainment, it shd. do fairly well if it recovers from the knock down blow which it received from its inauspicious start.

Pray accept our good wishes for a prosperous and happy year, my dear Daly, and convey the kindest regards of myself & my wife to Mrs. Daly. / Believe me, / Yours always / Arthur W. Pinero.
P.S. *The Hobby-Horse*, acted now some 60 odd times, is doing well, considering we are in the midst of the holiday times which are very bad for the comedy houses. It pleases the upper classes better than the pit.
Augustin Daly.

63. TO H. A. JONES

[Ax/8; Pe/38] Garrick Club.   28th. Jany. 1887.
[Pinero here refers to *Dandy Dick* and some last-minute hitch in its production. The play was preceded at 8:00 by a one-act play, *The Nettle* (Court, 13 October 1886), by Ernest Warren.]

My dear Jones.

In the first place—Mrs. Pinero asks me to tell you that she wrote
(I fancy yesterday) to you and to Mrs. Jones, addressing her missives
to the hotel in Cecil St. They will reach you at some time or another.

For my own part, accept my hearty thanks for the kind message
you sent me. Give my warmest acknowledgments to Mrs. Jones and
to Mr. and Mrs. Hatton. You did well not to come to Town—I don't
remember such an hour as we had last night, from 7 to 8. However,
with a somewhat curtailed but a very good tempered audience at the
Court, we got safely thro' our difficulties.

I hope to see you soon that I may be able to thank you for many
kindnesses.

Our best regards to you and to Mrs. Jones, with kisses to Myra.
Believe me, / Yrs ever / Arthur W. Pinero.
Henry Arthur Jones Esq.

64. TO H. A. JONES

[Ax/10; Pe/29; Pe/40] Hotel Royal Danieli, / Venice.

17th. April 1887.

[Current theatrical events on both sides of the English Channel were of
continued interest to both Pinero and Jones. This visit to the continent
was typical of many made by Pinero.

Francillon by Dumas fils was produced at the Comédie-Français,
Paris, on 17 January 1887. *Held by the Enemy* by William Gillette
(1855–1937) was produced at the Princess's on 2 April 1887. Jones's
Vaudeville play was *Heart of Hearts* produced on 3 November 1887.
Also produced at the Vaudeville, on 3 July 1883, was James Schonberg's
adaptation *Narcisse the Vagrant*.]

My dear Jones.

Your right-welcome chatty letter is like the buz of a friendly voice
at the end of a Telephone: I don't think I have ever before admired
your handwriting so thoro'ly.

```
┌─────────────────────────────┐
│                             │
│        Mrs. P               │
│                             │
│     Returns Thanks          │
│                             │
│    for Kind enquiries       │
│                             │
└─────────────────────────────┘
```

Thank God, my wife, and the doctor, I am—save for an appetite I am obliged to conceal from Hotel and Restaurant proprietors: it is so awful— quite myself. Indeed I am much better than myself. I am convinced there is nothing like an occasional illness—so that it be a severe one—to set a man up and keep him in decent health. Furthermore, to be ill (if one is to be ill) on one's holiday is a good idea—it doesn't interrupt work. Altogether I am quite satisfied with myself, in my capacity of an Interesting Convalescent.

———————————

I wish we could all have met in Paris. We didn't see *Francillon* but I bought the book. I quite share your envy at the existence of an audience that can listen respect and learn. But, given the existence of such an audience, is *Francillon* worthy stuff to feed them with? Clever! To its very backbone, of course—but, what else? Nothing more than any of our English plays—an Entertainment. Try to dignify it by deducing a moral; it can't be done. A woman maintains that a wife is justified in meeting her husband's infidelity with her own. The provocation is given, the lady affords but two hours entertainment— mostly of a conversational kind—and the curtain is rung down. The only moral here—a trite one—is that a woman never means what she says. For the play to have done something—to have taught something— the lady should have kept her word, lived happily ever afterwards or have ultimately died in the gutter: I haven't worked out the natural consequence of such an act. Yes—I admire the French audience—as an audience of listeners—as much as any man, but I sometimes wonder whether this model audience is illused by the stuff it is doctored with or (awful thought!) whether the model a[udience] creates the noxious dose it swallows so willingly.

I have read no accounts but good ones of *Held by the Enemy* and I am heartily glad to understand that you have an interest in its well-doing. Of course you are anxious about your Vaudeville play and will be more so as time advances. I wish you the safe deliverance I should wish myself under such circumstances—may you come up smiling.

Will you, for me, thank Mrs. Jones warmly for her kind note which I was pleased indeed to receive. I can, to my regret, say nothing for the moral character of *Narcissus* or for the propriety of his appearance—we depend however upon the vitiated tastes of two people who have been "going it" in Paris for the warmth of his reception.

We leave here on Wednesday for Milan, thence by Lucerne Basle and Paris for Home. I have, despite my illness, enjoyed myself but I am quite homesick—and business sick, for my letters &c &c are accumulating. We shall meet very soon I hope—till then Au Revoir; and accept, my dear Jones, my warmest thanks for the kind feeling which dictates your letter.

Mrs. Pinero joins me in all warm regards to Mrs. Jones. Believe me / Sincerely yours, / Arthur W. Pinero.
Henry Arthur Jones Esq.

65. TO THE EDITOR, THE *TIMES*

[Pp/37] Garrick Club.   Sept. 9 1887.
[Pinero's letter, published on 10 September 1887, p. 10, was prompted by the destruction of the New Theatre, Exeter, which burned down on 5 September 1887 with the loss of a hundred lives. Until the universal introduction of electricity as the means of lighting, the threat of fire in a theatre remained a constant, imminent danger.]

Sir,
    The destruction of the Exeter theatre is naturally producing so many plans for securing the safety of audiences that there seems to be a risk of the practicable being buried under the weight of the impracticable. It is in the hope that my proposal may survive this risk

that I venture to suggest a method for lessening in some degree the chances of panic.

It is admitted that when all known precautions for preserving the safety of playgoers are employed, when iron curtain, electric lighting, and numerous doorways are provided, there still remains the greatest danger—the confusion of a frightened body of people, with the possibility of loss of life even in the absence of a positive peril. To meet this danger it has always been the praiseworthy custom of the theatrical manager to print upon his bill of the play either a detailed statement of the facilities of egress or a diagram showing the means of exit afforded by the building. The fault of the first system is that a printed announcement of the fact that the occupants of a certain part of the house may disperse themselves through a special doorway leading to this court or to that alley may miss the mark altogether; in the moment of alarm the playgoer is likely to find that he has failed to possess himself of the information, or, having gained it, that he is ignorant of the geographical position of the localities mentioned or the doors which lead to them. The diagram system is equally delusive; the plan of the house is always a complicated affair, and at its best not likely to remain in the recollection of a fear-stricken person.

What I would venture to suggest is that it should be the duty of the manager or stage manager of the theatre to appear every night in front of the curtain, previous to the commencement of the principal play, for the purpose of explaining to all sections of the audience the available means of egress. This explanation, made clearly and formally, should be aided by the voices of the doorkeepers in the several parts of the house, each of whom when the particular door in his keeping is indicated should prove by the word "Here!" that he is at his post.

Extravagant as this plan may appear at first glance, I cannot help thinking that it is the best in the field for carrying straight to the minds of audiences the actual position of the doors of the theatre. It would inform playgoers directly of the extent of the precautions taken on their behalf; it would keep the manager constantly alert; and, while it tended to allay apprehension during the performance of the play, in the event of accident the likelihood of blind panic would be considerably modified. / I am, Sir, your obedient servant, / ARTHUR W. PINERO.

94

66. TO AUGUSTIN DALY

[Ax/6] 64 St. John's Wood Road, / NW.   18th. Sept. 1887.
[Pinero held back *The Profligate* for the opening of John Hare's new theatre, the Garrick, on 24 April 1889. The play was not produced by Daly.]

My dear Daly.

Since writing you my letter of a few days ago, which I accompanied by a copy of my play *The Profligate*, I have entered into an arrangement to put the piece upon the shelf for about a year. My reason for doing this is that at that time I shall have an opportunity of producing it under favorable circumstances with regard to theatre and cast, and I consider it wiser to wait for this rather than risk a very delicate play amongst uncongenial surroundings.

The Profligate therefore is not—until after its production here—in the market and I shall be much obliged to you if, in the meantime, you will regard the fact of its existence as a confidential matter between ourselves. / With best regards, / Sincerely yours, / Arthur W. Pinero.
Augustin Daly Esq.

67. TO AUGUSTIN DALY

[Ax/6] 64 St. John's Wood Road, / NW.   19th Octr. 1887.
[Daly staged *Dandy Dick* in New York from 5 to 31 October 1887. Daly was also interested in Pinero's *The Squire* and *The Weaker Sex* (referred to here as *Comedy*). *The Squire* was revived by Hare and Kendal at the St. James's on 16 June 1888, by Daly in New York on 19 February 1889, and by the Kendals at the Fifth Avenue, New York, on 13 October 1890. On *The Weaker Sex* see letters 47 and 68.]

My dear Daly.

I am sorry to hear that the second night of *Dandy Dick* did not carry out the promise of the first: I hope however, and shall hope till I know to the contrary, that the piece has rallied & that it may yet prove a success. Clayton, who plays the Dean here and for whom the part was written, acts it with such unction and irresistible good humour that the notion of an eminent cleric in trouble has never offended our audiences. Perhaps Mr. Fisher is a little too serious and sentimental. But however that may be I can quite understand that certain types of character drawn specially for an English audience lose much by being transplanted and I expect the Dean and Mrs. Tidman are strange monstrosities to your people. Mrs. Tidman here is understood to bear some resemblance to our Duchess of Montrose whose racing name is "Mr. Manton." As I have said I hope *Dandy Dick* has sufficient buoyancy to make a fair success with you yet. I am quite sure you have done everything in your power to make it a "go" and that you have been staunchly aided by your company.

The Profligate.

I am extremely pleased that you think so well of this play and thank you very heartily for your suggestions which I will bear in mind. I fear I can make no structural alterations but I will keep my eye on the sermonizing propensities of the heroine and on the hurrying up of the climax to Act III, at rehearsal. The piece will be produced (as I think I told you) at the beginning of next season.

The Squire.

I have already written you about this.

The Magistrate.

Yes—I think I may well take a weekly royalty now, relying upon you that it shall be a fair one. Many thanks for your trouble.

Comedy.

I will send this out to you within the next fortnight.

Hoping to hear better news in your next, believe me / Sincerely yours, / Arthur W. Pinero.
Augustin Daly Esq.

68. TO AUGUSTIN DALY

[Ax/6] 64 St. John's Wood Road, / NW.   3rd. Novr. 1887.
[Daly did not produce *The Weaker Sex* because the Kendals were given the American rights to it and staged it at the Fifth Avenue, New York, on 17 February 1890.

Pinero's "new play" was *The Cabinet Minister*, produced at the Court on 23 April 1890. (The new Court Theatre opened on 24 September 1888.) The same play was a failure at Daly's, New York, running only from 12 to 18 January 1892.]

My dear Daly.

By registered Post I send you the comedy I have mentioned in
my letters—*The Weaker Sex*. I think you will consider there is some
good in it but, as I wrote it three or four years ago, the material is not
used perhaps as dexterously as it might be.

The history of the piece is this—it was done for the St. James's
theatre and accepted by Hare & Kendal. Shortly afterwards Kendal
found among a bundle of plays sent to the theatre one containing a
plot (the complication of the love of mother & daughter) which bore a
resemblance to mine. He communicated the circumstance to me and
I instantly withdrew my play from the theatre, not caring for a
repetition of *The Squire* annoyance where the author of a worthless
play used me as a medium for advertising his unsaleable wares. I did
however shortly afterwards meet the author of the piece bearing a
likeness to mine, and who turned out a very civil fellow, and for our
mutual benefit we read each others plays. Structurally they resembled
each other—in treatment of course they were wholly dissimilar. We
exchanged letters acquitting each other of anything but being victims
of coincidence. Since that time my work has been lying in my desk, and,
as far as I know, his had shared the same fate. A few weeks ago I
unearthed *The Weaker Sex* and it struck me that if it contains any good
at all it shapes itself in the direction of yr. company:—

Lord Gillingham.	Fisher.
Bargas.	Lewis.
Dudley.	Drew.
Lee.	Skinner.
Green.	Gilbert.
Lady G.	Miss Dreher.
Lady Vivash.	Miss Rehan.
Mrs. B-Chewton.	Mrs. Gilbert.
Sylvia	Ingénue.
Rhoda	Ingénue.

This is my excuse for sending you a work which has faults enough
and to spare but in which you may discover some merit. You know
my infirmity—when I have done a play my critical faculty (if I have
any at all) entirely leaves me and out of the good and bad material I
know not which is the bad and which the good. If you can see yr. way

clear, by cuts and any other form of alteration, to improve *The Weaker Sex* I shall be glad to trust to yr. judgment. If you don't like it at all send it back to me.

———————————

I am about to start on my new play for the Court Theatre (the new Court, to be built opposite the old house). While it must be bright & amusing I shall try to make it less farcical than its predecessors and I shall keep yr. company in my mind. If I can keep out of it what is exclusively *English* I will do so—my notion at present is to do a play which while its basis is broadly humourous is in treatment natural and refined. One's intentions are always good—but, alas!— / Sincerely Yours, / Arthur W. Pinero.
Augustin Daly Esq.

69. TO CLEMENT SCOTT

[Ax/15(ii); P/25] 64 St. John's Wood Road, / NW.   16th Dec. 1887.
[Sir Charles Wyndham (1837–1919) was an actor, manager, and drama-tist; he managed the Criterion (1875–1899) and Wyndham's (see Ray-mond Mander and Joe Mitchenson, *The Theatres of London*, London, 1961, pp. 217–221). While at the Criterion Wyndham produced several of H. A. Jones's plays, *The Bauble Shop* (1893), *The Case of Rebellious Susan* (1894), *The Physician* (1897), and *The Liars* (1897). For a brief history of Wyndham's close association with Robertson's *David Garrick*, see Adams, *Dictionary of the Drama*, I, 381.]

Dear Scott.
I send you some extracts from the Hamburg papers referring to the production of *The Magistrate* in that city; the play has been done too in Vienna and in many other places in Germany, it seems always with success.

Perhaps you will think the matter of the connection between the English and German stages of sufficient importance for a line or two in your valuable dramatic notes.

The Gilbert and Sullivan operas have already made a stand in Germany—but there you have music which is a universal language. Wyndham has triumphed over many difficulties with *David Garrick*, but Davy comes to us from the French and to the French (I think) from

the German. *The Magistrate*, for what it is worth, is purely English and makes its way without aid from music or sensational effects of any kind. But the only importance it has in my mind is that it is the thin end of the wedge to open up some position for Englishmen on the German stage. The French keep us out—which considering the state of their stage just now they need not do for their own profit—and we are so busy in borrowing from the German that we forget to take our own wares to Berlin. But I hope the time will come—is coming—when the Englishman, like the Frenchman, will write his plays for all nations. The consciousness, when a man is writing a play, that he is working for the amusement of a few thousand middle-class English people, is not favourable to the development of Dramatic Art. That's why this German business seems of some importance—if the English writer's reach spreads, his thoughts might run out with his arm. Forgive this long scrawl. With best regards, I am / Faithfully yrs, / Arthur W. Pinero.
Clement Scott Esq.

70. TO H. A. JONES

[Ax/10; Pe/40] 64 St. John's Wood Road, / NW.   22nd. March 1888.
[Jones's congratulations were on the production, the previous evening, of *Sweet Lavender* (see headnote to letter 47).]

My dear Jones.
    Many hearty thanks to you and Mrs. Jones for the kind thought which prompted your telegram of yesterday. The play went well enough with its first audience—whether it will attract the public, in a substantial way, to the theatre I can't even guess. But it escaped immediate annihilation and I am thankful for small mercies. With kindest regards, believe me / Sincerely yours, / Arthur W. Pinero.
Henry A. Jones Esq.

71. TO T. MALCOLM WATSON

[Ax/12] 64 St. John's Wood Road, / NW.   3rd. April 1888.
[The two plays on which Pinero congratulated T. Malcolm Watson (1853–1929), a dramatist and drama critic of the *St. James's Gazette*,

Standard, and *Daily Telegraph,* were *Held Asunder* (Prince of Wales's, 3 April 1888) and *"Wanted, an Heir"* (St. George's Hall, 2 April 1888).]

Dear Sir.

I was glad to-day to see your play so attentively listened to and so well received. Mrs. Rowlands tells me that *Held Asunder* is your first work upon a large canvas: I can congratulate you upon the promise it gives and the encouragement its reception should hold out to you. I am pleased also to read of the success your smaller play has just met with at the St. George's Hall. / I am, Dear Sir / Faithfully yours, / Arthur W. Pinero.
T. Malcolm Watson Esq.

72. TO MRS. LEIGH MURRAY

[Ax/8(ii)] [64 St. John's Wood Road, / NW.]   1st. May 1888.
[Mrs. Elizabeth Leigh Murray (1815–1892) began her London career with Madame Vestris at the Olympic and the Haymarket. Her benefit was taken at the Haymarket on 9 May 1888 and included *The First Night* (Princess's, 1 October 1849) by Alfred Sydney Wigan (1814–1878). Lewis Wingfield (1842–1891) was a theatrical designer.]

Dear Madam.

Mr. Lewis Wingfield wrote to me a few days ago asking if I would play "The Author" in *The First Night* on the occasion of your Benefit. With great regret I begged to be excused because I felt that such an appearance on my part would not be in the best possible taste and therefore of no service to the object in view. In declining Mr. Wingfield's request I was however guided solely by my conviction that an actor should not under any circumstances play a part to which his recognized character off the stage lends the principal quality.

I trust that you will not misunderstand my action and that you will accept my assurance that I have every sympathy with the Benefit which is to be given to you—a Testimonial well earned by an honorable and distinguished career. / I am, dear madam / Yours most faithfully / Arthur W. Pinero.
Mrs. Leigh Murray.

73. TO WILLIAM ARCHER

[A/3(i)] 64 St. John's Wood Road, / NW.   11th. June 1888.
[William Archer (1856–1924), who became a lifelong and close friend
(and critic) of Pinero's, was a Scottish journalist and critic who worked
as a newspaper reporter in Edinburgh before moving to London in
1878. He was drama critic of *Figaro*, the *World*, *Tribune*, and the *Nation* and was largely responsible for introducing Ibsen into England,
besides promoting native English drama (his *English Dramatists of Today*, London, 1882, was a seminal work). Archer also wrote plays, his
most successful being *The Green Goddess* (St. James's, 6 September
1923). *The Squire* was revived at the St. James's on 16 June 1888.]

Dear Mr. Archer.

Mr. Hare asks me to send you the enclosed voucher for two stalls
for Saturday night and to say that he is extremely pleased to place the
seats at your disposal.

I know the criticism upon *The Squire* in *English Dramatists* very
well, and have naturally never suspected that it is not entirely your
own. But it is written as it were with your blood if not with your ink,
and I would almost rather that now-a-days you should not see the play.
Apart from its own faults it is hastily revived and where the cast is
new it is rough and perhaps unsuitable.

If Mrs. Archer would like a Box for a morning performance of
Sweet Lavender I can send it at once—the seats for the night
performances are gone for some time ahead. I am almost disappointed
that it is so since it keeps me from claiming the fulfilment for yr.
promise that you wd. see the piece again. However I will send seats
upon the first opportunity. In the meantime perhaps Mrs. Archer
might care to spend a Saturday afternoon at the theatre. / I am, / Most
faithfully yours, / Arthur W. Pinero.
William Archer Esq.

74. TO WILLIAM ARCHER

[A/3(i)] 64 St. John's Wood Road, / NW.   18th. June 1888.
[Typically, Archer sent Pinero his opinion of the revival of *The Squire*,
both encouraging and critical (see also letter 75). Pinero's reference
to Hardy's *Two on a Tower*, published 1882, recalls the plagiarism

controversy surrounding the original production of *The Squire* (see letters 32–37).]

Dear Mr. Archer.

Accept my hearty thanks for your kind and, to me, most interesting letter. I wont trouble you with a long reply, though I hope to have, someday, an opportunity of talking the matter over with you. It will satisfy my mind for the present to tell you that you do not detect in my play half the number of flaws which I feel it contains and which gave me many unhappy moments on Saturday night.

By-the-by (but please don't answer the question) have you ever read a novel by Mr. Thomas Hardy called *Two on a Tower*? But that I am sick to death of the question of my robbing Mr. Hardy I could contribute the fact of its existence as an interesting addendum to the old charge of plagiarism. *Two on a Tower*, born a year after *The Squire*, contains the central motive of my play—the unmarried wife and the coming baby—of which there is no hint in *Far from the Madding Crowd*. / I am, dear Mr. Archer / Most faithfully yours, / Arthur W. Pinero.
William Archer Esq.

75. TO WILLIAM ARCHER

[A/3(i)] 64 St. John's Wood Road, / NW.   Monday [18 June 1888?].
[Archer's criticism was directed at *Sweet Lavender* in which Maude Millett (1868–1920) played Minnie Gillfillian. She later played Ellean in *The Second Mrs. Tanqueray* (St. James's, 27 May 1893).]

Dear Mr. Archer.

Of course—you are quite right about *collapsed*. I think I felt how wrong it was when I wrote it but I wanted one word and *parted* seemed weak, so I put down *collapsed* and it escaped correction. I will change it directly I can. I fear Miss Millett wd. not be able to unlearn the error. Do you know of this peculiarity in actors and actresses? They can seldom put a mistake right after they have "studied" and rehearsed it. I ought to have reminded you of this when we had our talk about acting—it goes towards my theory I fancy; or doesn't it?

Please accept my thanks for your letter: I am gratified at yr. taking

so much interest in my work. / I am, dear Mr. Archer, / Sincerely yours, / Arthur W. Pinero.
Wm. Archer Esq.

76. TO HENRY IRVING

[A/4] Garrick Club, / WC.   19th. June 1888.
[Pinero, after leaving the Lyceum Company, remained a good friend of Irving's, often saw him perform, and wrote his impressions and opinions of Irving's work. Dame Ellen Terry (1848–1928), the famous actress and Irving's leading lady at the Lyceum beginning in December 1878, played Ellaline in *The Amber Heart* (Lyceum, 7 June 1887; revived special matinée, 23 May 1888) by Alfred Cecil Calmour (1857–1912). Irving played Macaire in *Robert Macaire* (Victoria, 3 December 1834; revived Lyceum, 23 May 1888) by Charles Selby (1802?–1863).]

Dear Irving.
    We are much indebted to you for your kind hospitality last night and for the favorable chance you afforded us of witnessing the delightful woes of "Ellaline" and the heroic mendacity of "Maccaire." For those who are willing to accept the dramatic remnants which make up the latter play for what they are, and not quarrel with them for what they are not—which is a favorite exercise of modern criticism—there is much in the drama to interest, to amuse, and at moments to absorb. Behind all the grim grotesqueness of your Maccaire there is a suggestion of real humanity which makes him a creature to be remembered; it is a thousand pities that the play gives you an opportunity only to suggest and not to embody. Believe me, with renewed thanks, to be / Most faithfully yours, / Arthur W. Pinero.
Henry Irving Esq.

77. TO H. A. JONES

[Ax/10; Pe/40] 64 St. John's Wood Road, / NW.   30th. Sept. 1888.
[Pinero's play was *The Weaker Sex* (see headnote to letter 47).]

My dear Jones.
    Accept my warmest thanks for your kind thought of me on Friday.

The piece was rapturously received by its audience and as ardently abused by the press on the following morning; I have left the poor thing to fight for its life between the two factions.

––––––––––––––––

I am disappointed to have missed you when you have called—we shall meet, I hope soon. Mrs. Pinero joins me in all kind messages to Mrs. Jones, and with best regards to you believe me to be / Sincerely yours / Arthur W. Pinero.
Henry Arthur Jones.

78. TO HENRY IRVING

[A/4] Marine View, / Rottingdean, / Sussex.   25th. Dec. 1888.
[Joseph Hurst was Irving's box-office manager. Irving revived *Macbeth* at the Lyceum on 29 December 1888.]

Dear Irving.
    Mr. Hurst has sent me on your behalf seats for the first performance of your revival of *Macbeth*. I have been surveying the occasion with longing eyes but being confined to work here had given up thoughts of being present. The temptation is however too strong for me and I intend coming to town for the night.
    I beg that with my thanks for your kind thought of us in this matter you will accept my earnest wishes for the success of the revival. I cannot conceive that there is anyone who does not wish it well. Those who regard the stage with distrust must see in this work at least the drama divested of everything they maintain to be harmful and meretricious, while the lovers of the stage must rejoice that in your production there is yet another reminder of the highest use and purpose of the theatre. / Believe me / Most faithfully yours, / Arthur W. Pinero.
Henry Irving Esq.

79. TO R. M. FIELD

[Ax/11(i)] 64 St. John's Wood Road, / NW.   1st. March 1889.
[This letter is one of several similar business letters between Pinero and Field. *Sweet Lavender* played at the Boston Museum in January

and February 1889, the year which marked Field's twenty-fifth anniversary as manager of the theatre.]

Dear Mr. Field.

Very many thanks for your letters of the 15th and 18th February, the latter with Returns and Draft (£70.3.5.) for the seventh week of *Sweet Lavender*. I am perfectly satisfied with the success of the play at your theatre and am glad that it has been an assistance—a creditable one, I hope—to you in your present season. I don't quite know when I shall next perpetrate another *serviceable* play—ie. one calculated to please all publics—but I hope it may not be long hence, in order that I may have the pleasure of doing business with you again soon. / Believe me / Sincerely yours / Arthur W. Pinero.

80. TO H. A. JONES

[Ax/10] 64 St. John's Wood Road, / NW.   25th. April 1889.
[Pinero here acknowledges Jones's letter of congratulation on the production of *The Profligate* at the Garrick. Jones's *Wealth* was produced at the Haymarket on 27 April 1889. Arthur Blunt or Blount was better known as Arthur Cecil (see headnote to letter 12).]

My dear Jones.

I was glad to receive your letter of the 24th. No sympathy is more precious than that which comes from the comrade beside whom one stands shoulder to shoulder.

It is a great regret to me that I cannot be at the Haymarket on Saturday night! I leave London on Saturday morning with Arthur Blunt for a two or three weeks jaunt in the country. But Mrs. Pinero will represent me and I shall look forward to a letter from her telling me of the complete success of your play. I shall be with you in thought and shall share some of your desires and anxieties.

Please thank Mrs. Jones for her kind note, and believe me to be, with every good wish for you both, / Sincerely yours / Arthur W. Pinero.
Henry Arthur Jones Esq.

81. TO CLEMENT SCOTT

[Pep/35] Weymouth.   7th. May 1889.
[Pinero's alteration of the ending of *The Profligate* had aroused some
debate in theatrical circles, and here he offers his explanation. His
letter was published in the *Theatre*, n.s. XIII (June 1889), 324–325.]

I feel that Mr. Hare, in his friendly anxiety to spare my shoulders,
has laid a burden upon his own which I am not justified in allowing
him to bear. The alteration of the ending of *The Profligate* was made
by me very willingly, and I am unfortunate if I conveyed to Mr. Hare
the impression that I was making any sacrifice of my convictions.
Indeed, I could never allow the consideration of mere expediency to
influence me in dealing with subjects upon which I feel deeply and
write with all the earnestness of which I am capable.

I had long settled the form of my play when a friend for whose
judgment I have great respect raised through Mr. Hare a question for
my consideration. Could not the moral I had set myself to illustrate
be enforced without distressing the audience by sacrificing the life of a
character whose sufferings were intended to win sympathy? Reflection
convinced me that such a course was not only possible but was one
which in no way tended to weaken the termination of my story, whilst
it promised to extend that story's influence over the larger body of the
public.

This sparing of the life of Renshaw has in no way distorted my
original scheme as it affected the other characters of the play. Murray's
love remains unrewarded; Janet suffers for her partnership in
Renshaw's sin, and passes away; Wilfrid's boyish passion shares the
fate of most boyish passions, and is left to become a memory; Renshaw
pronounces his own doom—than which not even the death penalty
could be heavier—in the speech which has for its burden "She knows
you!"—all these things are as I always intended they should be. The
forgiveness of Renshaw by Leslie was from the first part of my scheme,
and this softening of the wife towards her husband arises now, as it
did originally, through the good offices of Murray.

I am aware that in dealing with the destinies of many of the
characters in *The Profligate* I have not been guided by the usual and
often valuable mechanism of stagecraft; but it has been my purpose to
yield unresistingly to the higher impress of truth, and from the truths

of life as they appear to my eyes I have never wavered in any degree. /
I am, Sir, your obedient servant, / ARTHUR W. PINERO.

82. TO R. M. FIELD

[Ax/11(i)] White Hart Hotel, / Salisbury.   14th. May 1889.
[Even though *The Profligate* was a success in London, Pinero was re-
luctant to accept American offers to stage the piece, as letters 82–86
and 103 show.]

Dear Mr. Field.
        I owe you many apologies for allowing your letters to remain so
long unanswered. Immediately after ridding myself of *The Profligate*
I went into the country; I was much in need of rest and quiet and in
pursuit of this have felt bound to neglect my correspondence. Let me
now acknowledge your letters of April 11th, 15th, and 30th, the second
of which contained a draft for £23.11.5.
        The admirable photograph[s] duly reached me; I *acknowledged
them by letter immediately*. This letter must in some way have
miscarried. The pictures of *Sweet Lavender* in Boston have, I need
hardly say, great interest for me and they will always be a pleasant
reminder of our friendly dealings together.
        The Profligate is a great success in London. I think however that
in London will be found the beginning & the end of its popularity.
The London people have been led to expect such a play from me
by those who are good enough to believe that I can produce something
out of the beaten track of stagecraft, and *The Profligate* has been
welcomed with enthusiasm. I fear however that out of a London
theatre the play would not obtain a public large enough to reward
the great care and specially selected cast which will always be necessary
for its production.
        At present I do not, I am sorry to say, see anything coming from
my workshop which I shall be able to offer you for next season. But
you may rely upon me to let you have any play of mine at all likely
to serve the purpose of yr. theatre. I hope it will not be long before
we resume our pleasant business relations.
        With kindest regards to Mrs. Field and yourself, Believe me, /
Sincerely yours / Arthur W. Pinero.
R. M. Field Esq.

83. TO AUGUSTIN DALY

[Ax/6] Exeter, / Devon.   15th. May 1889.
My dear Daly.

I have been resting in the country since the production of *The Profligate* and have allowed my correspondence to get into arrear. I find therefore that I have not yet acknowledged your letters of April 3rd. and 15th., the former enclosing me draft for balance of *The Squire* fees, the latter a draft for German performances of *The Magistrate*. Many thanks. Your cablegram respecting *The Profligate* I acknowledged briefly.

As to your proposition with regard to a good brisk comic play, when I find myself in possession of one it will give me great pleasure to offer it to you. I wish I could set to work to construct and write such a piece with a view to the requirements of your theatre, but you will understand how many home claims there are upon me and I am desirous as my position becomes more assured and as only the best work is looked for from me to spare myself as much as possible. I have been writing original plays at the rate of two or three a year for nearly ten years. I want as soon as I am able to do so to restrict myself to one play a year and no more.

The Profligate.

I read in one of the theatrical papers that there is a chance of your coming to England for your holiday. Is this so? It would relieve my mind if you could see this play acted in London and then talk the matter over with me. I feel a great difficulty in making up my mind on the point of the advisability of representing *The Profligate* in America at all. The play is in some respects a pet child of mine and I am at any rate too fond of it to run the risk of an ignominious failure with it in America. The piece is a complete success in London— that you may have heard—but I feel that perhaps its success begins and ends here. It is not altogether well acted in London but I have been many months in getting together the cast, such as it is, and the labour of obtaining a respectable representation of the play has been great. Assuming that *The Profligate* is a work likely to suit yr. public I may be pardoned if under the circumstances I doubt the probability of obtaining a fitting representation for it without my direction. Perhaps therefore, my dear Daly, you will send me your views as to the cast of the play you would suggest for America. Do you propose to produce it at your own theatre? I cannot feel that yr. admirable company shapes in any way towards such a play.

As I have said I wish I could talk the matter over with you. In the meantime I know you will understand the motive which prompts me to write in this strain. It would be serving no good purpose, yours or mine, to produce *The Profligate* for the sake of producing it; and it would I am certain stand no chance of success without a most carefully selected cast and the completest interpretation of my views.

In the earlier part of this rambling note I find I have used the term "ignominious failure." I hope you will understand that I do not suggest that anything produced under yr. management and interpreted by yr. company deserves such a fate. I merely wish to emphasize the risk that *The Profligate* runs of being totally misunderstood by your public. / Sincerely Yours / Arthur W. Pinero.
Augustin Daly Esq.

84. TO R. M. FIELD

[Ax/15(i)] 64 St. John's Wood Road, / NW.   26th May 1889.
Dear Mr. Field.

Many thanks for your letter of the 14th enclosing me a draft for £19.18.7. which winds up the New England Tour of *Sweet Lavender*. I sincerely trust that no loss has befallen any person concerned.

The Profligate.

I have already written you on this subject. My fear is that nothing but possibly an artistic success could arise from the production of this play and that only in the event of its representation by a carefully selected cast. The piece is an entirely serious one containing absolutely no comedy, and I do not think that under any circumstances we could hope for a public response such as we were fortunate enough to gain for *Sweet Lavender*.

However I will let you know what arrangements, if any, I arrive at with reference to the play in N' York. Mr. Daly has the refusal of the piece for that city, but I shall not have it produced there at all unless I can obtain a cast which quite pleases me. This I do not see in my mind's eye at present. / With kind regards / Sincerely yours, / Arthur W. Pinero.
R. M. Field Esq.

85. TO AUGUSTIN DALY

[Ax/6] 64 St. John's Wood Road, / NW.   27th. May 1889.
[Jessie Millward (1861–1932) had acted with Irving at the Lyceum before becoming William Terriss's leading lady at the Adelphi from 1885
onward. They toured America together in 1889 but did not play *The
Profligate*.]

My dear Daly.
     Your cablegram reached me this morning. It would be a matter
of great regret to me were I to be the cause of any upset in your
arrangements and what I have written and do write to you is simply
from a sense of what is due to you, to myself, and to my work. I do
not want *The Profligate* to be added to the already sufficiently long
list of plays of my writing which have succeeded here and failed in
America. Unfortunately I cannot spare the time to do what you kindly
suggest—i.e. come to N' York to produce *The Profligate*. If I were able
to superintend personally the casting and the production of the
play many scruples which I now entertain would be removed—
because I hold that where an Author is a practical man a play gains
many chances of success from his help and direction. In this I don't
think you are likely to disagree with me.
     You may consider, without any doubt on the subject, that you have
the right of the refusal of the N' York production of *The Profligate*.
This is already an agreement between us and I beg you wont think
that I am in treaty with any other persons. In answer to all the
applications I have had from America I have stated that I am dealing
with you in the matter. But I, on my part and in my own interests,
want to know what is to become of my property and how it is to be
treated. In the first place I want, naturally I think, to have the
names of the ladies and gentlemen proposed for the cast. At present
I don't see, in my mind's eye, your company in *The Profligate*. But I
am open to reason and to the force of argument.
     Do you propose Miss Rehan for the young wife? The very essence
of the character of Leslie Brudenell is that she is a young fresh
girl—not a hoyden nor a romp, nor an artificial ingénue, but a
presentment of genuine simple earnestness. Do you really think that
Miss Rehan—of whose talents there is no warmer admirer than
myself—would do for Leslie? I ask your views on the subject. Recollect,

I am not opposing you because you have not yet said anything which I can oppose. I don't say that Miss Rehan cannot be earnest—indeed this is her most admirable quality—but her earnestness is strong, dominant, forcible; the earnestness, in point of fact, of a woman and not that of a girl.

Again, I do not think that admirable comedian Mr. Drew is at all the man for Renshaw—perhaps however you do not suggest this.

Terriss tells me he has written to you about the play. I hear you and he are doing business together. Do you think it would be a good move to produce the piece with him and Miss Millward as the husband and wife at your house or some other high class N' York theatre?

I look forward to hearing from you explicitly—in the meantime I hope you wont think that I am wilfully desirous of taking the play from you. I should like you to have it, and that it shd. be a success for both of us.

Did you gather from the critiques that I have altered the end of the piece?—I save the husband's life now and finish it less painfully. / Sincerely Yours, / Arthur W. Pinero.

86. TO AUGUSTIN DALY

[Ax/6] 64 St. John's Wood Road, / NW.   10th. June 1889.
[*The Profligate* closed on 27 July 1889 and reopened on 2 October 1889; during this break in the run, Hare and the Garrick Company performed the piece in Manchester, Birmingham, and Liverpool. Kate Rorke (1866–1945) became a leading actress, most notably at the Criterion and the Garrick. She played Leslie Brudenell in *The Profligate* and later took the title role in Shaw's *Candida* (first public performance, Court, April 1904). Johnston Forbes-Robertson (1853–1937; knighted 1913) acted with the Bancrofts and Irving before joining Hare at the Garrick. There he played Renshaw in *The Profligate* and other leading roles in Pinero plays staged there—*Lady Bountiful* and *The Notorious Mrs. Ebbsmith*.]

My dear Daly.

Yours of May 31st. to hand. I am very glad to read that you are coming to London and hope that we may be able to arrange a meeting.

My intentions at present are to spend August in Switzerland but I might get back sharp in time to catch you here or in Paris.

It is not yet decided whether we shall close the Garrick during August & re-open with *The Profligate* in September or face the empty season to avoid breaking the continuous run. August is a wretched month here as you know for any plays but Adelphi dramas & the like. I heartily hope you will have an opportunity of seeing *The Profligate* acted here. It is not that you will see good acting—far from it!—but you will better judge than from the reading the enormous difficulties in the way of getting the piece played with absolute conviction & reality on the part of the actor. Where this is attained, as in the case of Robertson & Miss Rorke, the piece creates a deep impression—deep enough indeed to carry the weight of mediocrity & absurd staginess inflicted upon us by the other actors in the cast. As it is our receipts from the play from 24th. April (date of production) to 31st. May, when my accounts were last made up, have been £7,421.12.2.

I have already written you at length on the subject of my misgivings as to the casting of *The Profligate* with your company, and will not inflict them upon you further in this. I do hope I shall see you when you are in London. In the meantime, of course, I will have scene models & prompt book &c prepared so that no hitch may occur on my side. / Sincerely Yours / Arthur W. Pinero.
Augustin Daly Esq.

87. TO WILLIAM ARCHER

[A/3(i)] The Granville, / St. Lawrence-on-Sea, / Ramsgate.

30th. June 1889.

[Ibsen's *A Doll's House* was written in 1878–1879 and produced in England at the Novelty on 7 June 1889. From the evidence of this letter there seems little doubt that Pinero had attended that performance, but this does not invalidate the claim he makes in letter 330—that he was not influenced by Ibsen at the time of writing *The Profligate*—since the latter play was written at least two years earlier, in 1887.]

Dear Archer.

Many thanks for your kind thought in sending me the Ibsen article; I have enjoyed it very much.

It is a small matter—but I cannot take your friend Rank to my bosom. If it is only an avowal of friendship and gratitude which Rank makes to Nora—he may have inherited ambiguity among other dreadful complaints—why does she promptly abandon her intention of placing herself under a monetary obligation to him? A mere protest of friendship on Rank's part would have encouraged her to appeal to him; and we know that Mrs. Helmer had a little intuition in these matters. / Most faithfully yours, / Arthur W. Pinero.

88. TO H. A. JONES

[Ax/10; P/28; Pe/40] 64 St. John's Wood Road, / NW.

15th. Octr. 1889.

[Pinero, it would seem, had more experience at this time of negotiating foreign royalties than did Jones, and this is his reply to Jones's request for guidance in such matters. Jones's *The Middleman* was produced at the Shaftesbury on 27 August 1889.]

My dear Jones.

I intended to walk round to you this morning to answer your question in person, but letters and bothers kept me in till there was no time but for the necessary "constitutional." So I must reply to yours in this fashion but hope to have a talk with you ere long.

I am to have 45% of the fees paid for *The Profligate* in Germany, and something rather less for *Sweet Lavender* which is supposed to require more "adapting." This adapting is a serious point and one—if the German market is to be regarded as a solemn business—upon which an English author should be firm. They may adapt *Sweet Lavender* till it is sage and onions for all I care; but *The Profligate* I have stipulated shall be merely translated. Let me advise you to treat *The Middleman* in the same way. Don't let 'em adapt it! They may tell you that certain phrases of our life and manners are not within the ken of the Germans and that your Pottery should be a Printing Press, or a loom, or a mangle. But make them drink your liquor from the pot of your own baking. (The real old Tatlow, in point of fact). I think you'll agree with me it is far better to be associated with a good play which the Germans *can't* understand than with a bad one which they can.

I may tell you that I have never yet soled my boots out of German fees. *Der Blaue Grotte* (*The Magistrate*, adapted!) is a popular play

and is always being acted in cities with extravagant names. The fees however are less extravagant—possibly they too are adapted ere they reach / Yours ever sincerely / Arthur W. Pinero.
Henry A. Jones.

89. TO CLEMENT SCOTT

[Ax/15(ii); P/25] 64 St. John's Wood Road, / NW.   21st Oct. 1889.
[Thomas William Shafto Robertson (1858–1895) was an actor-manager. T. W. Robertson's *War* was produced at the St. James's on 16 January 1871.]

Dear Scott,
    You may think it worthy a little note in your Friday's column that the present Mr. T. W. Robertson has just presented me with some interesting—and to me very precious—relics of his father's work. They comprise a printer's proof of *War*, with numerous corrections in the author's handwriting, and the written outline of a projected comedy, plans for its incidents and characters, and some notes of dialogue. Hare, Coghlan, Bancroft, and Clarke were to be provided for—but the play never went further than this rough memorandum of seven pages. Mr. Robertson gives me these remains bound in two little volumes with the inscription "To Arthur W. Pinero—a reminiscence of my father for whom he has so often expressed his admiration." / I am, dear Scott / Most faithfully yours / Arthur W. Pinero.
Clement Scott Esq.

90. TO THE EDITOR, THE *DAILY TELEGRAPH*

[Pp/24] Garrick Club, / WC.   Nov. 9, 1889.
[John Hollingshead (1827–1904) was a journalist, drama critic, manager, and dramatist and at various times worked on the *Cornhill*, *Household Words*, *Daily News*, and *Punch*. From 1868 he managed the Gaiety, staging there (15 December 1880) the first Ibsen play in London, *Quicksands; or, The Pillars of Society*. In his letter (*Daily Telegraph*, 9 November 1889, p. 5) Hollingshead said that he could not believe Pinero was in favor of restrictive legislation for music halls, as a newspaper report of some of Pinero's remarks indicated.

On the Empire Theatre see Mander and Mitchenson, *Lost Theatres of London*, pp. 67–72. Pinero's letter was published on 11 November 1889, p. 3.]

Sir,

I cordially agree with my friend Mr. Hollingshead that this question of dramatic privileges is not one to be settled by managers of theatres or music halls, nor, I would add, by playwrights. It is as one of the public, with qualifications of knowing something of theatres and music halls, that I venture to cry out against what I believe to be a steadily-growing injury to the art of the drama. With the shopkeeping aspect of the matter I have nothing to do.

Mr. Hollingshead justly maintains that forty millions of tax and rate paying people have the only voice that should be listened to on this subject; but the writer of your article goes further when he states that the public at large support the music-hall manager in demanding the right to sandwich the drama between the dance and the ditty. May I ask upon what occasion, and through what medium, the public have expressed sympathy with such a demand? I have it upon excellent authority that the entertainment, as at present constituted, at the Empire Theatre draws more money nightly than is taken at any other place of amusement in London. Is not this the voice of the people? Where is the evidence of public clamour for "harmless little operatic and dramatic sketches" at the Empire Theatre?

As a matter of fact, the commerce between theatre and music hall is no new movement; it has been insidiously developing for many years, and its recognition by legal measures would consolidate, not create it. The tendency of this commerce is to render indistinguishable the line between music hall and theatre. Already the music hall supplies the fashion of our pantomimes and of that which we still persist in calling burlesque; by-and-by it will strike the keynote of the drama. / Your obedient servant, / ARTHUR W. PINERO.

91. TO THE EDITOR, THE *DAILY TELEGRAPH*

[Pp/24] Garrick Club, / WC.   Nov. 14, 1889.
[In his letter (*Daily Telegraph*, 14 November 1889, p. 5) Jones regretted that Pinero was against the opening of music halls for plays. He

thought Pinero was right to be alarmed at music-hall methods being used in the theatre, but thought drama was pulling free of the halls, citing Irving, Tree, Hare, Willard, Wyndham, Terry, and Thorne as examples of good managers who would not suddenly betray the drama. Jones also believed that the music halls could not be changed without changing the tastes of the patrons, an impossible task. He wanted to open up the music halls so that the resulting competition would stimulate drama. Other correspondence on this topic included letters from Justin Huntly McCarthy (15 November 1889, p. 5), Arthur Lloyd (16 November 1889, p. 3), and another reply from Jones (18 November 1889, p. 5) in which he said he did not think the theatre would be swamped by popular taste, but he would support a national theatre (although there was a danger this could become stuffy and doctrinaire). Pinero's letter was published on 15 November 1889, p. 5.]

Sir,

The sole argument of Mr. Henry Arthur Jones's liberal and temperate letter is based upon an unfortunate assumption. Mr. Jones evidently believes that there exists and flourishes a compact and impregnable body of theatrical managers able to preserve the serious drama at any cost and against every vicissitude. A glance at the internal economy of playhouses will show that Mr. Jones's view of matters is sanguine and unsound, and that, although we have gentlemen controlling theatres who are ardent, cultured, and ambitious, it is not capable of proof that these gentlemen are fortified against the roll of the great wave of vulgarity. Mr. Jones's experience has been happy, but I fear somewhat superficial, if he has not discovered that our theatrical managers are, so far as the serious drama is concerned, the merest "struggle-for-lifers"—the higher their aim the more desperate is their fight with what is foolish and trivial; and they may be swamped by the flood of "popular taste" at any moment. It is easy enough to mark, as Mr. Jones does for the purpose of his argument, a line of cleavage; but who is to see that this line is maintained, and that it is not shifted backward and backward until it preserves absolutely nothing? In a recent magazine article Mr. Jones, with characteristic honesty, admits that even he has within the last three years produced a play animated not by his furthest notions of what a play ought to be but by simple expediency. Yet this play saw

light at one of those theatres now placed by Mr. Jones on the right
side of that line of cleavage by which the abode of serious drama is
"sharply marked and steadily preserved."

I am almost glad to find myself differing from my friend Mr. Jones
for the pleasure of adding him to about half a dozen out of a hundred
of my opponents who find it possible to state their own views without
labelling my desire to protect earnest dramatic art as illiberal,
impertinent, and idiotic. If Mr. Jones will now devote his fluent
and eager pen to advocating the subsidising of some of our theatres,
I will willingly take my place behind him and trudge at his heel.
Subsidised art is protected art, but the pill is coated. Has Mr. Jones
the hardihood to join me in urging the administration of this
medicine? Subsidise for the service of the serious drama but one
English theatre, and I shall regard with greater equanimity the
prospect of entrusting the people's play to the care of those managers
of music-halls who, on their own piteous avowal, have found
themselves incapable of keeping what is unseemly out of a business
which they profess to understand. / Your obedient servant, /
ARTHUR W. PINERO.

92. TO CLEMENT SCOTT

[Ax/15(ii)] 64 St. John's Wood Road, / NW.   3rd Dec. 1889.
[Scott's article was "The Modern Music-Hall," *Contemporary Review*,
LVI (November 1889), 683–690.]

Dear Scott.

My best thanks for the loan of the *Contemporary* article—its
manliness compels sympathy. It is only in fixing the method of reform
that I presume to differ from the majority. But whatever shape that
reform may take, I am afraid little of it is possible till the half-
publican, half-pugilist music-hall manager becomes actually a manager,
abolishes the "turn" system, and animates and controls the
entertainment he deals in. Given a capable person of this sort it would
be possible to create out of the rough material of "the halls" a guise
of harmless lightness and lightness which could feed an appetite which
I take—though I dare say I'm wrong—to be quite distinct from the
dramatic appetite.

Everybody, I am sure, must thank you for your paper in the *Contemporary*. / Very truly yours / Arthur W. Pinero.
Clement Scott Esq.

93. TO H. A. JONES

[Ax/10; Pe/40] Helvetia, / 25 The Leas, / Folkestone.

3rd Feby. 1890.

[The clock was a present for Jacob Thomas Grein (1862–1935), drama critic of, at various times, *Life*, *Sunday Special*, *Sunday Times*, *Financial News*, and the *Illustrated London News*. He is best known as the founder of the Independent Theatre (1891) and was responsible for the interchange of much drama between Britain and Europe.]

My dear Jones.

The old clock is a splendid idea—pray let me leave it to you to carry it into effect. Let me know my share of the expense.

Thanks for your suggestion about a French *Profligate*. Sometime ago Mr. Grein asked me if I had any objection to it; but I've heard nothing since, so presume it wont work. If it be worth while however to attempt to fight the prejudice of the Frenchman I dont think my form of writing would do much towards it. Dramas of strong effects would do more. It is possible perhaps to translate, for the intelligence of the Gallic mind, a British Railway accident, or a house a fire, or something of that kind. But there is no French dramatic author who really understands the English language, and I think, no French audience likely to be improved by English sentiment. I fear you will find this so. / Kindest regards / Yours ever sincerely / Arthur W. Pinero.
Henry A. Jones Esq.

94. TO AUGUSTIN DALY

[Ax/6] Helvetia House, / 25 The Leas; / Folkestone.

25th. Feby. 1890.

[Daly had suggested that Pinero help rehearse his company in *The Profligate* during their visit to the Lyceum that summer. The suggestion never materialized and Daly returned the promptbook of the play to Pinero in June 1890.]

My dear Daly.

Very many thanks for your letters of Feby. 8th. and 10th. It will give me great pleasure to rehearse *The Profligate* with your company here and to render every assistance. As to your preliminary production of the piece in Philadelphia and Boston, by all means—in Philadelphia. But I have promised to let Mr. Field have the refusal of that and some other plays in Boston; and, although I count the Boston verdict upon a play as of higher value than that of Philadelphia, this arrangement with Mr. Field prevents my allowing *The Profligate* to see light for the first time in Boston. I trust you will not feel inconvenienced by this. Mr. Field and I are upon friendly terms on the one hand, and, on the other, my business transactions with him have always resulted profitably and satisfactorily.

I look forward to meeting you in London where I hope you will have a brilliant season. / Kindest regards and good wishes. / Sincerely yours / Arthur W. Pinero.

Augustin Daly Esq.

95. TO WILLIAM ARCHER

[A/3(i)] 64 St. John's Wood Road, / NW.   24th. April 1890.

[The "book of the words" would be a privately printed prompt copy of *The Cabinet Minister*, produced the previous evening at the Court. George Louis Palmella Busson Du Maurier (1834–1896) was an artist and author of the novel *Trilby* (1894). Du Maurier illustrated editions of Thackeray's *Esmond* and Foxe's *Book of Martyrs* as well as worked for *Punch*, to which Pinero refers here. His son was Sir Gerald Hubert Edward Du Maurier (1873–1934), an actor-manager noted for his acting in J. M. Barrie's *What Every Woman Knows* (Duke of York's, 3 September 1908) and *Dear Brutus* (Wyndham's, 17 October 1917). He managed Wyndham's from 1910 to 1925.]

My dear Archer.

I send you the "book of the words" with great pleasure. Thanks for your kind note. I've seen one newspaper this morning and shall be careful not to open another for the next fortnight—and then it shall be only the *Mining Journal*, or something of that sort.

I offer *The Cabinet Minister* as a small and early study in the school of your Du Maurieresque comedy. But my one newspaper is utterly ignorant of the Society which the play illustrates! The Strathspey is treated as a kind of introduced Ballet and not as a dance natural to a Highland Ballroom! This is appalling! Odds French farce and Melodrama, as Bob Acres would say! / Faithfully yours / Arthur W. Pinero.

William Archer Esq.

96. TO H. A. JONES

[Ax/10; Pe/40] 64 St. John's Wood Road, / NW.   24th. April 1890.
[Pinero and Jones never saw themselves as rivals but simply as fellow workers, as this letter and number 97 show.]

My dear Jones.

Accept my heartiest thanks for your kind and welcome message. *The Cabinet Minister* will, I think, fulfill its modest purpose.

I hear nothing about Grein's clock! Has he got it, or does he continue timeless? And what is the precise sum I owe you? All these things weigh on me and bear me down.

After the middle of May I emerge for a month or two and become a gilded butterfly. Then I hope we shall meet more frequently. / My best regards to you and to Mrs. Jones. Believe me / Sincerely yours / Arthur W. Pinero.

Henry A. Jones Esq.

97. TO H. A. JONES

[Ax/8] 64 St. John's Wood Road, / NW.   22nd. May 1890.
[Jones's *Judah* was produced at the Shaftesbury on 21 May 1890; it ran for 123 nights.]

My dear Jones.

Let me be among the first, or at any rate not with the last, to congratulate you on your great success of last night. No one has better cause to be pleased at so thorough a demonstration of the usefulness of the modern dramatists' calling than have your fellow workers. / Believe me / Yours always sincerely / Arthur W. Pinero.

Henry A. Jones.

98. TO CLEMENT SCOTT

[Ax/15(ii); P/25] Highercombe, / Grayswood, / Nr. Haslemere, /
Surrey.   29th. July 1890.
[Emil Pohl (1824–1901) was a German author of several books on
drama. Dr. Oskar Blumenthal (1852–1917) founded the Lessing Theatre in Germany in 1888, where Sudermann's first play, *Die Ehre*, was
produced (1889). The author of many books, Blumenthal was also co-
author of *Im Weissen Rössel*, better known as *The White Horse Inn*.]

Dear Scott.

Will you permit me to correct the statement that Mr. J. T. Grein
has just arranged for the introduction into Austria of the first play of
English workmanship ever produced in that country? *The Magistrate*,
under its German title of *Die Blaue Grotte*, has long been a popular
play in all the important Austrian theatres and is at this moment
in further process of adaptation into the Bohemian or Tcheco-Slavonic
language for performance at the National Theatre at Prague.
Whether *The Magistrate* was the first English piece done in Austria
I cannot say, but I should think not.

Sweet Lavender, translated by Emil Pohl, has just seen light in
Germany and will follow the same course as *Die Blaue Grotte*; so
also will *The Profligate* upon which the well-known Dr. Blumenthal,
the literary theatrical manager of Berlin, is at work for production
in the autumn. *Sweet Lavender* too is in course of translation into the
Italian for representation at Florence and elsewhere.

I hope you will have a pleasant and restful holiday. I have fixed
myself here till the beginning of the new year, for both work and play.
We are on the top of a hill with a fine view into three counties. /
With kind regards, I am / Very truly yours / Arthur W. Pinero.
Clement Scott Esq.

99. TO R. M. FIELD

[Ax/15(i)] Highercombe, / Grayswood, / Nr. Haslemere, / Surrey.
8th Sept. 1890.
[Pinero's "new task" was *Lady Bountiful* (Garrick, 7 March 1891); the

manuscript in the Humanities Research Center Library, the University of Texas at Austin, is dated 1890.]

My dear Mr. Field.

The engraving has reached England safely and has been forwarded to me here. This is a country place we have taken for some months and where letters will find me *till the end of the year.*

The gift you send me, and which I gratefully welcome is another reminder of the pleasant link of friendship binding us to you and Mrs. Field. When you next visit London you will find your picture upon our wall; and I trust that, in the meantime, you will not allow it to attain much additional age.

I saw the Kendals about a week ago; they have just resumed work at Manchester with a very successful performance of *The Squire.* For myself, I am about to shed the first drop of ink over a new task which I should like to complete about Christmas; and you, my dear Mr. Field, are starting, I hope, upon another season of prosperity and honors / With every good wish, and our kindest messages to Mrs. Field, believe me / Most faithfully yours / Arthur W. Pinero.
R. M. Field Esq.

100. TO HENRY IRVING

[A/4] Highercombe, / Grayswood, / Nr. Haslemere, / Surrey.

19th. Sept. 1890.

[H. C. Merivale's *Ravenswood* was produced at the Lyceum on 20 September 1890 and ran until 20 February 1891 (99 performances).]

Dear Irving.

Please count me among those who, though forced to be absent from the Lyceum on the first night of *Ravenswood*, are heart and soul in your new venture. For your sake, for poor Merivale's, and for our own, I hope for a grand success. / Believe me / Ever yours faithfully / Arthur W. Pinero.
Henry Irving Esq.

101. TO R. M. FIELD

[Ax/15(i)] Highercombe, / Grayswood, / Nr. Haslemere, / Surrey.
27th. Oct. 1890.

[This letter clearly indicates a cooling in the relations between Pinero and Daly, and further correspondence is only occasional. Daly produced *The Squire* on 10 October 1882; the Kendals revived the play in New York at the Fifth Avenue on 13 October 1890.]

My dear Mr. Field.

Your letter of the 10th. addressed to London was allowed to lie there till just now and was not forwarded to me till to-day. So I have thought it best to cable you in answer to your question "Revive *Magistrate* Eight per cent."

With regard to Mr. Daly's position in the matter, I may tell you that that gentleman has held *The Magistrate*, *The Squire*, and other of my plays for some years, but only by right of a friendly arrangement with myself. Latterly however Mr. Daly has thought proper to treat me in a very high-handed cavalier manner. After keeping *The Profligate* by him for a long time he returned it to me with a curt communication that he had discovered that I had lost faith in his company &c. This was in answer to an enquiry on my part as to his views in reference to that play. I then had occasion to again approach him, which I did with every courtesy, as to the Kendals offer to play *The Squire* in America. He refused permission point-blank (assuming a right which he never had) stating that as I evidently could not let him play any of my new pieces he could, this season, revive two of my old ones.* By this time I felt I had had enough of Mr. Daly so I replied by granting Mr. & Mrs. Kendal the right to produce *The Squire* (which they have done with great success) and I now, in the same fashion, give you permission to revive *The Magistrate* at your theatre this season, if you choose to do so, for Eight per cent on the gross receipts.

If you like I will advise Mr. Daly that I have granted you this licence, or you may yourself inform him that you hold the play by direct leave from me. Please take the course you consider best.

Lady B is likely to be done in the early part of next year—too late for America this season.

By-the-by, would you prefer a graduating scale of per-centage for the revival of *The Magistrate*—say six, eight, and ten per-cent according to the fluctuation of receipts? Would this make it easier for you?

Daly has the models of *The Profligate* scenery—I should like to relieve him of them could I find a good excuse. If you think of doing the play—which I do not urge—you can have the use of these models. / With all good wishes and kindest regards to you and to Mrs. Field. / Yours sincerely / Arthur W. Pinero.
R. M. Field Esq.

The Squire and *The Magistrate*.

102. TO WILLIAM ARCHER

[A/3(i)] 64 St. John's Wood Road, / NW.   21st. Dec. 1890.
[Archer's history of William Charles Macready (1793–1873) was published in 1890 as part of his three-volume series *Eminent Actors*. Frederick Robson (Thomas Robson Brownbill; 1822–1864) was noted for his acting of comedy, farce, and burlesque at the Olympic in the 1850s. Edmund Kean, the famous actor, lived from 1787 to 1833.]

Dear Archer.

Accept my hearty thanks for the gift of your history of Macready— it was a kind thought which prompted you to send it to me. I sat my fire out last night reading two chapters with keen enjoyment—but what warmth there is in these old theatrical ashes! Who, after his death, is more interesting than the player?

I wish you would someday think of doing a short life of Robson. When the few now living who saw him act are gone there will be no trace of him, for his private live was mean and wretched. It seems certain that the common little man was the next stroke of real genius after Kean and, up to this time perhaps, our last. His story would scarcely belong to the scenes which include the austere Macready but it might be an interesting study of a veritable peak of nature.

Mrs. Pinero joins me in sending all kind Christmas messages to Mrs. Archer, to yourself, to Tom Archer and to Arthur Larkspur. / Very faithfully yours / Arthur W. Pinero.
William Archer Esq.

103. TO JOSEPH HATTON

[A/16] 64 St. John's Wood Road, / NW.   14th. Jany. 1891.

[Joseph Hatton (1841?–1907) was a journalist, novelist, dramatist, and editor of the *Gentleman's Magazine, Sunday Times,* and the *People.* Edward Smith Willard (1853–1915) was an actor-manager; he played Captain Skinner in H. A. Jones's *The Silver King,* and later, as co-manager of the Shaftesbury with John Lart, Cyrus Blenkarn in Jones's *The Middleman.* After playing in Jones's *Judah* Willard left England for America. Hatton's daughter Bessie performed with Willard at Palmer's, New York, on 29 December 1890 as Lady Eve Asgarby in *Judah.* On 4 February 1891, at the same theatre, she played Percy Tellant in her father's play *John Needham's Double.* Pinero was currently rehearsing *Lady Bountiful.*]

My dear Hatton.

   I reciprocate very heartily your kind wishes for the New Year—my wife joins me in seasonable messages to Mrs. Hatton, Miss Bessie, and yourself.

   Tomorrow morning *The Profligate* will be sent off to you. The scheme for turning it into a novel seems to me a very good one—supposing you can get the copyright. Read the play and see if it stirs you at all in the way of story-telling.

   As to Willard—if he wanted a play and thought this one likely to serve him I would, through you, treat with him, with pleasure; but it must on no account be thought that I ask Willard to represent *The Profligate* or any other play of mine. Indeed I have great doubts whether the play would serve him or he the play. The part of Renshaw is not a star part and it might disappoint his present audience to find him absent from the stage so much. And another matter is that, with the exception of Willard and your daughter, the company at Palmer's Theatre as at present constituted could not deal with *The Profligate.* However, of course I am "open to an offer." Terms for New York, 10%. Or 5% on the first 3000 dollars, 10% on the next 1000, and 15% on all over these amounts each week.

   This is a hurriedly written scribble, my dear Hatton—only a mere business letter. By and by, I shall have an opportunity of acknowledging the very kind interest you take in this little matter. I am glad you think of doing something with *The Hobby-Horse* and *The Rector*.

Your daughter's success must have pleased you very much and made your present visit to America a happy and memorable one. Please convey to her my warm congratulations. I miss her from the play I am now rehearsing, but I could not have given her, at this moment, so thankful a task as she is now discharging—she is the gainer therefore, I the loser.

I am cutting your message to Hare from your letter and am sending it to him by post, having forgotten to deliver it verbally—he will be glad to receive it. / With every good wish and warm greeting, believe me to be / Yours always sincerely / Arthur W. Pinero. Joseph Hatton Esq.

104. TO R. M. FIELD

[Ax/15(i)] 64 St. John's Wood Road, / NW.　　21st. April 1891. [Pinero was writing *The Times* which was produced at Terry's on 24 October 1891. Daniel Frohman (1851–1940) was an American theatre manager, who managed the Old Lyceum, New York, from 1885 to 1902, Daly's from 1899 to 1903, and the (new) Lyceum beginning in 1902. He produced several of Pinero's and Jones's plays.]

My dear Mr. Field.

A hastily written note to acknowledge your cablegram of yesterday and to tell you that I will most certainly reserve for you the Boston rights of the play I am writing for Terry's Theatre provided Terry himself does not visit America with it immediately after its London run. I have no reason to anticipate such an arrangement; I merely make the reservation.

The piece is of a comedy character throughout—but it will be less kind than my farces have been hitherto and I think, and hope, more human.

I hope Mr. Frohman passes my news on to you. Theatricals are very bad this season in London—only burlesque and melodrama do well. *Lady Bountiful* is much admired by our refined playgoers but they are not sufficient in number to do more than half-fill the theatre. And the expenses are £120 nightly. But there is no reason that I can see why the play should not do far better, commercially, in your country. You have not, I hope, quite turned your back upon the

healthy play! / Yours / Arthur W. Pinero.
R. M. Field Esq.

105. TO H. A. JONES

[Ax/10] 64 St. John's Wood Road, / NW.   Saturday [August 1891].
[Jones had complained of the demands of actor-managers for plays to
be written to suit them, even to the extent of altering an already
written play. Jones wanted a play to be performed exactly as it had
been written and claimed he had experienced difficulty in this respect
with Willard over *The Middleman* and *Judah*. This experience led
Jones to attempt his own management at the Avenue in October 1891
(see the *Era*, LIII, no. 2760, 15 August 1891, 13, and no. 2761, 22 August 1891, 13).]

My dear Jones.
    I hope that a stupid sort of paragraph which appears in the *Era*
of today doesn't mean that relations between you and the Shaftesbury
Theatre management are in any way strained. Willard is to be one of
the Luncheon party next Tuesday, and it would be a great regret to
me to place you or him, or both, in an uncomfortable position. Don't
trouble to acknowledge this if, as I hope, all is well. / Yours / AWP.

106. TO CLEMENT SCOTT

[Ax/15(ii); P/25] 64 St. John's Wood Road, / NW.   21st. Sept. 1891.
[*The Times* was the first of Pinero's plays to be published simul-
taneously with the production of the play. "Such a course, I have felt,
were it adopted as a custom, might dignify at once the calling of the
actor, the craft of the playwright. It would, by documentary evidence,
when the play was found to possess some literary value, enable the
manager to defend his judgment, while it would always apportion
fairly to actor and author their just shares of credit or of blame. It
would also offer conclusive testimony as to the condition of theatrical
work in this country" (Pinero's "Introductory Note" to *The Times*,
Boston, 1892, p. vii).
    Evidently the final date for the production of *The Times* remained
uncertain for some time; eventually it was produced on 24 October,
not 17 October as Pinero mentions here. William Heinemann (1863–

1920) founded his publishing house in 1890, publishing the works of, among others, Stevenson, Kipling, Wells, Galsworthy, Maugham, and Pinero. Robert Browning's *A Blot in the 'Scutcheon* was first produced at Drury Lane on 11 February 1843. His *Strafford* (Covent Garden, 1 May 1837) had been written especially for Macready.]

My dear Mr. Scott.

I wish I had known that your Dramatic Column was to have made so early an appearance; a fortnight ago, on making enquiries about it, I was told that you did not start the gossip till Oct. I fear I have now nothing that is new to say in reference to my play which is to be done at Terry's Theatre save that although it has been announced for the 10th. Octr. the date of production is more likely to be the 17th. of that month. The cast has already been published. The piece will be described as a comedy but it may perhaps be found to lean more to the side of satire than of sentiment.

I hope you will consider it worth some little comment that I intend on the first night of *The Times,* and at the subsequent performances, to offer the book of the play to the public. It will be the first of the series of my pieces which Mr. William Heinemann is about to publish in monthly installments. *The Profligate* will form the second vol: and, very likely, *The Cabinet Minister* the third. Since Macready's time (we remember the way in which *The Blot on the 'Scutcheon* was hurried through the press so that it might be ready for the production) such a thing as publishing a new dramatic work as an accompaniment to its first representation has not, I believe, occurred. / With all good wishes, I am / Sincerely yours / Arthur W. Pinero.
Clement Scott Esq.

107. TO WILLIAM ARCHER

[A/3(i); Pe/36] 64 St. John's Wood Road, / NW.   25th. Oct. 1891.

My dear Archer.

Your friendly letter is most welcome. I often think that I will write to you and ask you to join me in a walk upon the northern heights but then I remind myself of your constant hard work—for you are not one who labours in fits and starts—and I refrain. But there are matters, in which I think we are both interested, which I should hugely enjoy talking over with you.

Pray do not imagine, my dear Archer, that you are ever likely to write anything about myself which will in the slightest degree diminish the esteem in which I hold you as a writer or the warm feeling I have for you as a friend. None the less am I gratified by the concern you express upon this point. But, as a matter of fact, I have for years believed you to be an absolutely honest critic and, much as I have regretted at certain times falling under your critical displeasure, this belief has taken much of the sting out of your reproofs without, I hope, lessening their value. With your present aims believe me I fully sympathise though it has struck me that in your earnest, persistent search for one object you run the risk of missing all others, and that you and the school you have created are perhaps too inclined to accept the latest formula in art, whatever that formula may be, as the only true one.

As for myself, I am sadly conscious that I disappoint you and many good friends. You speak of the tastes or traditions which influence me and I feel the censure which is here implied. Yet when some years ago I started my attempt to purge the popular comic play of something worse than mere vulgarity I had little tradition to guide me while my tastes, in this connection at any rate, though they may have been simple hardly deserve to be more severely described. I thought the work would be really serviceable to the theatre and I set out upon it with some, very likely misdirected, enthusiasm. As far as I can gather my reward is only this— blame for not having done something else. However I hope I shall by and by turn out work which may take rank on a different platform. Of one thing I am certain, that you and many others wish me well and for this I am unaffectedly grateful.

Mrs. Pinero joins me in sending kind messages to Mrs. Archer. We often talk of the boy. / Believe me, always / Sincerely yours / Arthur W. Pinero.
William Archer Esq.

108. TO H. A. JONES

[Ax/10; Pe/40] 64 St. John's Wood Road, / NW.   25th. Oct. 1891.
[Pinero could now acknowledge Jones's congratulations on the produc-

tion of a play more tangibly, and sent him a copy of *The Times*. Jones's own new play was *The Crusaders*, produced at the Avenue on 2 November 1891.]

My dear Jones.

I heartily thank you for your good wishes and I appreciate the kind thought underlying them. I would send you a book by this post but I have only paper-covered copies in the house and you must have one with a smart binding. One shall be sent to you tomorrow: it is good of you to ask for it.

Your hour of anxiety is approaching—for, whatever the work and the conditions under which it is presented—the production of a new piece is rather a terrible business. At least I find it so. I hope everything will go smoothly and successfully with your undertaking. / Sincerely yours / Arthur W. Pinero.
Henry Arthur Jones Esq.

109. TO R. M. FIELD

[Ax/11(i)] 64 St. John's Wood Road, / NW.   27th. Octr. 1891.
[Field continued to produce Pinero's work regularly at the Boston Museum; both *The Schoolmistress* and *Lady Bountiful* appeared there in the last quarter of 1891.

T. W. Robertson's *Home* was first produced at the Haymarket on 14 January 1869. The Kendals played at the Star, New York, from 12 to 31 October 1891 and included *Home* and Pinero's *The Ironmaster* in their repertoire.]

My dear Mr. Field.

The strain on my time for the last two or three weeks has obliged me to put all my regular business matters aside and now I find myself deeply in your debt for letters and other kindnesses.

In the first place, accept my best thanks for the cuttings from the Boston journals, for the admirable photographs of your company and for the large coloured poster relating to *The Schoolmistress*. Further let me acknowledge your news of the production of the play and your remittance for fees due on the first week's performance. It is a great regret to me, for your sake as for my own, to hear from you that theatrical affairs are still depressed. I have been hoping that this season would see an improvement in this respect on your side and ours. However, perhaps things will pick up as we get further onward.

I have to-day sent you a copy of *The Times*—not a *stage* copy, but the work as prepared for the library; it forms vol:1 of a series of my plays which are being issued monthly to the reading public. *The Times* was produced on Saturday night and received with great warmth by the audience. Whether it will go out to the wide body of the public remains of course to be proved—at present, the box-office shews signs of a success. You shall hear from me further on the question of American representation of the play. In the meantime please glance through the book: you may, and very likely will, come to the conclusion that the thing is useless for your side.

I am sorry to see it reported that the Kendals have met with their first rebuff in America on their production of *Home*. I hope it isn't true. / With kindest regards to you and Mrs. Field / Yours most truly / Arthur W. Pinero.
R. M. Field Esq.

110. TO AUGUSTIN DALY

[Ax/6] Hotel de France & de Bath, / 239 Rue St. Honoré, / Paris.
21st. Novr. 1891.
[On *The Cabinet Minister*, see headnote to letter 68. *Monsieur l'Abbé* by Henri Meilhac (1832–1897) was produced at the Palais-Royal, Paris, on 18 November 1891, *Mon Oncle Barbassou* by Emile Blavet (1838–1924) and Fabrice Carré (1855–1921) at the Gynnase, Paris, on 6 November 1891.]

My dear Daly.

I should like you to do *The Cabinet Minister* and the arrangement you suggest, that you produce the play next season, is perfectly satisfactory to me.

I think I told you that *The Cabinet Minister* will form the third vol: of my published plays and will be issued therefore next month. You do not regard this, I hope, as a drawback. The piece is hardly one which the pirates will favour. You will be interested to know that *The Times* is doing very finely here while the book is just going into its second edition, having rapidly exhausted its first large edition of

5000 copies. Up to the present therefore I am not dissatisfied with my publishing scheme though of course I am not pledged to continue it if I find my interests jeopardized.

As to terms for *The Cabinet Minister*—some time ago you offered me, I think, 9% for any play of mine which you might produce. As this particular piece is a rather expensive one to mount you may perhaps wish to modify this figure. I am open to reason. Would you prefer a graduating scale of per-centage, say from 5% to 10%? or what?

There is nothing very interesting going on here theatrically. I saw the first performance of *Monsieur l'Abbé* at the Palais-Royal—the eternal mother-in-law again and not a good edition of her. *Mon oncle Barbassou* is a good comic play but I doubt if it would be possible to cleanse it without ruining it utterly. / Yours sincerely / Arthur W. Pinero.
Augustin Daly Esq.

111. TO R. M. FIELD

[Ax/15(i)] Hotel de France & de Bath, / 239 Rue St. Honoré, / Paris.
26th. Nov. 1891.

Dear Mr. Field.

Accept my best thanks for yours of the 17th., which reached me here this morning, with its enclosures of press-criticisms upon the Boston production of *Lady Bountiful*. I am sure that this production is in all respects an admirable one and that it considerably increases my already vast debt of gratitude to you and to the company of the Boston Museum. May your outlay, artistic and pecuniary, meet with fair reward!

Let me know whether you think *The Times* of any value for America or whether it is, in your opinion, too strictly local. In London the play is, up to the present moment, a great success. / With kind regards and every good wish, I am, dear Mr. Field, / Yours most truly / Arthur W. Pinero.
R. M. Field Esq.

112. TO J. F. McEWEN

[Ax/15(i)] 64 St. John's Wood Road, / NW.   8th. March 1892.

Dear Mr. McEwen.

The account you have of me is quite accurate. The name of John Daniel Pinero may not appear regularly in the Law List after '65; I think however you will find that it crops up again at intervals, though in this I may be mistaken. As a matter of fact, my father was very negligent in the matter of taking out his annual certificate; the year was often far advanced before he attended to it. To be included in the Law List a solicitor must take out his certificate by a certain date—some time in January, is it not? My father continued to qualify himself in the irregular way I describe up to '69 or '70. By that time nearly all his old clients were dead, or had departed from other causes, and he entirely ceased to practice.

I really believe that I became my father's right hand *before* I was ten years old. But I have to get such facts as this from my mother, who is not at hand to prompt me, and so I am vague on the point. I know however that I was always a very old little boy. / Yours very truly / Arthur W. Pinero.
J. F. McEwen Esq.

113. TO R. M. FIELD

[Ax/11(i)] 64 St. John's Wood Road, / NW.   19th. April 1892.
[Pinero was currently writing *The Second Mrs. Tanqueray*, but had nothing else with which to meet Field's request for a new piece for the Boston Museum.]

My dear Mr. Field.

I am very glad to know there is a prospect of seeing you and, I hope, Mrs. Field this summer.

On the question of business, I fear there is no prospect of my being able to offer you anything for next season. The play I am at work upon is not one likely to suit the palate of an American audience. However, when it is finished you shall read it—don't imagine I want to rob you of a play or myself of the chance of a production at your theatre. But I don't expect I shall have finished the piece by the time you visit us.

When will you get your audience in trim for receiving a really serious play? I don't claim much for *our* audience but it is too bad of your people to turn a deaf ear and a closed pocket to everything that isn't farce or melodrama.

I write hurriedly having just returned from an Easter holiday to find a mass of correspondence to be dealt with. / Kindest regards / Yours sincerely / Arthur W. Pinero.
R. M. Field Esq.

114. TO CLEMENT SCOTT

[Bx/15(ii)] 64 St. John's Wood Road, / NW.   23rd. May 1892.
[Pinero here adds to W. E. Chapman's history of the difficulties *Jim, the Penman* (Haymarket, 25 March 1886) had reaching the stage. The piece was written by Sir Charles Young (1840–1887). Lady Monckton lived from 1837 to 1920. Marion Terry (1852–1930) was variously a member of the Bancroft's Company at the Prince of Wales's and the Haymarket and Alexander's Company at the St. James's. She appeared at the Court with Clayton in the early 1880s and acted in *The Magistrate*.]

Dear Scott,

I see that Mr. Chapman in his letter to *The Daily Telegraph* mentions our poor friend John Clayton in connection with the wholesale rejection of *Jim, the Penman* by the London managers. During the latter years of his life I was, in business matters, in Clayton's confidence. About the beginning of the year '85 he told me that he had a play by Sir Charles Young in his possession, a play in which he had the firmest belief. He gave me an outline of the story of *Jim, the Penman* and added "if that piece is properly produced it will be a very great success." *Jim, the Penman* however came to Clayton saddled with the condition that the part of Mrs. Ralston was to be acted by Lady (then Mrs.) Monckton, an actress whose excellent qualities were then unknown and perhaps unsuspected. Clayton, having, as I have said, the firmest belief in the play, did not consider himself justified in displacing his own leading lady, Miss Marion Terry, by Mrs. Monckton and felt compelled therefore to return *Jim, the Penman* to its author. Does not this throw some light on the cause of the wanderings of Jim before he found his resting place? / I am,

Dear Scott / Yours very truly / Arthur W. Pinero.
Clement Scott Esq.

115. TO WILLIAM ARCHER

[A/3(i); Pe/36] 64 St. John's Wood Road, / NW.   25th. May 1892.
[Tom Archer (d. 1918) was Archer's only child.]

My dear Archer.

Now that you remind me of it, I think I *have* said something of
the kind. A few years ago the native authors were working with a
distinct and sound aim and with every prospect of popularising a
rational, observant home-grown play. Then came the Scandinavian
drama, held up by the New Critics as the Perfect drama and used by
them as a means of discrediting native produce. Just for the present
everything is knocked askew; the English dramatist has little influence
and the public, urged to witness *A Doll's House*, patronises the Empire
Theatre of Varieties!

I wish we were to rest in Surrey this summer, but we have settled
nothing except that we move from this house into a larger one in
Hamilton Terrace at the end of July. So we shall probably spend our
holiday in trying to make a little furniture go a long way.

Next week I shall run down to Westgate to get on with my work.
I wonder whether you could spare time to spend a day with me there?
I would put you up and look after you: the blow would do you good.

Mrs. Pinero joins me in sending kind messages to Mrs. Archer
Tom Archer—and to Arthur Larkspur. / Sincerely yours / Arthur W.
Pinero.

116. TO R. M. FIELD

[Ax/15(i)] 70A Hamilton Terrace, / NW.   21st. Augt. 1892.
[Pinero's "serious play" was *The Second Mrs. Tanqueray* which, because of production difficulties, was staged after *The Amazons*, referred to here as "my next job." Pinero is incorrect in saying *Mayfair*
was produced in 1886; the date was 31 October 1885 (see headnote to
letter 26). Sardou's *Maison Neuve* was produced at the Vaudeville,
Paris, on 4 December 1866.]

My dear Mr. Field.

I am very glad to hear from you. But I have been expecting to *see* you. You were to turn up, according to a former letter of yours, at the end of July. Either you changed your mind or I must have misunderstood your communication. At-any-rate I am disappointed at missing a meeting with you this summer. I have changed my address, as you will notice; we have now a nice roomy house not very far from the little cottage where we have had the pleasure of seeing you and Mrs. Field. The two old engravings you so kindly gave me now hang in my writing-room: I value them very much.

The serious play I have been so long engaged on will (D.V.) be in the hands of the printers in about a week's time. I will send you a copy in due course; but I can hold out no hope that you will find it a play suited to the tastes of American audiences. However, my next job will be of a lighter kind and perhaps this will give me the satisfaction of seeing another play of mine represented at your theatre.

I send you a copy of *Mayfair*, my adaptation of Sardou's *Maison Neuve*, produced some years ago ('86) at the St. James's Theatre. I don't think you've ever read this. Of course anybody can perform the *Maison Neuve* and it has been frequently adapted, but *Mayfair* is more than half my own original work. The copy I send you is from my M.S.: I would let you have a prompt-book if you thought anything of it. / Our kindest regards to you and to Mrs. Field / Yours always truly / Arthur W. Pinero.

117. TO EDWARD F. SPENCE

[Ax/11(i)] 70A Hamilton Terrace, / NW.   24th. Octr. 1892.
[Pinero sent similar letters to Clement Scott and Moy Thomas. Edward F. Spence (1860–1932) was drama critic of, at various times, the *Westminster Gazette*, *Sketch*, and *Scotsman*. Sir George Alexander (George Alexander Gibb Samson; 1858–1918) was a very successful actor-manager. He joined Irving at the Lyceum in 1881 and took over management of the St. James's in 1890; he was noted for his productions of Pinero and Oscar Wilde (1854–1900). Alexander placed the following notice in the *Times* (25 October 1892, p. 8): "Mr. Alexander has much pleasure in further intimating that at some time during the season, commencing with a series of afternoon performances, a new modern

serious play by Mr. Pinero will be presented." These matinee performances never materialized.]

Dear Sir.

In tomorrow's paper Mr. George Alexander announces a play of my writing for production at his theatre during the season. Will you let me add to Mr. Alexander's announcement by telling you that this play, on which I have been long engaged, has a modern setting but that its interest is of an entirely serious kind—also that it is in four acts and called *The Second Mrs. Tanqueray*? / I am, dear sir, / Yours most truly, / Arthur W. Pinero.
Edward F. Spence Esq.

118. TO GEORGE ALEXANDER

[Cx/16; Pe/32] 70A Hamilton Terrace, / NW.   28th October 1892.
[This, and subsequent letters to Alexander (through to letter 127), deal with casting problems for *The Second Mrs. Tanqueray*. Olga Isabel Nethersole (1870–1951) had played Janet in *The Profligate*, and later, in May 1895, took over the role of Agnes in *The Notorious Mrs. Ebbsmith* (Garrick, 13 March 1895).]

My dear Alexander,

I can only say that I hope we shall not be debarred from the privilege of soliciting Miss Nethersole's services. With every consideration for our friend Hare, as Miss Nethersole had already made advances in your direction for an engagement I don't think it was necessary to refer to him. However, even if he engaged her he might underlet her. / Yours / P.

119. TO GEORGE ALEXANDER

[Cex/16; Pe/32] [63 Hamilton Terrace, / NW.]   21st. Dec. 1892.
[Alexander's "present success" was R. C. Carton's *Liberty Hall* (St. James's, 3 December 1892) which prevented the early production of *Mrs. Tanqueray*. Winifred Emery (1862–1924) appeared with Hare and Irving before marrying, in 1888, Cyril Maude (1862–1951). She became Maude's leading lady when he took over the management of the Haymarket in 1896.]

The great drawback, to my mind, is the delay it would occasion me in putting into evidence such work as I have been labouring at during the present year. The fittest time to begin rehearsing a play is, in my opinion, the day after it is finished.

It strikes me, my dear Alexander, that in the enjoyment of your present success, and in the contemplation of the almost assured freedom from risk and anxiety for the rest of this season which this success gives you, you may feel *The Second Mrs. Tanqueray* to be a little bit of an encumbrance. If you should entertain any such thought you will not, I hope, hesitate to express it. Should you even care to go so far as to discuss the advisability of entirely quashing our agreement, so that you may be relieved of what is now perhaps a burden and I given the freedom of trying my luck elsewhere, I will meet you, or see you here, at any time you appoint.

One of the dangers of waiting for Miss Emery is that one could get no absolute assurance that she would be able to act next season. Her health might be poor—a dozen chances might intervene. / Pardon this untidy scribble, / Yours sincerely, / Arthur W. Pinero.

120. TO GEORGE ALEXANDER

[Cex/16; Pe/32] [Westgate-on-Sea]   24th Jany. 1893.
[Olga Nethersole was playing the Comtesse Zicka in B. C. Stephenson (1839–1906) and Clement Scott's *Diplomacy* (Prince of Wales's, 12 January 1878), revived by Hare at the Garrick on 18 February 1893. Mrs. Beerbohm Tree (née Helen Maude Holt; 1863–1937) married Sir Herbert Draper Beerbohm Tree (1853–1917) in 1883 and was closely associated with his theatrical career, notably during his management of Her/His Majesty's from 1897 onward. Tree mounted lavish Shakespearean productions and was knighted in 1909.]

Will Hare allow Miss Nethersole to act in your theatre in the morning while she is appearing in *Diplomacy* at night? I do wish heartily I could bring myself to see her in the part, but I writhe when I think of it. There are so many elements in Paula which would direct attention, I fear to the indisputable maturity. I wish on your side you could imagine Mrs. Beerbohm Tree as Ellean. This I fancy would be a good thing.

As to incidental music, I can't see that anything of this sort is required. Don't you think "incidental" scraping vulgarises a piece that doesn't belong to either "the kettle-on-the hob" or "the Blood-on-the-Breadknife" order of play? But of course I am open to any suggestion you are kind enough to make.

121. TO W. L. COURTNEY

[Ax/11(i)] 63 Hamilton Terrace, / NW.   15th. Feby. 1893.
[William Leonard Courtney (1850–1928) was a journalist, reviewer, dramatist, and editor of *Murray's Magazine* and the *Fortnightly Review*. Arthur Chudleigh (1858–1932) was an actor-manager and from 1888 to 1897 joint proprietor with Mrs. John Wood of the Court. The new Court piece was *The Amazons*; the other Court farces were *The Magistrate*, *The Schoolmistress*, *Dandy Dick*, and *The Cabinet Minister*. The full cast of *The Amazons* was Fred Kerr, Elliot, J. Beauchamp, Quinton, Compton Coutts, R. Nainby, Weedon Grossmith, Rose Leclercq, Ellaline Terriss, Pattie Browne, Marianne Caldwell, and Lily Hanbury.]

Dear Mr. Courtney.
    Mr. Chudleigh tells me that you have been good enough to ask for some particulars of the new Court piece.
    The piece will be described as a "whimsical play." It forms the fifth of the series of farces done by this hand for the old and the new Court Theatre. Though the characters of the present piece appear in modern garb, the slight story told is likely to be found more fantastic than its predecessors. The setting is mainly sylvan—the scene of the first and second acts shews a park, that of the third act the interior of the mansion it surrounds. Miss Rose Leclercq will be seen as the titled mother of three fair daughters to be represented by Miss Hanbury, Miss Terriss, and Miss Browne. Mr. Elliot will be a gallant young French gentleman, Mr. Fred. Kerr a young Englishman fresh from the University, and Mr. Weedon Grossmith a nobleman of ancient lineage. / Yours most truly / Arthur W. Pinero.
W. L. Courtney Esq.

122. TO HENRY IRVING

[A/4] 63 Hamilton Terrace, / NW.   8th. March 1893.
[The "little play" was *The Amazons*.]

My dear Irving.

A thousand thanks for your most kind remembrance. The little
play seemed to please the not very exciting audience in Sloane Square
last night and there is every promise that it will fulfil its modest
purpose. / Your message was truly welcome. / Always sincerely /
Arthur W. Pinero.
Henry Irving Esq.

123. TO GEORGE ALEXANDER

[Cx/16; Pe/32] 63 Hamilton Terrace, / NW.   16th Mar. 1893.
[*Liberty Hall* continued to play at the St. James's, although Pinero was
obviously anxious to get Alexander to set a definite production date
for *Mrs. Tanqueray*. Washington Irving's story of Rip Van Winkle
dates from 1819–1820; Dion Boucicault the elder's dramatic adaptation
was produced at the Adelphi on 4 September 1865, and H. B. Farnie's
comic opera at the Comedy on 14 October 1882. In 1893 Pinero was
chairman of the Royal General Theatrical Fund, which held its annual dinner on 25 May at the Hotel Metropole, London.]

My dear Alexander,

I think we might perhaps as well say now that *The Second Mrs.
Tanqueray* will go into the evening bill as soon as your present play
has run its course. As you have the machinery for such deeds, will you
see to the paragraphing of the announcement?

If the Rip idea strikes you as having something in it you would
do wisely, I believe, to follow the notion up. Get hold of the Boucicault
play and the libretto of the more recent opera and compare them
with Washington Irving's story. I will read these things too, if you like,
and, should my engagements prevent me from actually doing the work
for you, you shall at least have the benefit (! ?) of my advice in the
matter.

I am very glad to hear that you will reply for the Fund at the
Dinner. This is excellent. It is good of you to close your theatre on the

occasion, and for the great aid this affords me I thank you most heartily. / Believe me, / Yours always, / P.

124. TO GEORGE ALEXANDER

[Cex/16; Pe/32] [63 Hamilton Terrace, / NW.]   6th April 1893.
[The first major success of Janet Achurch (1864–1916) had been in the 1889 production of *A Doll's House*. Lily Hanbury lived from 1875 to 1908. Julia Neilson (1869–1957) was the wife of the actor Fred Terry (1863–1933). She later took the role of the Princess Pannonia in Pinero's *The Princess and the Butterfly*.]

I will start my tour of the playhouses tomorrow night at the Adelphi Theatre. . . .
She [Janet Achurch] is a little bit of a genius. . . . Miss Hanbury is a possible Paula—the best, the most attractive would be Miss Neilson. If Miss Emery will not bind herself for November it seems— should the production of the piece be postponed—that we must decide to put her out of our minds. I don't think that Miss Nethersole will be in Hare's Autumn bill unless he re-opens his theatre with a continuation of *Diplomacy*.

125. TO GEORGE ALEXANDER

[Cx/16; Pe/32] 63 Hamilton Terrace, / NW.   10th April 1893.
[In March 1893 Lena Ashwell (1872–1957) was playing the part of Dora Prescot in H. C. de Mille (1850–1893) and David Belasco's (1859–1931) *Man and Woman* at the Opéra Comique. Her career was established by her performance in H. A. Jones's *Mrs. Dane's Defence* (Wyndham's, 2 October 1900). At this time Maude Millett was a member of Alexander's Company and playing in *Liberty Hall*. She was cast as Ellean in *The Second Mrs. Tanqueray*. Mrs. Patrick Campbell (née Beatrice Stella Tanner; 1865–1940) was playing the part of Clarice Berton in G. R. Sims and Robert Williams Buchanan's (1841–1901) *Black Domino* at the Adelphi. Her career was established by the role of Paula in *Mrs. Tanqueray* and consolidated by that of Agnes in *The Notorious Mrs. Ebbsmith*.]

My dear Alexander,

We need not trouble ourselves, I think, any further about Miss Lena [Ashwell]. A profoundly uninteresting young person, it struck me. Up to the present your suggestion of Miss Millett holds the field. She has certain assured qualities, if not all that are necessary, for the part; and it would be unwise to entrust the task to a lady of smaller experience and less authority for the sake of some mere pictorial attribute.

Mrs. Patrick Campbell is playing in such a poor piece that it is difficult to form an estimate of her powers. She is however a very interesting actress, so much makes itself apparent. Whether in a theatre such as yours, and under such good influences as we should hope to bring to bear upon her, she could rid herself of a certain artificiality of style, engendered doubtless by her present situation and surroundings, is a riddle which I cannot pretend to solve. I should like you to see her; if you have another attack of influenza you might lay up in a box at the Adelphi! / Yours / A. W. P.

126. TO GEORGE ALEXANDER

[Cx/16; Pe/32] 63 Hamilton Terrace, / NW.   12th April 1893.
[Fanny Coleman (1834–1919) had played the Duchess of Berwick in Wilde's *Lady Windermere's Fan* (St. James's, 20 February 1892) and Crafer in *Liberty Hall*. She later played the Countess of Owbridge in *The Gay Lord Quex* (Globe, 8 April 1899). At this time Marion Terry was in the lead, with Alexander, in *Liberty Hall*.]

My dear A.

If you find yourself obliged to change your bill this season I think *The 2nd Mrs. T.* should no longer be denied her opportunity. Forgetting Paula for the moment, I am quite satisfied with the cast you propose. Miss Coleman is certainly not my notion of Mrs. Cortelyon but she is, as you say, a good actress and I recognise her claims as a member of your company.

Miss Neilson would be the thing, could we get her. Failing this, Mrs. Campbell would be an interesting experiment. Nothing but a collapse of *The Amazons* would set Miss Hanbury free; Tree has now no claim on her, as Chudleigh has bought her services by the sacrifice of Miss Leclercq.

Supposing Miss Neilson and Mrs. Campbell are absolutely unobtainable I suppose it would be impossible to restore Miss M. T. [Marion Terry] so reverently and artistically as to revive a sense of her original architectural proportions? / Yours ever, / P.

127. TO GEORGE ALEXANDER

[Cx/16; Pe/32] 63 Hamilton Terrace, / NW.   26th April 1893.
[Edward Seymour Hicks (1871–1949) was an actor, manager, dramatist, and the husband of Ellaline Terriss (1872–1971). James Nutcombe Gould (1849–1899) played in *Lady Windermere's Fan* and *Liberty Hall* and was cast as Misquith in *The Second Mrs. Tanqueray*. Walter Brandon Thomas, besides being a dramatist, was also an actor, manager, and composer. The role of Cayley Drummle finally went to Cyril Maude.]

My dear Alexander,

Hicks is a bright young actor. Would he look too much like a young man with a wig on?

I fear the natural sententiousness and solemnity of Gould. Read over the first act and note how bright and chirpy Drummle ought to be. In a very serious play a ray of brightness is invaluable.

What about Charles Adair? He is heavy in voice but has a sense of comedy. Or Brandon Thomas? He is only two or three feet shorter than Gould but in his composition there is a vein of sympathetic kindly geniality.

By-the-by, May 25th is the night of the R.G.T.F. Dinner. This would delay production till the Saturday.

I can't help thinking that Brandon Thomas is the best after Maude.

Are you sure Fanny Coleman is a little like Mrs. Cortelyon? Keep on telling me she is or I shall doubt it. Miss C. is so like a cook we once had. / Yours late at night, / P.

128. TO EDMUND GOSSE

[Ax/10] 63 Hamilton Terrace, / NW.   2nd. May 1893.
[Sir Edmund William Gosse (1849–1928; knighted 1925) was one of the

leading literary figures of the day, and worked at various times in the
British Museum, the House of Lords, and the Board of Trade.]

My dear Mr. Gosse,

Will you come to the St. James's Theatre on the night of May
27th. to see the production of *The Second Mrs. Tanqueray?* If you say
yes I will send you a couple of stalls in the hope that you will bring
Mrs. Gosse.

It is not my habit to ask folks to witness my work—I am now
asking only yourself, George Meredith, Henry James, and Heinemann
—but this play is a play for grown-up people, and you are amongst
the few grown-up people whose word I care for. / Yours faithfully /
Arthur W. Pinero.
Edmund Gosse Esq.

129. TO T. EDGAR PEMBERTON

[Ax/15(i)] 63 Hamilton Terrace, / NW.   18th. May 1893.
[One of Pinero's duties as chairman of the Royal General Theatrical
Fund was to solicit donations to the fund, and Pemberton was one of
the many people he approached. Thomas Edgar Pemberton (1849–
1905) was a dramatist, stage historian, and from 1882 to 1900 drama
critic of the *Birmingham Daily Post.*]

My dear Pemberton.

I am truly grateful to you for your donation to the Fund. But I
am very sorry to hear such poor news of your eyesight. It will be a
great regret to me if you are not at the dinner; in the first place, I
shall miss shaking you by the hand—in the second, I shall fear there is
no improvement in the eyes. I hope to get a better account of you
soon. / Mention me kindly to Mrs. Pemberton and believe me / Yours
sincerely / Arthur W. Pinero.
T. Edgar Pemberton Esq.

130. TO JOSEPH HATTON

[A/16] 63 Hamilton Terrace, / NW.   24th. May 1893.
[Pinero refers here to his play *The Second Mrs. Tanqueray* and Hat-

ton's book *Reminiscences of J. L. Toole* published in two volumes in 1892.]

My dear Hatton.

I've bought a typewriter and have half a mind to make it write to you—but the medium is too cold a one to fittingly acknowledge your truly friendly note.

First, my thanks to your Bessie for her generous gift to the Royal General Theatrical Fund. And thanks to you, my dear Hatton, for your contribution. It is especially kind of you, for you pay the penalty of your wonderful versatility pretty constantly I guess and—as Novelist, Dramatist, and Journalist—must always have your hand in your pocket.

I am grateful to you for your good wishes in respect of Saturday night. The play is a risky one and, at best, must offend many people. But it will be all right in the end—a long time hence, I mean—when we all settle down and review matters calmly and pleasantly.

Your new book is already in its second edition, I'm glad to see. So that's all right.

I wish you were coming to the dinner tomorrow. There will be a lot of people, but I shall miss many good friends who, from one cause or another, can't turn up. / Yours / Arthur W. Pinero.

131. TO EDMUND GOSSE

[Ax/10] 63 Hamilton Terrace, / NW.   29th. May 1893.
[Pinero received many letters of congratulation on the production of *Mrs. Tanqueray*; Gosse and Henry James (see letter 132) were two among the many.]

My dear Mr. Gosse,

Your kind words of consideration and encouragement touch me deeply and this, for the moment, is all I can say.

But I must add that it will always be a pleasure to me to remember that you, and Mrs. Gosse, were at the St. James's Theatre when Mrs. Tanqueray gave her first impudent nod to the public. / Believe me / Yours always faithfully, / Arthur W. Pinero.
Edmund Gosse Esq.

132. TO HENRY JAMES

[Ax/8(i)] 63 Hamilton Terrace, / NW.   30th. May 1893.
[Henry James's (1843–1916) *The Real Thing, and Other Tales* was published in 1893 and included "The Chaperon."]

My dear James.

I am very grateful to you for your kind note. I hope we shall soon meet and that you will not hesitate to find fault with me upon any point you reserve.

The Real Thing charmed and consoled me at a moment of much worry and mental tribulation. You do not need me to tell you that in "The Chaperon" you have the germ of a fine comedy for the theatre. / Yours always / Arthur W. Pinero.
Henry James Esq.

133. TO HENRY JAMES

[Ax/8(i)] 63 Hamilton Terrace, / NW.   3rd. June 1893.
[James's *The Private Life; Wheel of Time; Lord Beaupré; Visits; Collaboration; Owen Wingrave* was published in 1893.]

My dear James.

Your publishers have sent me, on your behalf, a copy of *The Private Life*. My heartiest, my best, thanks for this very kind thought of me.

I open your new book eagerly. *The Real Thing* gave me greater pleasure than has taken to me for many a day. / Yours always faithfully / Arthur W. Pinero.
Henry James Esq.

134. TO MRS. PATRICK CAMPBELL

[A/3(ii)] 63 Hamilton Terrace, / NW.   26th. June 1893.
[Actors and actresses did not always adhere to Pinero's scrupulous direction (see letter 61) and he employed various ruses to rectify this.]

My dear Mrs. Campbell.

Some good people who are, naturally, your admirers beg me to send you a line of injunction urging you not to allow the shrewish side of Paula's disposition to get uppermost. I accede to this request because I think I am serving your interests, as well as my own, in doing so. Constant repetition may lead you into developing too fondly—for that is the side of the character more easily reproduced perhaps—the termagant aspect of poor Paula at the expense of her more sympathetic, her equally natural and genuine, qualities.

A nod is as good as a wink to a gifted artist—and infinitely more respectful. So I content myself with writing these few words, begging you to read between the lines nothing but an expression of my gratitude and admiration. / I am, my dear Mrs. Campbell, / Yours most faithfully, / Arthur W. Pinero.
Mrs. Patrick Campbell.

135. TO WILLIAM ARCHER

[T/3(i)] 63 Hamilton Terrace, / NW.   27th June 1893.
[Eleonora Duse (1859–1924) was an Italian actress who gained international fame in the early 1890s. She played in *La Dame aux Camélias* (Vaudeville, Paris, 2 February 1852) at the Lyric on 24 May 1893. Réjane (Gabrielle Charlotte Réju; 1857–1920) was a leading French comedy actress.]

My dear Archer,
For many weeks I have been looking for an opportunity of writing to you to ask you to fix a Sunday for the projected walk. But whenever I have tried to arrange this business Mrs. Pinero has told me that she has accepted an invitation for the particular Sunday which I have desired to come to you to dine with the Smiths of Balham, or some other distinguished family. I now find that I am pledged for every Sunday until the time of our going away, so I can no longer hope to see you in Surrey before the Autumn. But I have a house at Southwold for ten weeks from the 15th July, and I am wondering whether it would be possible for us to persuade you and Mrs. Archer to spend two or three days with us. Let me have your views and if they are favourable to this plan Mrs. Pinero will write to Mrs. Archer on the subject. Southwold is not a beautiful place, but the air is wonderfully invigorating. I am going up there to think out some new work and shall not get my real holiday till the Spring. There are many things I should like to talk over with you.

I saw Duse in *La Dame aux Camélias* the other night; she moved me very deeply and I place her beside another goddess of mine, the adorable Réjane.

You will see I have started a Typewriter. This letter is dictated, but I would have you know that I occasionally operate myself and have already acquired a speed of about 10 words per minute. / Believe me, / Yours always faithfully, / Arthur W. Pinero.
William Archer Esq.

136. TO WILLIAM ARCHER

[A/3(i)] Southwold.   16th. Augt. 1893.
[Arthur Bingham Walkley (1855–1926) was drama critic of the *Star* (1888–1900), the *Speaker* (1890–1899), and the *Times* (from 1900). Ibsen's *The Master Builder* was first produced in England at the Trafalgar Square Theatre on 20 February 1893.]

My dear Archer.

You should have left it to me to get the little book, but it is nevertheless most kind of you to have sent it. I have read the letter to Mr. Walkley; it strikes me as being among the very best of your good things of this sort—please forgive me for saying so. Perhaps I don't quite agree with you in your Hawthorne-Ibsen comparison. Hawthorne does for me what Ibsen never does—makes me believe in the reality of wonders. The marble form—the actual thing in marble, I mean—is alive for me, or was when I commenced with him not so very long ago. I look for Macbeth's Witches on every heath—there is a Gretchen kneeling in a dark corner in every church in Germany. *The Master Builder* is more shadowy to me than any dream: I can almost put my fingers through the pages of the book. Nothing is a bit real after the play begins—you even end your admirably told story with the size of the curtains. Ibsen may be as symbolic as he pleases but he ought to make me feel the truth of his signs. How otherwise am I to be touched? As for these dolls, it is simply because we don't believe in the existence of Mrs. Solness that we laugh at them. The fact that *you* can make me admit the possibility of the dolls while Ibsen makes me guffaw at them goes to the root of the whole matter. It was Ibsen's business to make these dolls duly impressive, and he didn't do it. And there, I honestly think, you have an account of a great deal of his work—he is continually failing to make one believe in his dolls. One doesn't ask him for real people, one does demand real dolls.

We have a New York parson staying with us. He knows about your work and wants to meet you, but I fear he'd be gone before you come down again. / Yours always / AWP.

137. TO WILLIAM ARCHER

[A/3(i)] Stone House, / Southwold, / Suffolk.   24th. Augt. 1893.
[Clement Scott, in a series of articles in the *Illustrated London News* (CIII, no. 2835, 19 August 1893, 212; no. 2838, 9 September 1893, 329; no. 2839, 16 September 1893, 339), accused Pinero of using the German dramatist Paul Lindau's (1839–1919) play, *Der Schatten*, as the basis for *The Second Mrs. Tanqueray*. (On the developments of this incident, see letters 138–142).

Leon Kellner (1859–1928) was a German writer of, among other things, books on American literature and Shakespeare.]

My dear Archer.

I am infinitely obliged to you for your letter and for the trouble you have taken about the Lindau play. It was a good thought of yours to apply to Encyclopaedic Kellner: I had it in my mind to beg you to do so. I have not sought for information elsewhere.

The Second Mrs. Tanqueray was framed, in my head, in November '91. I sat down to it in January '92 and in February or March I read the first act to Hare. It may be, as you suggest, that Lindau's play is a recent one, but new or old I know nothing of it.

You kindly ask me whether you can do or say anything for me in this business. My dear Archer, I can suggest nothing. But I cannot help feeling certain that in such a matter I must have the good will and the good word of the honest workers for the stage. / Believe me / Yours always truly / Arthur W. Pinero.
William Archer Esq.

138. TO WILLIAM ARCHER

[T/3(i)] Stone House, / Southwold, / Suffolk.   28th August 1893.
[Sir George Henry Lewis (1833–1911; knighted 1893) was a famous criminal lawyer.]

My dear Archer,

Thanks for your telegram. Your information that the German play [*Der Schatten*] was produced in Vienna in the month of October 1890 places it, I fear, beyond hope that I shall be able to bring Mr. Scott to account for his malevolent attack upon me through the medium of the law—though, of course, I shall take Sir George Lewis's opinion upon this point, when I get it. I must leave myself in the hands of all fairminded men and trust, in some measure, to my past record.

As regards the likeness between the two plays, the question seems to be whether the story of a man who, having married a lady who had been seduced, finds his sister engaged to his wife's seducer is essentially like the story of *The Second Mrs. Tanqueray*.

I should like you, and indeed everybody, to read *Der Schatten*. Unfortunately I cannot read German.

I have not thanked you sufficiently for all your trouble and personal kindness to me nor do I intend, in words, to try to do so; you will take this, I beg, for granted. / Believe me, / Yours ever / Arthur W. Pinero.

P.S. I found another telegram from Cromer, when I reached home, addressed to my wife, containing the announcement that the *wound had healed during the night*! I imagine that Sherringham must be a dull little hole and the wound is weary of it.

139. TO WILLIAM ARCHER

[A/3(i)] Stone House, / Southwold, / Suffolk.   29th. Augt. 1893.

My dear Archer,

Again, thanks. The sketch for the plot of *Der Schatten* is interesting and instructive. I truly believe that I could hardly have accused my worst enemy of founding *The Second Mrs. Tanqueray* upon it.

By-the-by, you will very likely have forgotten *The Weaker Sex* and the coincidence—which I do not defend—which forms the kernel of that play. A young woman—Mary—I forget her maiden name—loves and quarrels with a man named Lyster. They part—he disappears—she marries Lord Vivash, bears a daughter, and in time becomes a widow.

The daughter grows to womanhood and, travelling abroad, meets, in Paris, one Ira Lee, falls in love and becomes engaged to him. Lee the Lyster aforesaid, comes to London and meets Mary Vivash at a party. Her love for him has grown rather than diminished with years and she confesses it to him, whereupon the man is presented to her by her daughter Sylvia as Sylvia's accepted suitor.

You will see here in this old play the same line of thought which directed the coincidence in *The Second Mrs. Tanqueray*. Such theatrical tricks are hardly perhaps to be excused—unless the way they are employed in *The Second Mrs. Tanqueray* pleads for them. My point is that these tricks are the common stock of playwrights and that the array of events which Lindau and I have marshalled together recently with some similarity I manoeuvred in much the same way nearly ten years ago. / Yours always / Arthur W. Pinero.

P.S. My negociations with the Deutsches Volkstheater are in their earliest stage and the director of that establishment may, as yet, know of my play but vaguely through his London representative. It would be an odd thing were *The Second Mrs. Tanqueray* to be done at the D.V.

140. TO GEORGE HENRY LEWIS

[Tux/2] Stone House, / Southwold, / Suffolk.   17th September 1893.
[Archer's article in the *World* is reprinted in William Archer, *The Theatrical 'World' for 1893* (London, 1894; reissued London and New York, 1969), pp. 202–213. Clement King Shorter (1858–1926) was a journalist and critic. From 1891 to 1900 he edited the *Illustrated London News* and from 1900 the *Sphere*; he also founded the *Sketch*.]

Dear Sir George.

I daresay you have seen the article in the current number of *The Illustrated London News*, written by Mr. Clement Scott, headed "Mr A. W. Pinero and Myself." Of course, I am entirely in your hands & if you tell me that this article is an Apology, & all that I can reasonably demand, I bow to your views. To my thinking, however, the article is as little like an Apology as anything could well be. It is true that Mr. Scott denies that he ever intended to charge me with being a plagiarist; it is true also that he has made this denial on three occasions—but the first of these denials was not made until after he had emphasised his original accusation by the publication of a paragraph in *The Daily Telegraph* of August 26th, until after I had publicly denied knowledge of the German play, until after he had been called to account in *The Evening News & Post* of August the 29th for his vindictive attack upon me. Whatever may have been Mr. Scott's intentions therefore in writing the original article (& there can be little doubt what those intentions were) he has yet to apologise for the tone in which that article was couched.

But what is as serious as the original article is that Mr. Scott still asserts that my play & the German play are so alike that the German play is shut out from representation in England, & this assertion is supported by the detailed comparison of the two pieces in his original article which contains the gross misstatement exposed by Mr. Archer in *The World* of September the 13th. This misstatement is still allowed to stand. I contend that Mr. Scott's assertion, supported by the above mentioned misstatement, that my play, in effect precludes the representation here of Herr Lindau's play is a libel, in-as-much as it asserts that the resemblance between the two plays is so extraordinarily close that the one is substantially the other.

I suggest therefore that Mr. Scott & Mr. Clement Shorter still have to apologise to me, firstly, for the original charge of plagiarism in *The Illustrated London News* of August 18th &, secondly, for the misstatement contained in Mr. Scott's comparison of the two pieces. And I say that this apology should appear as an explicit & formal apology only & not in the form of a verbose article by Mr. Scott in which the main issue is carefully mixed up with a lot of extraneous matter. / I am, dear Sir George / Yours most faithfully

141. TO WILLIAM ARCHER

[T/3(i)] 63 Hamilton Terrace, / NW.   26th September 1893.
[In September 1893 Pinero drafted a letter to the *Pall Mall Gazette* indicating that he was concerned only with establishing the truth over the plagiarism charges, and not with trying to suppress honest dramatic criticism. Archer's criticism of H. A. Jones's *The Tempter* (Haymarket, 20 September 1893) is reprinted in *Theatrical 'World' for 1893*, pp. 213–230.]

My dear Archer,

I saw George Lewis to-day. He says that Scott's "climb down" would render the bringing of an action a risky matter and advises me to accept Scott's suggestion that the business should be referred to him (Lewis). I *have* accepted this suggestion & Lewis has written to Scott telling him to call in Ely Place to-morrow. Should Scott not back out of his own proposal of arbitration, he & I will have to assemble before Lewis & state our views. It will be a disagreeable matter for me to meet the creature but if necessary it must be done; I have little doubt as to the result of an arbitration, should it take place. In the meantime the question of the letter to the P.M.G. [*Pall Mall Gazette*] as to gagging criticism may wait; very likely I shall come to you again about this later on. My most sincere thanks are yours for the trouble you have allowed me to put you to.

Your criticism of *The Tempter* is, as far as it has gone, a severe one. It has been stated as an imposing fact that Henry Arthur took "no less" than fifteen months to write this play. It can't be done in the time. / Yours always / Arthur W. Pinero.

William Archer Esq.

P.S. Will you, please, let me have *Der Schatten*? I may want to "put it in" as evidence.

142. TO WILLIAM ARCHER

[A/3(i)] 63 Hamilton Terrace, / NW.   30th. Sep. 1893.

My dear Archer.

Lewis informed Scott to-day that he must apologise, and so a formal apology will appear in next Friday's I.L.N. [*Illustrated London News.*] The terms of it were dictated by Lewis; it doesn't cover the whole ground but it is something to point to—and it is, or should be, a standing humiliation to Scott.

The ceremony of to-day struck me as being supremely ludicrous. The office seemed flooded with Scott's tears. *You* were the King Charles's Head of his discourse.

Of course I shall take your advice, but I am inclined to think that the letter to the paper as to my wishing to "gag" criticism would now appear superfluous. Having obtained a formal apology it would

be more dignified perhaps were I to let the matter drop. / In haste, /
Yours always / Arthur W. Pinero.

P.S. Just off to Brighton for a few hours—to blow Scott away.

143. TO WILLIAM ARCHER

[A/3(i)] Hotel de France & Choiseul, / 238–241 Rue St. Honoré, / Paris.
27th. Decr. 1893.

[*Gigolette* by Pierre Decourcelle (1856–1929) and Edmond Tarbé
(1838–1900) was produced at the Ambigu, Paris, on 25 November 1893.
La Duchesse de Montélimar by Albin Valabrègue (1853–1934) was produced at the Gymnase, Paris, on 19 December 1893. Henry Pettitt, a
dramatist, was born in 1848 and died on 24 December 1893. Myra,
later Mrs. Claude Neville Hughes, was Pinero's stepdaughter.]

My dear Archer.

I have not the slightest objection to the enclosed. Many thanks
for your kindness in asking me the question.

Last night, *Gigolette* at the Ambigu—a tearing melodrama of the
old Porte St. Martin pattern with one very fine, and equally objection-
able, scene stuck in the middle of it. But the whole far more vital
than that terrible *Mdme Sans-Gêne* at the Vaudeville.

The Gymnase piece is scarcely a success, I fancy; that impression,
and what you tell me of its chance resemblance to *The Times*, will
keep me from seeking *La Duchesse de Montélimar*'s acquaintance.

Poor Pettitt! I knew him, Horatio—so can say no more than that
he was a very, very good fellow. He was bred, theatrically, in a poor
school or it all might have been very different.

Mrs. Pinero joins me in sending kind messages to Mrs. Archer,
Tom, and yourself. Myra is at Nottingham, with friends, firmly
believing that she is enjoying herself. / Yours / Arthur W. Pinero.

144. TO THE EDITOR, THE *STAR*

[Pp/34] Ramsgate.   1 Feb. 1894.

[Louis Frederick Austin (1852–1905) was a dramatist, writer, sometime
secretary to Henry Irving, and drama critic of the *New Review*. His
article appeared in the *Star* on 31 January 1894, p. 1. Both he and
Israel Zangwill (1864–1926), dramatist and novelist, misinterpreted

Pinero's remarks made at the tenth annual dinner of the Playgoers' Club, held at the Criterion on 28 January 1894. Pinero felt obliged to defend himself with this letter, published 2 February 1894, p. 1. Rejoinders from Austin and Zangwill appeared in the *Star*, 3 February 1894, p. 1, and 5 February 1894, p. 1. Austin maintained there were differences in Pinero's intentions as expressed in his speech and in his letter. Pinero clarified his position in the *Star* for 6 February 1894, p. 1, stating that although there should not be "one standard of criticism for the professed critic and another for the amateur . . . the professed critic was not uppermost in my mind" when he made his initial remarks.]

Sir,—

Mr. L. F. Austin has every excuse for being wide of the mark in his article in *The Star* of Wednesday; he was not at the dinner of the Playgoers' Club. Nor can he have read a complete report of my speech, inasmuch as the newspapers, under pressure perhaps of other matters almost equally important, did not report that speech fully. If Mr. Austin had witnessed the ceremony of Sunday night he would, I fancy, have found no difficulty in gathering that my speech did not refer to the authorised dramatic reviewer of to-day, that it was directly aimed at a body of earnest young gentlemen who constitute themselves "the auxiliary critics of the drama." After dealing with a custom existing, or lately existing, with the Playgoers' Club of opening its debates upon current plays by the proposal of a vote of censure, I counselled these young amateur critics to seek the opportunity on all occasions of praising, to praise where they found evidence of good intention, however imperfectly that intention might be realised. Will anybody, will Mr. Austin, say that these were inappropriate words to address to a body of young, irresponsible critics? Trite, commonplace, yes—but to-day the commonplace of last week may be, to youth and inexperience, a revelation. And granted that the dogmas with which I illustrated my counsel to the Playgoers were misleading, which I deny, were they, under the special circumstances, dangerous? Finally, I protest against any attempt to put me in the position of a man with grievances. Had I grievances, I should not, I hope, display the poor taste of airing them at a convivial gathering. But I have no personal grievances whatever; no man has smaller cause for them. And will it be believed that even a writer of dramas is not always thinking about

155

himself? One word more. Clever as Mr. Zangwill is, I seem to have taxed his ingenuity too far in involuntarily imposing upon him the task of interpreting my obscurities. What I recollect best of a private conversation with Mr. Zangwill is the pleasure I felt at meeting him; I certainly had no intention of conveying to him that in my speech to the Playgoers' Club I had meant anything but exactly what I had said. / Yours, &c., / ARTHUR W. PINERO.

145. TO WILLIAM ARCHER

[A/3(i)] The Granville, / Ramsgate.   8th. February 1894.
[The book was Archer's *Theatrical 'World' for 1893*. Robert W. Lowe (1853–1902) was a theatre historian. Pinero's note to the *Star* was his letter published on 6 February 1894, p. 1.]

My dear Archer.

The book has "arrived safely," as the children say. I prize it very highly, and shall always do so, inasmuch as it is the only record in my possession of what I suppose stands to my account as the most creditable year in my poor theatrical life. Of the eulogy bestowed upon *Mrs. Tanqueray*, and of the little blame, not one scrap of evidence remains to me except this book. Indeed, beyond the plays which I often forget Heinemann is publishing—of these my set is incomplete!—your three reviews, the present one of '93 and its predecessors, are all I have in print to remind me that it is not now the year 1874 and that I am no longer sitting, all day and every day, in a very dull, dirty room in Lincoln's Inn Fields trying to screw up courage to cut myself adrift from the law and join you and Mr. Robert W. Lowe in Edinburgh.

I don't know how I got the impression that you radically differed from my after-dinner advice to the Playgoers' Club. But I did get it and included you, in a note to *The Star*, with those who certainly did so differ. It relieves me however to think that I said I had missed your article. / Believe me, my dear Archer, / Always yours truly / Arthur W. Pinero.

146. TO WILLIAM ROTHENSTEIN

[Ax/8(i)] [63 Hamilton Terrace, / NW.]   17th. April 1894.
[Sir William Rothenstein (1872–1945) was an artist known especially for his portraits. He was principal of the Royal College of Art from 1920 to 1935.]

Dear Mr. Rothenstein.

I should esteem it a compliment to be drawn by you. Let me know your wishes as to sittings and I will try to accommodate my time to yours. The morning, please.

I was looking at your work yesterday, at the Dudley Gallery. / Believe me / Yours most faithfully / Arthur W. Pinero.
Will Rothenstein Esq.

147. TO MRS. PATRICK CAMPBELL

[A/3(ii); P/22] 63 Hamilton Terrace, / NW.   21st April 1894.
Dear Mrs. Campbell.

When you count up the minor rewards which your acting in *The Second Mrs. Tanqueray* has brought you, you will not fail, I hope, to include in them the hearty appreciation of the author. But I beg your acceptance of this little broach, as a jog to your memory; for if you are kind enough to wear it occasionally it may serve as a reminder of my indebtedness to you. / Believe me / Yours always truly / Arthur W. Pinero.
Mrs. Patrick Campbell

148. TO H. A. JONES

[Ax/10] 63 Hamilton Terrace, / NW.   29th. April 1894.
[Jones's *The Masqueraders* was produced at the St. James's on 28 April 1894.]

My dear Jones.

My heartiest congratulations! And every acknowledgement of your real friendliness in sending a copy of your new play: I shall apply myself to it—I hope, tonight—with the keenest interest.

Don't forget your engagement for next Sunday evening. / Yours always / Arthur W. Pinero.

149. TO WILLIAM ARCHER

[A/3(i)] 63 Hamilton Terrace, / NW.   21st. May 1894.
[Edmund Yates (1831–20 May 1894) was a civil servant, writer, and editor of *Temple Bar* and *Tinsley's*. In 1874 he founded the *World* with Grenville Murray (1824–1881).]

My dear Archer.
      You must be in great sorrow at the death of poor Edmund Yates. But his end must have been painless; and the scene of the fatal stroke, the theatre, to which through his parentage and sympathies he belonged, seems to have been a fitting one. I know little of his faults or virtues in detail, but to me he was always a loveable man and I mourn him sincerely. / Yours always truly / Arthur W. Pinero. William Archer Esq.

150. TO WILLIAM ARCHER

[T/3(i)] 63 Hamilton Terrace, / NW.   27th May 1894.
[Elbridge T. Gerry (1837–1927), a lawyer and president of the New York Society for the Prevention of Cruelty to Children (1876–1901), found Gerhart Hauptmann's (1862–1946) *Hanneles Himmelfahrt* (1893; produced at the Fifth Avenue, New York, in May 1894) impious and a danger to the health and morals of the child actress Alice M. Pierce, aged 15, who was cast in the lead. An adult actress had to be found for the actual performance (see *New York Times*, 21 April 1894, p. 1.). Lewis Waller (William Waller Lewis; 1860–1915) was an actor-manager; he produced Wilde's *An Ideal Husband* at the Haymarket on 3 January 1895. Duse eventually performed a version of Hermann Sudermann's (1857–1928) *Die Heimat*, entitled *Magda*, at Drury Lane on 12 June 1895. In the same year the Ducal Company of Saxe-Coburg and Gotha gave a performance of *Die Heimat* at Drury Lane (25 May 1895).]

My dear Archer.
      It is very good news, this approaching association of yours with such a popular paper as the *Pall Mall Budget*. It will bring you and the general public closer together, and good will result, I am sure, all round.

Now as to what little assistance I can give you. Whenever I hear of anything at all likely to fit your column, or to suggest anything to you in the way of an idea for a paragraph in that column, I shall at once scrawl it off to you. Don't acknowledge any communications of this kind from me; in nine cases out of ten they will be worthless to you. I shall never expect to see again the stuff I send you, in any form. On the other hand, if you want to know anything that you think I can grub up for you, drop me a line and I will do my best.

Just now I am not going out very much and am not therefore in the way of gleaning gossip; but it will not always be so. I send you a cutting from an American paper; perhaps you have not read anything of the manifestation by Mr. Gerry against Hauptmann's *Hannele*. You, of course, are especially interested in this matter. Anything more comical than the man Gerry's attitude I can't imagine.

You will have been informed that during Tree's absence in America in the early part of next year the Haymarket Theatre will be managed by Mr. Lewis Waller. But I don't think it has been announced that the play upon which Oscar [Wilde] has recently been engaged is the motive for Waller's excursion into management.

If any announcement has been made that the Duse is likely to act Sudermann's *Heimath* during her season I have not seen it. Alexander bought the English rights of this play some time ago; with a generosity which at-any-rate is not founded upon business prudence he has given the Italian actress permission to represent the play in her language. *Il Seconda Signora Tanqueray* is not likely to see the light just yet. It is reported Duse fears a comparison might be made between the acting of her company and that of the English one. It is quite probable she may be right. Very likely, for instance, at the Italian Tanqueray's dinner-party, the waiters might appear to be in excess of the guests.

———

We all hope to see you and Mrs. Archer at Walden someday. Perhaps you will let me, by-and-by, when I feel myself free, ask myself down to you for a walk in your pretty country. / Yours always / Arthur W. Pinero.

151. TO GEORGE ALEXANDER

[Cx/16; P/32] 63 Hamilton Terrace, / NW.   26th July 1894.

[Alexander took the role of David Remon in H. A. Jones's *The Mas-queraders*.]

My dear Alec,

I had no opportunity last night, without running the risk of appearing to be merely complimentary, of telling you that I thought your acting of David Remon strong, sympathetic, and altogether delightful. No part that you have played, in my recollection, has brought out the grace and tenderness of your method so effectively.

As for the play I could see it again to-night with the utmost pleasure: I don't often get this feeling now-a-days. / Yours always / P.

152. TO WILLIAM ARCHER

[A/3(i)] Sea Grange, / Westgate-on-Sea.   5th. Octr. 1894.
[*Les Trente Millions de Gladiator* was written by Eugène Marin Labiche (1815–1888) and Philippe Emile François Gille (1831–1901). Pinero's Garrick play was *The Notorious Mrs. Ebbsmith*; "Carr's play" was *The Benefit of the Doubt*, staged at the Comedy which J. W. C. Carr was currently managing. Cibber was Pinero's dog. Johnston Forbes-Robertson played Sir Launcelot in Carr's *King Arthur* (Lyceum, 12 January 1895) and Lucas Cleeve in *Mrs. Ebbsmith*. *The Raiders: Passages in the Life of John Faa* (1894) was written by Samuel Rutherford Crockett (1860–1914); *Trilby* by George Du Maurier; *The Ebb Tide* (1894) by Robert Louis Stevenson (1850–1894); *The Manxman* (1894) by Sir (Thomas Henry) Hall Caine (1853–1931; knighted 1918); *Social Evolution* (1894) by Benjamin Kidd (1858–1916). Wilson Barrett (1847–1904) was an actor, manager, and dramatist who was very successful in melodrama. From 1881 to 1886 he managed the Princess's, playing Wilfred Denver in H. A. Jones's *The Silver King*. He later played Marcus Superbus in his own play *The Sign of the Cross* (Lyric, 4 January 1896), which ran for 435 performances. Justin Huntly McCarthy (1860–1936) was a dramatist and novelist. Harry Nicholls (1852–1926) was an actor long associated with comedy and pantomime at Drury Lane.]

My dear Archer.

It is very good of you to send me the information about *Les Trente Millions de Gladiator*, which information I am passing on to a

160

Boston manager who, doubtless anxious to prove that no adaptation exists, will not thank you for your pains. This is how enemies are made!

The play—the Garrick play—is still unfinished. But I am better in health than I have been for a long time and hope to really get the thing out by about Christmas. As a matter of fact, I have been very seedy for the last twelve months, though I haven't said anything about it. The Engadine has done me much good and I'm now in the highest spirits I can hope to attain. Carr's play is fully planned, and a bit of it written, so a great deal of work has been done—to bear creditable fruit, let us pray, by-and-by. I can't let anything go that is not at least up to my poor form—hence the delay. I want to talk to you, to gossip and ramble; it is "an age" since I last saw you. When I get back to town you must be kind enough to come and see me. I'm down here only to untie a knot in my work—alone, for at such times I am gloomy and depressing to those at home. Cibber especially hates me when I'm like that; he and Mrs. and Miss Myra shall receive your friendly message. Were they here they would desire to be mentioned kindly to Mrs. Archer.

I haven't sent you any "gossip" lately, noticing how your *Pall Mall* papers have developed into something more useful and, if I may say so, more dignified than mere chit-chat.

They "wish they may get" Forbes Robertson at the Lyceum— for Lancelot in *King Arthur*—but he is engaged to Hare for the season. I would not stand in the way of the Lyceum arrangement but—I have a partner, Mr. Jenkins. I mean, Mr. Hare.

I came down here with a load of light literature, such as *The Raiders, Trilby, The Ebb-Tide* and *The Manxman*—not that *that* is light literature, I would have you understand. I travel with Kidd's *Social Evolution*, letting it lie about to impress the landlady, but really *The Manxman* would have done for this purpose. I thought there was something wrong when all the writers rose as one man and hailed Hall Caine's latest brochure as the greatest book of the century. Caine still persists in dealing with Man instead of Mankind, and is doing for that island just what Scott didn't do for Scotland; he is ruining the place. Oh, the coarse, foul-mouthed, blathering, blasphemous folks he peoples it with! But it's a marvellous piece of industry, the whole thing. Dickens and Hardy and the French realists edited by the spirit of the late Nathaniel Hawthorne—the whole revised and arranged by

Wilson Barrett.

But *The Raiders*! There now, if you like! How fine these Scotsmen are! But *The Ebb Tide* is disquieting. The trick of it is becoming too apparent. That schooner again, and the mysterious cargo, and that blackguardly skipper. Only the flats don't jine so closely as usual. And yet I thank God for it, though it did keep me up half the night.

Trilby! dear, sweet, formless thing! I would not part with the memory of her for a wilderness of Manxmen!

No, I cannot make out why Justin Huntly has shaved away his moustache—unless, as Nicholls used to say in a Drury Lane pantomime after a similar act, "further disguise is useless!"

There, my dear Archer, this will teach you to think twice before writing to *me* again! / My best regards to you, and yours. / Faithfully / Arthur W. Pinero.
William Archer Esq.

153. TO WILLIAM ARCHER

[A/3(i)] 63 Hamilton Terrace, / NW.   29th. Nov. 1894.
[The Architectural Association met on 7 December 1894 for a meeting on "Municipal Subscription and People's Theatres"; Pinero was clearly contemptuous of some current proposals about municipal theatres. Archer's lengthy reply is reprinted in Wilbur Dwight Dunkel, *Sir Arthur Pinero: A Critical Biography with Letters* (Chicago, 1941), pp. 55–57.

Hermann Vezin (1829–1910), an American actor, came to England in 1850 and subsequently appeared with Charles Kean, Phelps, Irving, and Tree. (Wilhelm) Richard Wagner (1813–1883) built his famous theatre at Bayreuth in 1876.]

My dear Archer.

Yes, I meant to place my note to the Architects at your disposal. Their meeting is on Decr. 7th.: I don't know whether it is right to give you liberty to deal with the letter *before* the date of that meeting, but I leave this to you. If my honour demands it, I can always accuse you of breach of confidence.

The Architects amuse me; they sniff the chance of tendering for the creation of a Municipal theatre at Spinnymoor, or Hanley, or Burnley. I know that theatre—when it arrives. It is a circular thing of

162

red brick with stone facings, and stands in an inaccessible part of the town. It has many doors and is dangerously draughty. Critics go down from town to assist at the opening and to lunch. At night, Herman Vezin takes the stage in *Timon of Athens*. Afterwards, the building is given over to farcical comedy—of course, "genuine pure Family," as the grocers describe their inferior jams.

Your letter shews me that I have very poorly expressed myself in mine. I have no objection to an endowed theatre. (Aren't half our theatres already endowed—by "backers"?) I should rejoice with you to see a theatre "run" by a capitalist with non-commercial aims. It is the theatre under municipal *control* that terrifies me. But surely you will find this in my letter.

To say that England and America are behind countries possessing state-aided theatres in respect of plain-speaking drama is only saying that Englishmen are not Frenchmen or Norwegians or Russians. But what great new movement do we really owe to the state-aided theatre of any country? That of your Ibsen? or of Wagner—a dramatist? Who built the theatre at Bayreuth? Even the modern French dramatic movement—though I don't claim much for that—is found springing up outside the subsidised houses.

And what has kept Shakespeare going in this country—the state? / Yours always / Arthur W. Pinero.

P.S. I have something to say to Irving, but no time just now to say it, about subsidised theatres and the social and general status of the actor. Observe the actor in the land of the subsidised theatre!

William Archer Esq.

154. TO WILLIAM ARCHER

[A/3(i)] 63 Hamilton Terrace, / NW.   29th. Nov. 1894.
[The "coming play" was *Little Eyolf*. Archer published a translation of it in November 1894, which was produced at the Avenue on 23 November 1896.]

My dear Archer.

It has come upon me that I used a foolish expression in my letter to you this morning: I spoke of "your Ibsen." But I assure you—though it reads, to me now, like a poor little sneer—that I had in my mind only the thought of your gallant fight for Ibsen and that victory of his which in part belongs to you. It would not, of course, matter a row of pins if I did sneer at Ibsen and all his works, but I would rather not be suspected of being capable of doing so.

I am more than interested in the account you give of the coming play. And now don't you think that the time has arrived when a proper production can be afforded an Ibsen drama? You know my opinion of "side-shows." The great prize, to my thinking—as I remember saying at Margate to you—is the gaining of the great public. Ibsen should at least have as dignified and important a production as our stage can give. If I can be of any help I should be delighted.

Excuse this petty and incoherent letter. I am writing to you and dictating to the type-writer at the same moment. Try it. / Yours sincerely / Arthur W. Pinero.
William Archer Esq.

155. TO HENRY JAMES

[Ax/8(i)] 63 Hamilton Terrace, / NW.   31st. December 1894.
[James invited Pinero and his wife to see *Guy Domville* which was produced at the St. James's on 5 January 1895; the play failed, running only until 9 February. Hare's "latest production" was *Slaves of the Ring* by Sydney Grundy (1848–1914), best known for his play *A Pair of Spectacles* (Garrick, 22 February 1890). *Slaves of the Ring* ran at the Garrick from 29 December 1894 to 16 January 1895.]

My dear James.

Your kind letter ought to give me great pleasure—it is at once a compliment and the promise of real enjoyment. But I get no pleasure from it, only pain. For I can't come out on Saturday night. I am still behind-hand with my work for the Garrick Theatre—it should have been finished long ago, but it turned out a more perplexing job than I reckoned for—and now, to my dismay, Hare's latest production, upon which I depended for time to finish my difficult task leisurely, is, I greatly fear, a failure.

I do thank you heartily for your most kind thought of us. Mrs. Pinero will be at the St. James's and will afterwards give me an account of the, I sincerely hope, great success of your play. Greetings! And

every good wish for this triumph and for many others! / Yours most truly / Arthur W. Pinero.
Henry James Esq.

156. TO W. L. COURTNEY

[Ax/11(i)] 63 Hamilton Terrace, / NW.   1st. Jany. 1895.
My dear Courtney.

I hope I shall not inconvenience you by telling you, as I feel obliged to do, that I do not see my way clear to the fulfilment of my promise to furnish the *Fortnightly* with a criticism of Ibsen's *Little Eyolf*. The not very pronounced success (to put it mildly) of Hare's latest venture at the Garrick Theatre robs me of the possibility, which I had been craving for, of finishing my work for him deliberately and leisurely. But beyond this serious call upon every moment of my time during the present month, I find on re-reading Ibsen's play, that I could approach a dissection of that drama with so little cordiality that my criticism of it, in the result, might appear not only unappreciative but, to some people's minds, quite ungenerous. I hope you will sympathise with me in my perplexity and forgive me for disappointing you.

Perhaps you will someday give me the opportunity of dealing in your *Review* with some aspects of Ibsen's work, apart from his latest achievement—work for which I feel, in the main, considerable admiration.

With every acknowledgement of the compliment you have paid me, I am, my dear Courtney, / Always yours truly / Arthur W. Pinero.
W. L. Courtney Esq.

157. TO WILLIAM ARCHER

[A/3(i)] 63 Hamilton Terrace, / NW.   16th. Mar: 1895.
[Joseph Knight (1829–1907) was a drama critic and historian. He wrote for the *Athenaeum*, contributed to the *Dictionary of National Biography*, and edited *Notes and Queries*.]

Private.
My dear Archer.

I remember that I have omitted to answer a question of yours. No,

Mrs. Ebbsmith suffered no mutilation at the Chamberlain's office. *I* made a few cuts at rehearsal.

For my own satisfaction, I should like to make a personal explanation to you. You will have judged, from Scott's notice in the *Telegraph*, that he is in possession of a copy of the play. I authorized Hare to send him a book. One was given to Knight, another to Watson, a third I sent to *you*. With Scott I could hold no communication, but I felt that I ought in fairness to give him the advantage (?) enjoyed by other critics—Watson & Knight asked for books, to enable them to write in advance—and so I told Hare that if he liked to furnish Scott with a copy of the play I should offer no objection.

I make you this little explanation of an unimportant matter because I would not have you think me capable of any act which might be construed with a desire to curry favour with a man towards whom I have hitherto expressed feelings of contempt. As a matter of fact, though I was glad that Hare's theatre had the benefit of a favourable criticism in a popular journal—he is old fashioned enough to believe in the commercial value of such things—Scott's present praise filled me with as much disgust as his dishonesty and misrepresentation have done in the past.

Up till now, the "booking" at the Garrick beats the previous record of that house. / Yours sincerely / Arthur W. Pinero.

158. TO WILLIAM ARCHER

[A/3(i)] Tankerton Tower, / Whitstable, / Kent.   4th. Septr. 1895. [Pinero's play was *The Benefit of the Doubt* which he was writing for the Comedy, then under J. W. C. Carr's management. *Alabama* (Garrick, 2 September 1895) was written by the American dramatist Augustus Thomas (1857–1934). The Adelphi "specimen" was *The Girl I Left Behind Me* (Adelphi, 13 April 1895) by Franklyn Fyles (1847–1911) and David Belasco (1859–1931).]

My dear Archer.

I am glad to see your handwriting again. It is kind of you to want to know about my health. Yes, I have been seedy; a few weeks ago I caught a chill and tried to ignore it and work through it. The result

166

was something like a collapse and the doctor ordering complete rest. I lay in a chair, gazing at the sea, for a week and then returned to my desk, to find that a normal temperature absolutely declined to ratify the labours of "101 point five." So I have been much thrown back with my play and poor Jan [J. W. C. Carr] must be tearing his hair. But I am pushing along fairly well now.

I expect to be clear of it all by the end of this month and, as this house is mine during October, I have still some hope of seeing you down here before my tenancy runs out. I have had little of the pleasure of seeing my friends this summer.

I am interested in what you say of *Alabama*. The American drama —even the recent specimen at the Adelphi—delights me. Whatever its relation to life, it takes me more quickly out of myself than any other form of play I know of. But it *doesn't pay in England. Held by the Enemy*, as good a melodrama as I can remember, never "took salt." The reason is, I think, constitutional—the Englishman, in his heart, does not like the American. We accepted the nigger minstrel because we associated him with slavery, a matter in which we suppose ourselves to have behaved very finely. But we have no excuse for extending this spirit of sentimental patronage to America generally.

Mrs. Pinero and Myra send the kindest messages. They are both expert cyclists—bicyclists, not tricyclists, I must make you understand, or I shall get into trouble. I bought a new machine of a most superior kind a few hours before the doctor ordered me to cease riding for a time. But it stands in my dressing-room and is a great ornament. / Yours always / Arthur W. Pinero.

159. TO WILLIAM ARCHER

[A/3(i)] 63 Hamilton Terrace, / NW.   26th. Octr. 1895.
[The dramatization of Du Maurier's *Trilby* by Paul (Meredith) Potter (1853–1921) was produced at the Haymarket on 30 October 1895; it was first performed at the Theatre Royal, Manchester, on 7 September 1895. Dorothea Baird (1875–1933), an actress, married Henry Irving's son H(enry) B(rodribb) Irving (1870–1919) in 1896.]

My dear Archer.

I hope you will come and eat a meal with me some evening, soon. I will try you by-and-by when I return from Brighton where we are going for a short stay. It is so long since I had a chat with you.

Oh, but I shall be at the first performance, here, of *Trilby*! But then your mood will be a stern and unbending one. I must have you out of these serious moments.

Trilby—Miss Baird—came to me some months ago soliciting an engagement; a pretty, willowy creature—looking so honest and shabby, just unlike an actress. And now she has fallen on her feet—her bare feet—and I have lost the privilege of shewing the rose with the dew upon it! / Yours always / Arthur W. Pinero.
William Archer Esq.

160. TO WILLIAM ARCHER

[B/3(i)] 63 Hamilton Terrace, / NW.   Dec: 9., 1895.
[Pinero wrote a "Prefatory Letter" to Archer's *The Theatrical 'World' of 1895* (London, 1896). *The Benefit of the Doubt* was withdrawn on 27 December 1895.]

My dear Archer

It so happens that I intended writing you tonight. I want you to tell me whether you were in Edinburgh at the end of 1874—I mean, absolutely at the end. I should like to imagine, in writing my paper, that I may have passed you in the street on New Year's Eve, the Eve of 1875. Of course, if you were not in Edinburgh at that moment, it cannot be helped; it is too late now to remedy the mistake. I am going down to Westgate on Thursday, for a few days of reflection, and shall write my "Letter" to you while there. If the weather looks at all promising, what do you say to coming down there to see me on Sunday? I shall be at my old quarters—Sea Grange—and the bedroom you once before slept in shall be again at your disposal. We might have a good walk & talk under these circumstances.

Save for my disappointment at my failure to render Carr a business service, I am not much disturbed at the shabby result which has attended *The Benefit of the Doubt*. We did very finely for a few weeks, and then the business forsook its high figures, and despondency settled upon the authorities in Panton Street [the Comedy Theatre]. They have no money there to fight through the Christmas season with a serious play, and I could not find it in me to offer them a word of encouragement to do so. It is a little cheering to note that the worst week's receipts have never fallen below £700: but so high are the salaries that one is compelled to pay even to indifferent artists, that such a sum is not sufficient nowadays to enable a manager to keep a play in his bills.

By no means are cycling operations suspended. I rode out with my wife on Sunday morning, & shall take my machine to Westgate. My ladies send kind messages. / Yours always / AWP.

161. TO WILLIAM ARCHER

[A/3(i)] Hotel Chatham, / Paris.   16th. Jany. 1896.
[The "proof" was of Pinero's "Prefatory Letter." "Barrett's Cross" is a reference to Wilson Barrett's play *The Sign of the Cross* (see headnote to letter 152). George Bernard Shaw (1856–1950) was currently writing reviews for the *Saturday Review*, and Pinero here refers to Shaw's article "Plays of the Week," *Saturday Review* (11 January 1896), reprinted in *Our Theatres in the Nineties*, 3 vols. (London, 1948), II, 7–14. *Viveurs* (Vaudeville, Paris, 20 November 1895) was written by Henri Lavedan (1859–1940), *Amants* (Renaissance, 5 November 1895) by Maurice Donnay (1859–1945). Jeanne Granier (1852–1939) was a French actress taking her first role as a serious actress in *Amants*; she had previously played in light and comic opera.]

My dear Archer.

I return the proof, corrected, with hearty thanks for your suggestions. I venture only to let the sapphire surface of Duddington Loch remain undisturbed for I have seen the ice, there and elsewhere, when there has been no snowfall, of this hue on a fine, blue night. But if I find by-and-by that you have put your pen through the adjective I shall, after the first burst of grief, regard you no more maliciously than heretofore.

I am not surprised to hear that the majority of your brethren cling to Barrett's Cross fervently and hopefully. It comes to them as a sign that the good old crusted "British Drama" is still "going strong." As for Mr. Shaw, he may always, I fancy, be trusted to speak tolerantly of anything that doesn't encroach upon what he is pleased to consider his preserve.

Yes, I have seen *Viveurs!* and *Amants*, and two delightful nights I have had with them. In the first named, my dear Réjane gave you some moments of her best; in *Amants* Jeanne Granier steps from opera-bouffe to serious drama, and acts a most arduous part with an ease and an amount of resonance that are surprising. Even the frank indelicacy of many of the incidents of these plays is preferable to the Clapham-and-Brixton morality of our home-made article. *We* are in, if I mistake not, for a silly period—but it will pass. There is no finality, thank God, in any theatrical fashion. / I wish you were here. / Yours / Arthur W. Pinero.

162. TO H. A. JONES

[Ax/10; Pe/28; Pe/40] 63 Hamilton Terrace, / NW.
                                          Sunday [26 January 1896].
[Jones's "poor luck" was the failure of *Michael and His Lost Angel* (Lyceum, 15 January 1896), which ran ten nights only.]

My dear Jones.

I want to talk to you upon a little matter. I wonder if you would care to have a walk with me one morning. Next Friday would suit *me* for such a pleasant adventure—but, if you kindly fall in with my proposal, name your own day and hour, and tell me where we are to start from—this house or your own.

————————————

I do not trouble you with any expressions of sympathy over the poor luck at the Lyceum. You will have accepted the matter philosophically, I feel sure—recognising that the theatres are in for a silly period. But, of all fashions, theatrical fashions are the least durable—a condition of things which operates both for and against the earnest writer; at the present moment he must console himself with the reflection that the next change of public taste is likely to be to his advantage. / With kind regards to Mrs. Jones, I am / Yours sincerely / Arthur W. Pinero.
Henry Arthur Jones Esq.

163. TO GEORGE ALEXANDER

[Cx/16; Pe/32] 63 Hamilton Terrace, / NW.   18th Feb. 1896.
[Alexander lived at 57 Pont Street. He played Rassendyll in *The Prisoner of Zenda* by Edward Everett Rose (1862–1939), produced at the St. James's on 7 January 1896.]

My dear Alec,
   I have booked *Tuesday the 25th* for our talk. I will turn up in Pont Street at eleven o'clock on that day, unless I hear from you to the contrary.
   We had a delightful evening in witnessing *The Prisoner of Zenda*. It is a charming piece and most brilliantly put upon the stage. You and I must talk much about it when we meet: I watched everything with great care and am full of appreciation of the excellent work of actors and authors. I don't think you, as an actor, have been seen to greater advantage in any play you have produced.
   I compliment Mrs. Alexander, too, upon the ladies' dresses. They are most beautiful. / Yours always, / Arthur W. Pinero.
George Alexander, Esq.

164. TO WILLIAM ARCHER

[A/3(i)] 63 Hamilton Terrace, / NW.   26th. Feb: 1896.
[Pinero prepared this information on *Mrs. Ebbsmith* as evidence for an article Archer wrote in the *World,* in which Archer attacked Sydney Grundy's despairing attitude toward the state of the English theatre (see "Mr. Grundy's Crack of Doom," *The Theatrical 'World' of 1896,* London, 1897, reissued New York, 1971, pp. 41–58, especially pp. 46–47). Pinero adds further information in letter 166.
   Mrs. Campbell played the role of Agnes from 13 March to 11 May; the total receipts (given by Pinero) amounted to £14,168.11s. at an average of £244.5s. a performance. Olga Nethersole acted Agnes from 15 May to 14 June; the total receipts were £3,477.10.6. at an average of £124.4s. a performance.]

My dear Archer.
   I have had prepared for you a detailed account of the commercial results of the production of *The Notorious Mrs. Ebbsmith.* Note the

averages which I give you of receipts during the engagement of Mrs. Campbell and that of Miss Nethersole, and the average receipts of the entire run. Could any theatre in Europe do much better with a play—though it possessed treble the artistic worth of my poor work—of the character of *Mrs. Ebbsmith*?

You will observe that the vulgar public gave Miss N. a fair chance of interesting them. They came, and saw, and dwindled away.

A "good house" at the Garrick Theatre, I may tell you, is represented by £160–£200. The theatre does not fairly hold the large sums accounted for, but to a great success the people come so eagerly that stalls commanding little or no view of the stage are purchased gratefully, "top boxes" are at a premium, and a "packer" is employed in the pit for the purpose of fitting elbows into ribs. / Yours always / AWP.

165. TO GEORGE ALEXANDER

[Bx/9] 63 Hamilton Terrace, / NW.   Monday 9.3.96.
[Fay Davis (1872–1945), an American actress, came to Britain in 1895 and was a member of the St. James's Company from 1896 to 1901. She played Fay Zuliani in *The Princess and the Butterfly*, the play Pinero discusses here, and later Iris in *Iris* (Garrick, 21 September 1901).]

My dear Alexander

I am wondering whether it would be worth your while to see Miss Fay Davis, who is not engaged for next season, and, without pledging yourself to her in any way, interest her by telling her that there *might* be a part for her in my play at your theatre. Your managerial wisdom will suggest some way, if you feel so inclined, of obtaining from Miss Davis a promise that she will perhaps consult you before pledging herself definitely in another direction. She is, as I dare say you know, a charming young lady, with a very sincere quality in her acting—as evinced, at any rate, in her recitals. She is a great deal like the part I am writing—a character which I think I could perhaps bend even more in her direction. Even the slight trace of Americanism in her pronunciation I fancy I could, in a way, account for and get over.

Tomorrow or next day I shall send you the plan of the First Scene with a full written description of the scene and its properties.

I propose to do this with regard to every scene as the acts progress, so that you will always have some material by you to amuse yourself with at your leisure.

The First Act is finished and is, I think, a little like what I intended it to be—a lot of people of a light kind flitting in and out of a room. I think of it in my own mind as a Buzz of Bees. / Yours always, / Arthur W. Pinero.

166. TO WILLIAM ARCHER

[B/3(i)] 63 Hamilton Terrace, / NW.   March 26, 1896.
[This letter furthers the information Pinero gave Archer in letter 164. *The Second Mrs. Tanqueray* was revived at the St. James's on 20 June 1895 and ran for twelve performances. *The Idler* by Charles Haddon Chambers (1860–1921) was first produced at the St. James's on 26 February 1891 and revived on 4 July 1895 when it ran for six performances. Pinero was a keen bicyclist.]

My dear Archer,

I look forward with genuine pleasure, & with gratitude to you, to receiving the books you are sending me.

If you have another shot at Grundy, and I crop up again in the matter, you may perhaps care to avail yourself of some facts concerning the performances given by the Kendals in America of *The Second Mrs. Tanqueray*. (I am told that in his first article Grundy said that this play was merely "included in a repertory"—suggesting that as an attraction it was not sufficient to stand alone.) The Kendals have *always* travelled with a repertory, as Mr. Grundy, who has more than once contributed to it, well knows. Now for the facts concerning the Kendal-*Tanqueray* tour in America. The tour opened on Oct. 9, 1893, and closed at Albany on May 25, 1894. It embraced, therefore, 199 nights available for acting, and upon this tour, exactly *one hundred and thirty five* representations of my play were given. The Kendals repeated their performances of *Mrs. Tanqueray* on their '94–'95 tour, giving sixty-five further representations.

I trouble you with these figures to show you that Mr. Grundy is not over-scrupulous in making his case.

It is true that the revival at the St. James's Theatre did not do very well; but it occurred, you will remember, during very hot weather. It was followed by a reproduction of *The Idler*—a play surely after Grundy's own heart; and this shut the theatre, for after giving three or four representations of Chambers's play, Alexander, at a few hours' notice, terminated his season.

I am interested in your news of the purchase of an "Ormonde"; I should like to have a run with you very much. I would have you know that I went the whole length of Oxford Street yesterday, crossing Regent Circus even, without dismounting. / Yours always / Arthur W. Pinero.

167. TO HENRY IRVING

[A/4] 63 Hamilton Terrace, / NW.   23rd. Sep: 1896.
[Irving revived *Cymbeline* at the Lyceum on 22 September 1896; Ellen Terry played Imogen.]

My dear Sir Henry.

It is a great pleasure to me to receive your kind message. I met a friend, from abroad, in your theatre last night, felt bound to look after him, and so missed the privilege of offering my congratulations to you upon the success of *Cymbeline*. I hope to have an opportunity of telling you soon what I thought of your beautiful production; you are always very patient in listening to other people's opinions.

Iachimo was a *great* villain in your hands. And Miss Terry's performance would prove almost that the sweetness of girlhood may be a perpetual gift of the mind.

Humbly, I make a trifling suggestion—that, in the bedchamber scene, you would do well to act more *behind* the bedstead, standing perhaps upon an imperceptible platform. We should then lose none of your face as you bend over Imogen; and at certain times—the moment of triumph when the bracelet is removed, for instance—you would be saved the necessity of relaxing your watchfulness of the sleeping woman. A faint, uneasy movement, after the loss of the bracelet, on the part of Imogen might slightly change her position and be supposed to reveal to Iachimo the blemish upon her body.

One other point. Would it not be effective, in this same scene, if the light which falls upon the lower half of the woman were tinged with blue—coming, as it is supposed to do from the window—while the light upon her face and shoulders were alone kept white, as if proceeding from the taper? And that when Iachimo carries away the taper, to inspect the tapestry, the illumination of Imogen's face should, for the moment, be suspended or, at least obscured?

Your illustration of two passages in the play last night, one in Act I. sc. II, the other in Act II. sc. I, rendered plausible, even probable, important episodes which I—and I dare say many others—have always found difficulty in swallowing. / Believe me / Your faithful friend and servant / Arthur W. Pinero.
Sir Henry Irving.

168. TO HENRY IRVING

[A/4] 63 Hamilton Terrace, / NW.   21st. December 1896.
["Owing to a sprain received by Sir Henry Irving he will be unable to play for a few days, and the Lyceum Theatre will therefore be closed this evening, and to-morrow and Wednesday evenings" (*Times*, 21 December 1896, p. 11). Irving was playing Richard in *Richard III*, revived at the Lyceum on 19 December 1896.]

My dear Irving.
    We are deeply concerned at the news of you given us in this morning's paper. Your days of enforced idleness will, however, I sincerely hope, be but few; and during these days you must allow yourself to be consoled by the recollection of your splendid triumph, and by the knowledge that you are constantly in the affectionate thoughts of your friends. / Yours ever faithfully / Arthur W. Pinero.

169. TO GEORGE ALEXANDER

[Cx/16; Pe/32] 63 Hamilton Terrace, / NW.   22nd December 1896.
[Alexander's letter, complimenting Pinero on *The Princess and the Butterfly* which he had just read, is printed in A. E. W. Mason, *Sir George Alexander & the St. James's Theatre* (London, 1935), p. 120, and Dunkel, *Sir Arthur Pinero*, p. 61.]

My dear Alec,
    I was pleased to receive your telegram (which I ought to have acknowledged) and am more than pleased to read this morning, in your

kind letter, the very warm expressions you employ in reference to *The Princess and the Butterfly*. There are no pleasanter moments for the playwright than those in which he finds his manager in full sympathy and accord with him.

It will be a very great pleasure to me to visit you at Ovingdean. At present I am engaged only on Sunday, January 3rd. I shall wait to hear from you before making any other Sunday fixtures.

We spend Christmas at Brighton, at the Bedford—going down tomorrow and returning to town to-day week. Mrs. Pinero intends to write to Mrs. Alexander suggesting a luncheon or dinner, or some wild orgie of that kind.

A happy Christmas to you both, my dear Alec, and every warm friendly wish for the coming year! / Believe me, always, / Yours sincerely, / P.

170. TO GEORGE ALEXANDER

[Ax/9] 63 Hamilton Terrace, / NW.   Wednesday. 5.30.
[This letter could refer equally to Alexander's performance in *The Second Mrs. Tanqueray* or in *The Princess and the Butterfly*. The St. James's Theatre was in King Street.]

My dear Alec.

I am coming down to-night, if I may, to see as much of you, and as little of the piece, as possible. It is, as I have often assured you, positive pain to me to sit out a play of my own writing; and this feeling alone is the cause of my apparent neglect of you lately. Directly you play other men's pieces I shall turn up in King Street frequently.

I am sorry I appeared cold to you on Monday night. In my heart I didn't feel so, believe me. But it was at a party, and I like parties only one degree better than my own plays.

I shall turn up about 9. / Yours always / Arthur W. Pinero.

171. TO WILLIAM ARCHER

[T/3(i)] 63 Hamilton Terrace, / NW.   9th. June, 1897.
[Duse produced *La Dame aux Camélias* at the Renaissance, Paris, on 1 June 1897 and Sudermann's *Magda* on 7 June 1897. *The Second Mrs. Tanqueray* was announced for performance on 19 June 1897, but was

withdrawn because of the popularity of these other pieces (see *Le Temps*, 31 May 1897).]

My dear Archer,

The Duse has made a great impression in Paris in *La Dame aux Camélias* and in *Magda*, and she is advised by the manager of the Renaissance and by Madame Bernhardt that these pieces will remain sufficiently attractive to carry her through her engagement, and that it would be an unwise thing for her now to present herself in a play, the story and substance of which are unfamiliar to the Parisians. So, unless Madame Duse—who is a beautiful but irresolute creature—alters her mind, I do not go to Paris on the 18th. / Yours always, / AWP.

172. TO AUGUSTIN DALY

[Tx/6] 63 Hamilton Terrace, / NW.   13th. October 1897.
[The two plays to which Pinero refers are his collaboration with J. W. C. Carr, *The Beauty Stone* (Savoy, 28 May 1898), and his Court play *Trelawny of the "Wells"* (Court, 20 January 1898).]

Dear Daly,

I got back from Brussels last night to find your letter of October 9th waiting here. This will account for my apparent neglect of it. I am dealing this morning with an accumulation of correspondence, which explains my use of the typewriter; you will forgive it, I know.

I have been abroad with Mr. Comyns Carr, with whom I am collaborating over a long ago projected opera for the Savoy Theatre. My pen-and-ink share of this work will confine me to my room till Xmas. Then I shall have to go into the Court Theatre to produce the little play I have written for that house, and by the time I have got rid of this production I shall have, I expect, to turn in to the Savoy Theatre to superintend the staging of the opera. All this will—supposing everything goes smoothly—hold me fast until next Easter at the earliest, and then I shall be obliged to take a little rest. It seems to me therefore, on consideration, that I had better dismiss from my mind any notion of being able to start upon another play single-handed before the middle of next year; and that date is so remote that I cannot at this moment decide as to what idea would then be attractive to me to work upon. I think we had better leave the matter, for the present, like this, and I will write to you again by-and-by and let you know how my ideas shape.

I am sorry to have been away while you were at the Grand—particularly so as I fear I shall not be in London in November. It gave me great pleasure to read in the papers of Miss Rehan's unqualified success. / With cordial greetings and good wishes, / I am / Yours always truly, / Arthur W. Pinero.

173. TO L. S. IRVING

[A/4] 63 Hamilton Terrace, / NW.   31st. December 1897.
[Laurence Sidney Irving (1871–1914), actor, manager, and dramatist, was the youngest son of Henry Irving and showed much potential as an actor. He was drowned when the *Empress of Ireland* sank in the Gulf of St. Lawrence in 1914. His play, *Peter the Great*, was produced at the Lyceum on 1 January 1898 with Henry Irving and Ellen Terry in the leading roles.]

Dear Laurence.

My heart is with you, and will beat especially warmly for you tomorrow night. I hope *Peter the Great* will start you with a big stride upon a distinguished career—a career marked always by unwavering earnestness and steadfastness of purpose, worthy in fact of the name you bear. / I am, my dear old, young friend / Yours sincerely / Arthur W. Pinero.

174. TO WILLIAM ARCHER

[T/3(i)] 63 Hamilton Terrace, / NW.   25th January, 1898.
[Archer wrote to Pinero, congratulating him on *Trelawny of the "Wells."* Beerbohm Tree was playing Mark Antony in *Julius Caesar*, revived at Her Majesty's on 22 January 1898. Salomon August Andrée (1854–1897) was a Swedish engineer who attempted to discover the North Pole in a balloon in 1897. His body was discovered at White Island in 1930.]

My dear Archer,

I wish I could write you a long letter in answer to your very kind ones; but I am already at work again, and am obliged to make my acknowledgements to you in this chilly way. We shall meet soon, however, I hope, and then I shall be able to express myself with more warmth than the typewriter can suggest.

I read your *World* notice this morning with much gratification. It would be "quite out of place," as Miss Trafalgar would say, for me to thank you for the good things you write of me; I should think no more of doing this than I should think of blaming you for any adverse opinion you might at any time express. But I do feel entitled to say that, from what my people tell me of other criticisms, you are the only writer who has discovered the intention with which the little play was written. If all I hear be correct, the critics as a whole seem to be divided as to whether the piece is a weak farce or an imperfect realistic drama.

As to the acting. Those *real* views of mine which you invite must be breathed close to your ear. Some of it is, I daresay, better than you think it, and not so good as I think it; but it would be ungrateful of me, after working for a month with a company of actors who have at least done their utmost, were I to sit down and dissect the results in cold blood.

Poor Tree! His throat seemed very sore on Saturday night. But he is always sore, somewhere or another, about something. There was no critique in the *Star* last night, so Walkley is destroyed. Let this be a warning to all of you. If one could get further away from it all, how amusing it would be! I think that Andrée went up in his balloon, not to discover the North Pole, but to obtain an accurate survey of the actor-manager. / Yours ever, / AWP.

175. TO HENRY IRVING

[A/4] 63 Hamilton Terrace, / NW.   13th. April 1898.
[John Davidson (1857–1909) was a Scottish poet, dramatist, and novelist. His *Fleet Street Eclogues* was published in 1893, *Ballads and Songs* in 1894, and his adaptation of *Pour la Couronne* was performed, under the title of *For the Crown*, at the Lyceum on 27 February 1896. Edmond Rostand's (1868–1918) *Cyrano de Bergerac* was first produced at the Porte St. Martin, Paris, on 28 December 1897; Irving staged the play at the Lyceum on 4 July 1898.]

Dear Irving.

John Davidson, the poet, is about to approach you with a scheme of a drama he has conceived, of which he has written the first act. He is a shy creature, and I have undertaken to perform the unnecessary office of mentioning his name to you as being that of the writer of *Fleet Street Eclogues, Ballads and Songs*, etc., etc., and of the English version of *Pour la Couronne*. Pray forgive me for my intrusion; it is because Davidson is a considerable man, as well as a modest one, that I venture to write you in the matter.

I saw *Cyrano de Bergerac* played in Paris on Saturday night—a beautiful, a fine, thing. But the characters of Cyrano and Roxane have yet to be acted. I congratulate you on the possession of this piece. / With warm regards, I am, dear Irving, as always / Yours most faithfully / Arthur W. Pinero.

176. TO EDMUND GOSSE

[Ax/10] 63 Hamilton Terrace, / NW.   15th. April 1899.
[Gosse's congratulations were on *The Gay Lord Quex*, produced a week earlier (8 April) at the Globe.]

My dear Gosse.

Accept my warm thanks for your letter; it was a characteristically kind thought that prompted you to write it. Perhaps you guess there is no one from whom I would more gladly receive a pat on the back than from yourself. / Yours always truly / Arthur W. Pinero.

177. TO GEORGE ALEXANDER

[Cx/16; P/32] 63 Hamilton Terrace, / NW.   10th August 1899.
[Alexander proposed that Pinero write another play for him, and provoked this reply. Pinero did not work again with Alexander until 1906 when *His House in Order* was produced at the St. James's.]

My dear Alec,

I am glad to hear from you and to know that you have had an enjoyable and restful holiday. For myself, business has kept me in town much later than I care for; but we are off on Saturday morning to our old haunt—Maloja. Somewhere about Sept. 12th we shall drop down to Cadnabbia; thence I go to Turin, (to assist at the production, in Italian, of *Quex*! an odd experience) and finally, to amuse my step-daughter, to Venice. All being well I shall be home again by the middle of October.

Accept my hearty thanks, dear Alec, for your suggestion that I should write a play for the opening of your remodelled theatre. I have such pleasurable associations with the old house that I cannot reconcile myself to the title—the *New* St. James's. May it, at any rate, resemble the old in the fame and fortune it brings to its tenant.

Coming to the dry bones of your proposal, I consider it best to be quite open and candid with you. If my words bear a curt and abrupt look pray ascribe it to the limitations imposed by a hurriedly-written letter. Frankly, dear Alec, I don't think that you and I go well together in harness; or, rather, I do not feel happy in running in tandem with you, myself as wheeler to your lead. I know you take a pride in being an autocrat in your theatre; it is a natural pride in a position which you have worthily won for yourself. But I also have won—or have chosen to usurp—a similarly autocratic position in all that relates to my work. I hope I do not use my power unfairly or over-bearingly, but I do exercise it—and any other condition of things is intolerable to me. In my association with you on the stage I have always felt that you have resented my authority. In the case of our last joint venture the circumstances which led up to it were of so unhappy a character that I resolved to abrogate this authority—to reduce it, at any rate, to a shadow. But, at the same time, I did not relish my position and determined—even before I started upon a campaign which I foresaw could not be otherwise than full of discomfort and constraint—that I would not again occupy it. To put the case shortly, there is not room for two autocrats in one small kingdom; and in every detail, however slight, that pertains to my work—though I avail myself gratefully of any assistance that is afforded me—I take to myself the right of dictation and veto.

In face of this explanation, my dear Alec, (longer than I intended it to be) I trust you will forgive me for declining your offer, and will believe that this prompt candour on my part is exhibited in a spirit of fairness to yourself as well as from a desire to explain my own attitude.

Notwithstanding the foregoing I am, I assure you, none the less obliged to you for your proposal. By making it you pay me a compliment, one I appreciate thoroughly. / I am, my dear Alec, / Yours always truly, / Arthur W. Pinero.

178. TO WILLIAM ARCHER

[A/3(i)] The Granville Hotel / Ramsgate.   19th Jany. 1901.
[James K. Hackett (1869–1926) was a Canadian actor-manager who, while leading man at the Lyceum, New York, had played Lamorant in *The Princess and the Butterfly* (23 November 1897).]

My dear Archer.

Thank you for letting me read Mr. Hackett's approving word. I have asked Mr. Rice to send you a parcel of photographs, so that you may select one you consider suitable for the purpose. That with the monumental necktie has already been reproduced—in the special edition of *Quex*. Should you think an entirely new picture preferable, there is another view of the necktie—as seen from the East—taken at the same sitting and not perhaps beneath the dignity of the *Pall Mall* or, indeed, any other magazine in the world.

I have been brooding over the point you raise about the tendency of modern drama to gravitate towards hig'lif, and cannot help believing that the cause goes deeper than mere imitation of French models—that it is to be found, in fact, in the very root of drama. From the Greeks onward the dramatist has always drawn his inspiration, at any rate borrowed his method of expression from the lives of people of exalted station. Nothing, of considerable merit, but low comedy has ever come from the study of low life. As for tragedy, there is none that can be properly so esteemed in low life, because there is no height from which a common person can fall—consequently no irony of circumstance nor refinement of suffering. One is not greatly stirred by the sorrows, appropriate as one thinks, of those of humble condition; one is rather surprised and amused by the prosperity of the lowly—and then you get comedy, but not even then high comedy. / Yours always / Arthur W. Pinero.

I return to town tomorrow.

179. TO WILLIAM ARCHER

[Tu/3(i)] 63 Hamilton Terrace, / NW.   22nd January, 1901.
[Pinero's "Real Conversation" with Archer appeared in the *Pall Mall Magazine*, XXIII (1901), 388–399, and, as part of a complete collection, in *Real Conversations*, published in 1904. Captain Robert Marshall (1863–1910) wrote *His Excellency the Governor*, produced at the Court on 11 June 1898 and published in 1901.]

My dear Archer,

If ninepins have feelings they must resemble mine upon reading the first of your *Real Conversations*. But I will not ask you to alter your report save in two trifling instances. The first is at the bottom of page 9, where my allusion to the success of "a military play" might be misconstrued by an ill-natured reader—and who, to employ the late Lord Tennyson's phrase, "imputes himself"—into a sneer at what, by all accounts, is a very charming play written by my friend Captain Marshall of whom I am a cordial admirer. Please steer me clear of any misconception in this regard.

The other point occurs at the bottom of page 47, where I am made to say that one of the difficulties of presenting dramas of middle-class or low life lies in the circumstance that the majority of our actors are society people incapable of interpreting any aspect of life but that of fashion and frivolity. This I never said, nor do I think it for one moment. One can more easily get from our actors an imitation of low than of high life; while the most truly refined artists of my time—Coghlan, Bancroft, Wyndham and Irving—were not recruited from the ranks of society at all, but were middle-class men who went through the ruck of provincial apprenticeship. I believe the cause of the drama's constant dealing with the "Upper Classes" is to be found elsewhere. (See my hastily scribbled note to you of Sunday.)

I hope you will be able to supply yourself with another cue for your admirable paragraph about a school of acting, commencing on page 50. / With warm regard, / I am, / My dear Archer, / Yours always truly / A NINE-PIN-ERO.

180. TO MRS. PATRICK CAMPBELL

[A/3(ii)] 63 Hamilton Terrace, / NW.   28th. February 1901.
[Mrs. Campbell leased the Royalty from February 1900 to November

1901 and revived *The Notorious Mrs. Ebbsmith* there on 27 February 1901.]

My dear Mrs. Campbell.

Thank you for your very kind message. It was pleasant to hear, late last night, that the play had gone smoothly and well. That you should, after a lapse of some years, have repeated your former triumph is a feat of which you may well feel proud. For the rest, I heartily hope that the revival will serve the commercial interests of your theatre.

With the greetings of an old comrade—if I may presume to so describe myself—I am / Yours always faithfully / Arthur W. Pinero.

181. TO EDMUND GOSSE

[Ax/10] 39 Fourth Avenue, / Hove.   5th. November 1901.
[Pinero was working on *Letty*, produced at the Duke of York's on 8 October 1903. Gosse published *Hypolympia or, the Gods in the Island: An Ironic Fantasy* in October 1901.]

Alas, my dear and constant friend, I am out of London, intending to work here unbrokenly till the spring, and dare not even for a moment revert to the pleasures of the town. Your invitation is a terrible temptation to me; but I am one of those pitiably weak creatures who by an unnatural austerity render themselves capable of strong deeds. In which condition of outwardly-imposing, but really most unhappy, resolution I subscribe myself / Yours always admiringly / and faithfully / Arthur W. Pinero.
My hearty congratulations on your latest, delightful, achievement.
Edmund Gosse Esq.

182. TO MISS LAWRENCE ALMA-TADEMA

[Tx/19(ii)] 14 Hanover Square, / W.   19th June, 1902.
[Miss Lawrence Alma-Tadema (d. 1940), a writer and the daughter of the painter Sir Lawrence Alma-Tadema (1836–1912), invited Pinero to sign a letter protesting the censorship of Maurice Maeterlinck's (1862–1949) *Monna Vanna*. This piece was first produced at the Nouveau Théâtre, Paris, on 17 May 1902, and an adaptation by Alfred Sutro (1863–1933) was given a private performance at the Bijou, Bayswater,

on 19 June 1902. The first licensed performance in England was the Queen's on 21 July 1914. The man primarily responsible for withholding the license was George Alexander Redford (d. 1916), Examiner of Plays for the Lord Chamberlain from 1895 to 1911.

Pinero declined to sign the letter, which appeared in the *Times* on 20 June 1902, p. 7, supported by such people as Archer, Hardy, Jones, Meredith, Swinburne, and Yeats.]

Dear Miss Tadema,

I am surprised to hear of the taboo by our Reader of Plays of the proposed public representation in the French language of Maurice Maeterlinck's drama, *Monna Vanna*. I have not, however, read *Monna Vanna* and I do not, therefore, feel myself entitled to sign the letter of protest to the *Times*. Beyond this, I doubt the advisability of attaching to it the names of English Dramatic Authors. It is a matter, I consider for the action of the literary and theatrical critics.

Very likely it will be necessary ere long to thresh-out the whole question of the Dramatic Censorship in this country. And, without being in the least Protectionist, I am of opinion that the point had better be raised, when occasion shall arise, over a prohibited work of English growth. Maeterlinck's *Monna Vanna* already has existence and cannot be greatly affected by the vagaries of British puritanism. / I am / Yours very truly / Arthur W. Pinero.

183. TO THE EDITOR, THE *TIMES*

[Pp/37] 14 Hanover Square, / W.   Sept. 4. 1902.
[Sir Edward Richard Russell (1835–1920) was the editor of the *Liverpool Daily Post*, a former M.P., and president of the Institute of Journalists. He was created First Baron Russell in 1919. *The Gay Lord Quex* was revived at the Duke of York's on 6 May 1902 and provoked Russell to make adverse comments about the play during a public address. Pinero's response was published on 5 September 1902, p. 6.]

Sir,

I observe from your issue of to-day that Sir Edward Russell has been administering to the members of the Institute of Journalists at their annual conference some grandmotherly admonitions on the subject of the drama and theatrical criticism. This would not concern me greatly had not Sir Edward taken the occasion, in enforcing the familiar injunction that writers and spectators should always be on the side of the angels, to declare that my comedy, *The Gay Lord Quex,* is one which, on the score of flagrant immorality, is deserving of the severest censure. I have not the advantage of being a constant reader of Sir Edward Russell's remarks upon the current drama, but I am aware that his predilections incline to a class of production not of late years much in vogue upon our stage. Here Sir Edward has my sympathy, for it must be a sad matter for so earnest and industrious a critic as he has proved himself to be to find in the autumn of his critical life his gods displaced, to see work which he has loudly acclaimed either forgotten or treated with deliberate neglect. What I venture to complain of is that Sir Edward Russell in his chagrin at the mustiness of his ideals should allow his vexation to tempt him into unfairness towards work with which he is not in accord—work, perhaps, to which he brings, almost of necessity, an imperfect understanding.

My object in departing from my practice of refraining from intruding myself upon the readers of the Press is to challenge Sir Edward Russell to substantiate by extracts from my play (it is published) his charge against me of deliberate immorality. I challenge him to demonstrate by such extracts, if justly made, the "hard vileness" of Lord Quex; I challenge him to show that neither that character nor the play in its entirety displays "desire or preference of what is chaste," that, in short, the play contains "no suggestion for any feeling for the right side in life and conduct." That the comedy does not belong to the school of composition which labels each of its characters "wolf" or "lamb"; that it seeks to depict men and women as they are— not wholly virtuous nor wholly evil—I am prepared to admit. But I may remind Sir Edward Russell of the accepted *dictum* that a man should be judged by the good that is in him; and by this standard the Marquis of Quex is not, I submit, an unamiable personage. Lord Quex will not, I am convinced, be condemned utterly by intelligent and liberal-minded people because of his lapses—any more than Sir Edward Russell is to be so condemned on account of his present variation from truth, good feeling, and good taste. / I am, Sir, your obedient servant, / ARTHUR W. PINERO.

184. TO THE EDITOR, THE *TIMES*

[Pp/37] 14 Hanover Square, / W.   9 Sept. 1902.
[Russell in his reply (*Times*, 9 September 1902, p. 8) maintained his criticism was fair, that he had previously praised *The Profligate*, that he found *The Gay Lord Quex* a "non-moral" play and therefore condemned it. Russell also rejected Pinero's challenge to substantiate his charges by quoting extracts from the play. This rejoinder from Pinero was published 10 September 1902, p. 10.]

Sir,

It would have been more prudent if Sir Edward Russell had taken a day or two longer to frame his excuses. As it stands, his defence will not do at all. Not only does he seek to put aside my challenge under the mild plea that it is "unreasonable," but he now says "the character of the manicurist, Miss Fullgarney, is none the less *womanly, loyal, and chivalrous* because of its volatility; and there is one moment at the end of the bedroom scene when Lord Quex is moved to *warm admiration of these qualities.*" (Quex's attitude goes considerably beyond mere warm admiration, by the way; a circumstance which Sir Edward Russell has apparently forgotten.) "Nor, indeed, is it likely that he would ever be insensible to the characteristics of a 'brick' or a 'trump' conspicuously displayed." (Quite so.) "But is there any other indication of a moral feeling in him *except that, being about to marry a pure young girl, he declines to recur to the illicit embraces of the lady in high life* who so egregiously tempts him back to her?" A valuable exception truly. The italics are mine; the inconsistencies Sir Edward Russell's.

And this is written by the critic who a few days ago thought it fair to tell the members of the Institute of Journalists that my play contains "no suggestion of any feeling for the right side in life and conduct." Really, Sir Edward!

The Profligate, which appears to have won Sir Edward Russell's commendation, saw light in 1889. Much water has flowed into the Mersey since then. / I am, Sir, your obedient servant, / ARTHUR W. PINERO.

185. TO THE EDITOR, THE *TIMES*

[Pp/37] 14 Hanover Square, / W.   12 September 1902.
[Russell's second reply (*Times*, 12 September 1902, p. 5) accused Pinero of resorting to "enigma" and refused to subscribe to the opinion that people now "regard sexual sin in the cool and easy manner of Lord Quex." Russell further maintained that *The Gay Lord Quex* was "isolated by undesirable Restoration *morale* from the drama of the day." Pinero's final riposte was published on 13 September 1902, p. 14.]

Sir,
     Like Mr. Dick and King Charles the First, Sir Edward Russell cannot keep the Restoration out of his memorials. The word has a sufficiently alarming sound, and there ends the appropriateness of its application to the present question.
     A last remark. Those who have followed this controversy with interest or amusement, or both, will not have failed to notice the significant fact that Sir Edward Russell has evaded my direct challenge. He repeats his charge against me, though with a growing disposition towards the "more removed ground" of academic debate, but to justify it otherwise than by platitude and generality would be "unreasonable." So that this does not escape your readers I am satisfied.
     To make clear my objectionable enigma, what I intend to convey is that since the production of *The Profligate*—the period is fixed by Sir Edward's mention of the play; I do not suggest that *The Profligate* had anything to do with the movement—our drama has taken strength, drawn closer to life, advanced. As obvious is it to me that Sir Edward Russell is among those who have stood still. He may say, with a certain Sir Chichester Frayne in *The Gay Lord Quex*, "There are not many of us left; we are a dwindling band."
     Tendering you, Sir, my acknowledgements of your courtesy in affording the hospitality of your columns to a discussion not of the first importance, / I am your obedient servant, / ARTHUR W. PINERO.

186. TO WILLIAM ARCHER

[T/3(i)] 14 Hanover Square, / W.   23rd September, 1902.
[Pinero was preparing an address on Stevenson as a dramatist which he delivered to the Philosophical Institution, Edinburgh, on 24 February

1903. *Deacon Brodie; or, The Double Life* (Pullan's, Bradford, 28 December 1882; Prince's, 2 July 1884), *Beau Austin* (Haymarket, 3 November 1890), and *Admiral Guinea* (Avenue, 29 November 1897) were plays written by Stevenson and William Ernest Henley (1849–1903). Balfour's *Life of Stevenson* was published in 1901.]

My dear Archer.

I find myself, without much premeditation, going to Paris tomorrow. I shall not be away long; you shall hear from me directly I return and then, if you please, we will have our projected walk which I shall greatly enjoy.

I have read *Deacon Brodie* and *Beau Austin* and have made some pencil notes in the margin. *Deacon Brodie* I can get nothing out of for reading purposes—though I am open to suggestion. It is nothing but well-written melodrama, to my thinking, and unfortunately the drama is of a stale and conventional sort. What strikes me chiefly from my reading of *Beau Austin* is that Stevenson's (and Henley's) idea of writing a play was that it should be full of fine speeches. I can fancy them sitting together and saying "This or that would be a capital opportunity for a good speech," and Stevenson subsequently telling Henley what a splendid "speech" he had just written. It is all rhetoric, beautifully done but with no blood in it. And they all talk alike; even the Beau speedily lays aside his paint and patches and becomes as sentimental as the rest of them. I shall take *Admiral Guinea* with me to Paris. In it, if I recollect aright I shall find some speeches with grit in them—but still "speeches."

I read that you have had a birthday. You are getting quite a collection of them. My warm regard to you on these occasions and always. / Yours / Arthur W. Pinero.

P.S. In Graham Balfour's *Life of Stevenson*. vol. 2., page 3., you will find the following:—

> "The reception of *Deacon Brodie* had been sufficiently promising to serve as an incentive to write a piece which should be a complete success, and so to grasp some of the rewards which now seemed within reach of the authors. They had never affected to disregard the fact that in this country the prizes of the dramatist are out of all proportion to the payment of the man of letters, and already in 1883 Stevenson had written to his father: The theatre is the gold mine; and on that I must keep an eye."

This supports my idea that Stevenson lightly turned to the drama as a means of getting money easily and quickly, never dreaming of the study and pain and weariness that go to the making of even a "popular" play.

187. TO WILLIAM ARCHER

[A/3(i)] Overstrand Hotel, / Overstrand, / Norfolk.

28th. October. 1902.

[Pinero here refers to *The Letters of Robert Louis Stevenson*, ed. Sidney Colvin (London, 1900), I, 271–272 and 328.]

My dear Archer.

I am still on the hunt, you shall hear with what result later. In the meantime here are some extracts from letters relating to theatrical matters, not without interest. The letter to Henley of May 1883 should, I think, be read by the light of the letter to the elder Stevensons of September '84. I do not understand that R. L. S. yearned for "money enough to write a play" in order that the play should be a fine thing. He wanted money enough to enable him to break off from his hum-drum work so that he might turn with ease and freedom to the sort of composition which would speedily produce "some of the ready." And it is noteworthy in this connection to observe that whenever plays are mentioned Stevenson appears to have been at a low ebb pecuniarily; when his people, or his publishers, send him a cheque dramatic prospects seem instantly to drop into the background.

The Encyclopedia Britannica is at the service of the Institution named in your last. You will hear from Mr. Rice on the subject; I am asking him to take your instructions. / Yours always / Arthur W. Pinero.

188. TO IRENE VANBRUGH

[Pp/39] 14 Hanover Square, / W.   9th October, 1903.

[Irene Vanbrugh's own note to this letter reads: "This letter from Pinero came after the first night of *Letty*. The 'little man' referred to was my husband, who had had an accident to his eyes." Dame Irene

Vanbrugh (1872–1949), the famous actress, was the wife of Dion G. Boucicault the younger (1859–1929), an actor-manager. They met while appearing in *Trelawny of the "Wells"* and were closely associated with many of Pinero's later plays. Boucicault, "Dot," was responsible for the productions at the Duke of York's from 1901 to 1915 and managed the New from 1915 to 1920; he also worked in Australia (the 1880s and 1923–1924) and South Africa (1923).]

Dear Irene,

Thank you for your charming little note. It is good of you to have disturbed your first day of rest by writing to me.

Most warmly do I congratulate you on your triumph. I should have been heart-broken, I may now tell you, if the material furnished you had not enabled you to make it. As it is, today I feel ten years younger—for my unfulfilled promise to you has weighed heavily upon me for many, many months.

Your success amply rewards me.

I am glad to know that your little man—that is your good man—is not to suffer more than temporary inconvenience from the bad eye. It fills me with remorse to think that the mishap has been occasioned by his devotion to the cause.

"Soot! Feel happy!" / Your faithful friend, / ARTHUR W. PINERO.

189. TO WILLIAM ARCHER

[A/3(i)] 14 Hanover Square, / W.   13th. Octr. 1903.
[Archer sent his (customary) congratulations and opinion of *Letty,* which led to this lengthy explanation. Nevill Letchmere in *Letty* was played by H. B. Irving. Walkley's review of Duse appeared in the *Times,* 12 October 1903, p. 6.]

My dear Archer.

Thank you for your kind letter.

You are quite right in your view of the character of Letchmere. I have attempted to draw, not the mere, gross "man about town," but a creature of refinement and some culture—a man who, as you put it, is superior mentally to his conduct. (Note the difference, in the opening scene of the play, between Nevill and Crosbie.) Letchmere lives in rooms furnished with almost feminine delicacy, possesses a library, has musical tastes—and, unconsciously perhaps, quotes Milton! Undoubtedly one of his marked characteristics is a persistent, ironic, verbal playfulness. I thought I had made this clear; evidently I haven't. And yet I can't understand how anybody can believe that when Letty (in Act II) cries out scornfully "a moral lecture!" and he replies "I am conscious of the incongruity but repeat the admonition"—I can't understand, I say, how anybody can believe that Letchmere doesn't know—that *I* don't know—that he is sounding a phrase in a spirit of grim, ironic humour. The note may be a false one but it is not struck by me carelessly. The same observation applies to his response to Hilda's question at the restaurant, "You'll excuse my leaving off talking?" He is watching Letty and Mandeville, with what emotions we may guess, but his prompt reply to Miss Gunning is "I mourn the loss but recognize the necessity." Again, when Hilda in the Fourth Act, says "Mr. Mandeville did get testy at the restaurant, didn't he?", his reply is "The limit of irritability justified by our licensing laws was slightly exceeded." Isn't it obvious that this is a joke—especially when one remembers what did occur at the Café Régence? I repeat, is it reasonable to suppose that I believe these to be purely "natural" expressions? They are second nature to Mr. Letchmere, but that is all.

And do all men talk nothing but the simplest colloquialisms, even in these days? The men of my acquaintance—certain of them—do not, at any rate.

Not that Letchmere cannot drop into an easier mode of talk— indulge in slang too!—upon occasion. And here I want you to notice this—that I have attempted throughout (not only in this play but in others) to make the difference between the spontaneous utterance and the utterance which is the outcome of deliberate thought. Thus, when Letchmere is describing the bucket-shop to his sister he is on his verbal stilts. The bucket-shop is a matter he has pondered over, a subject his mind has dwelt upon. But directly he talks to Florence about her association with Drake he becomes, conversationally, another man. So it is in his conversation with Mandeville in the same act; yet, directly Mandeville has taken his departure, Nevill is sufficiently "natural" to say to Letty "Oh, bother her party! I look to you to manage that we are left alone, my dear." No verbal playfulness, no ornate diction, here. And again, in his scene on the "leads," his rounded phrases are the formal telling of a tale which his thoughts have previously put into shape. Very different is his remark about the street-organ—the organ being an incident of the moment—"The porter in Grafton Street has my orders, &c."

It is the same with Marion. "How you preach!" says Hilda. And Marion does preach; she is unrolling thoughts that are crammed away in her brain, polished and complete. The music of the street-organ is not ground-out much more mechanically. And so it is with Letty. When she says (page 19) "To my imperfect intelligence, it seems to me, &c." she is simply repeating what she has said to herself, if not to others, a hundred times. Her description of the "dome of solid gold" is another instance of this. Yet she is "natural" enough when she discovers that Nevill is a married man. "You might have mentioned it before, &c." The diction is not very lofty, on either side, at that point.

The story of Iris's downfall, as delivered by her to Trenwith, is carried out in much the same spirit. It is little more than a recital of phrases she has already framed. She "feels" every word she speaks, but she has spoken them, or something like them, to herself previously.

And so on, and so on. I could give you an illustration of what I mean by the difference between the spontaneous utterance and that which proceeds from carefully formulated thought from almost every page of my later work. But I have wearied you sufficiently.

I am told that Mr. Walkley is going to pitch into my literary methods in wholesale fashion. If he does so, I shall be tempted to remind him that, in his rhapsody of Signora Duse in Monday's *Times* he finds that all the delicacy of his own literary style, and all the resources of his scholarship, are inadequate without a quotation (unacknowledged) from my play. She is "alive all over," he writes, referring to the Duse. See *Letty*, page 27! / Yours always / Arthur W. Pinero.

190. TO H. A. JONES

[Ax/10] 14 Hanover Square, / W.   12th. Jan: 1904.
[Jones's new play was *Joseph Entangled* produced at the Haymarket on 19 June 1904.]

My dear Jones.

As you are about to produce a new play—for which I wish the best of good fortune—I assume you are paying one of your rare visits to this country. I wonder whether you feel inclined to fulfil your kind promise to lunch with me one day and have a chat by my fire-side. It would be good and comrade-like of you to do so. Name your *own* day, but don't let it be next Thursday.

I hope that Mrs. Jones and all your boys and girls are well. / Believe me / Yours ever / Arthur W. Pinero.

My luncheon hour is 1.30 and I would suggest that you come *here*, for comfort.

191. TO T. MALCOLM WATSON

[Ax/12] 14 Hanover Square / W.   14th. Jan: 1904.
[A benefit matinee for Clement Scott was held on 23 June 1904 at His Majesty's; it realized £1,200. Scott died on 25 June 1904.]

Dear Mr. Watson.

You may include my name in the list of the Committee organising the performance to be given in aid of Mr. Clement Scott. I sincerely regret the necessity for such a performance. / Yours very truly / Arthur W. Pinero.

192. TO WILLIAM ARCHER

[A/3(i)] 14 Hanover Square, / W.   8th. Feb: 1904.
[Archer's scheme for a national theatre was eventually published in 1907 as *A National Theatre, Scheme and Estimates*. His co-author was Harley Granville-Barker (1877–1946), an actor, writer, and director. He managed the Court and Savoy theatres with John Eugene Vedrenne (1867–1930) and was responsible for introducing many foreign plays into Britain, as well as productions of Shakespeare, Shaw, and Galsworthy.]

My dear Archer.

It is very good of you to present me with a copy of *Real Conversations*. I add it to a nice little company of books especially valued by me as coming from your hand.

I am greatly interested in what you and your young friend are doing in relation to the preparation of a scheme for a National Theatre, and I count it a privilege—which you may rely, of course, upon my not abusing—to be taken into your confidence. Let me have the Draft when you will, and I'll read it carefully; and then perhaps you will sup with me here one night in the old way and discuss the matter afterwards at the fireside. As to your begging-letter, whenever you send it, it shall receive a prompt response.

I am sorry you have a cold, but it can be nothing to mine. *Mine* was caught at that dreadful, fever-laden spot, Paestrum—good heavens, you sent me there, now I come to think of it!—and I cannot depend upon losing it before the Spring. And there's no knowing when we shall have a Spring in England; so my case is a bad one. / I look forward gladly to hearing from you again. / Yours always / Arthur W. Pinero.

193. TO WILLIAM ARCHER

[T/3(i)] 14 Hanover Square, / W.   16th June, 1904.
[The "volume" was the draft on a national theatre. Arthur James Balfour (1848–1930) was Conservative Prime Minister of Britain from 1902 to 1905. Edward Grey, First Viscount Grey of Fallodon (1862–1933), was a Liberal M.P. and Secretary for Foreign Affairs from 1905 to 1916. He was later British ambassador to Washington and chancellor of Oxford University.]

My dear Archer,

Your parcel came to hand all right yesterday. The volume is got up in a nice, blue-booky way, as befits the serious purpose. I am wondering now how, and in what direction, the charge of condite is to be fired.

I met Mr. Balfour at dinner a few weeks ago—since you stayed with me at Tunbridge Wells—and managed to turn the talk towards the subject of a National Theatre with a school attached to it. Mr. Balfour airily observed "Englishmen can never be *taught* anything." This was, of course, applied to the school rather than to the theatre, but it shewed the attitude that such men take with regard to matters outside the political game. Balfour left the room shortly after this weighty pronouncement—over which I had a wrangle with him—having to return to the House; and I remarked to Sir Edward Grey, who sat on the other side of the table, that we evidently had nothing to look for from the present Government and that we must fix our hopes

upon the next one. Grey gave us one of his wan smiles and said
nothing. / Yours ever / Arthur W. Pinero.

194. TO WILLIAM ARCHER

[T/3(i)] 14 Hanover Square, / W.   24th June, 1904.
[Benjamin West (1738–1820) was an American painter who, in 1763,
settled in London where George III became his patron. He became
president of the Royal Academy in 1792.]

My dear Archer,

I think it is not at all improbable that the medical gentleman
you mention was a member of the family to whom I owe my second
name. My paternal grandfather was Mark Pinero. He was a solicitor
and lived in Charles Street, Cavendish Square, and, for a country
residence, at Kingsbury, Middlesex. He was born 14th March, 1762.
He married, at a date upon which I cannot for the moment put my
finger, a Miss Margaret Wing, a daughter of a Deputy-Teller of the
Exchequer. She had to my knowledge a brother—Captain Thomas
Wing, R.N. who, as a youth, was on board the "Victory" at Trafalgar—
and a sister, Frances. Young Wing figures in Benjamin West's picture
of "The Death of Nelson" now hanging in Greenwich Hospital;
another portrait of him is in my dining room here. I have also his
full-dress sword; and had, until the moths deprived me of it, his
cocked-hat.

In none of the papers which I have by me is there any mention
of a Wing other than Thomas, Margaret, and Frances. But, of course,
there may have been another brother, or some family connection,
who practised medicine in Norfolk or Suffolk. And I am the more
inclined to believe that this was so because my father's sister, Margaret
Elizabeth—born August 10th, 1797—married a gentleman of the name
of Bunn and lived and died at *Ipswich*. This is, at least, an odd
coincidence.

I can add nothing to this precious information but I will send
your kind note on to my mother. She may be able to furnish further
particulars. / Yours always / Arthur W. Pinero.

195. TO WILLIAM ARCHER

[T/3(i)] 14 Hanover Square, / W.   2nd November, 1904.
[The "Real Conversation" is preserved in typescript in the British Museum (Add. MS. 45294) and contains some rather cynical remarks on the poor reception of Pinero's *A Wife without a Smile* (Wyndham's, 12 October 1904). Pinero also maintained that, whatever he wrote, he was criticized for not producing something else. His "new task" was *His House in Order* (St. James's, 1 February 1906); in his "Real Conversation" he had referred to his farces as chicken and his serious dramas as beef.]

My dear Archer,

I thank you sincerely for your great kindness. But, to be quite honest, I do not think I should like this "Real Conversation" to appear at the present moment. I would prefer that anything of the kind should be delayed until the play is withdrawn—an event which I don't fancy is very far off. I shall then have something to say, supported by documentary evidence, which I think will interest both you and your readers. That I should sit down now, in the face of such insult and opprobrium as has been poured upon me, and chat to you in the calm way in which you have made me talk does not accord with my sense of the fitness of things. I am not angry but I am exceedingly indignant.

What seems to be happening is this. Our "houses" at the theatre were very great up to the end of last week but, so far as I can ascertain, the audiences have been composed mainly of people who have come to search for the indecent suggestions discovered by certain gentlemen of the press. And in many instances people have left the theatre expressing dissatisfaction at not finding evidence of indelicacy. The middle-class playgoer—i.e. the dress circle man and his wife and daughter—has never been near us at all and shews no signs of coming. He has been frightened away by the bogey. The libraries (Bond Street Speculators) having tried without avail to get a ten per cent commission out of us, are now not only working for us but are working against us. In these circumstances, I cannot see a very long career for the little piece.

Don't forget that you have promised to give me a walk some day. / Believe me, / Yours always faithfully / Arthur W. Pinero.

P.S. I should like you to be the first to know that I have settled upon my new task. It is to be Beef.

196. TO EDMUND GOSSE

[Tx/10] 14 Hanover Square, / W.   21st February, 1905.
[The protest (*Times*, 27 February 1905, p. 6), signed by Barrie, A. C. Bradley, W. S. Gilbert, Gosse, Murray, Pinero, Walkley, and others, was against a scheme to erect a Shakespeare House in London as a memorial to Shakespeare because it would duplicate facilities in Stratford. George Gilbert Aimé Murray (1866–1957) was an Australian scholar and professor of Greek at Glasgow and Oxford universities.]

My Dear Gosse,
    I send you the typewritten copy of your draft letter of protest. Like yourself with regard to the letter drawn by Archer and Murray, I agree with it in the main; but I think it might be strengthened and made more explicit here and there without giving it the slightly vitriolic character of Archer's protest.
    I wonder whether you could leave your library to-morrow for a little while and lunch with me, say at half-past one, in the Grill Room of the Prince's Restaurant in Picadilly? We could then talk the thing over. In the meantime, shall I telegraph to Archer saying:—"Gosse preparing modified protest. I agree. Instruct me."
    You attach only four signatures to your letter but I assume you propose to append as many names to it as can be obtained. We don't want to be likened unto those everlasting tailors of Tooley Street. / Yours always / Arthur W. Pinero.

197. TO GEORGE ALEXANDER

[Ax/9] Stillands, / North Chapel, / Sussex.   19th Sep: 1905.
[Pinero, as ever, was concerned to get the right cast for his play (*His House in Order*), and in this, and letters 198, 200–202, he discusses various possibilities.
    Alexander was rehearsing in *The Prodigal Son* (Drury Lane, 7 September 1905) by Hall Caine. Iris Hawkins (b. 1893) was cast as the boy, Derek Jesson, in *His House in Order*. Arthur Bourchier (1863–1927) was an actor-manager, who helped found the Oxford University

Dramatic Society (O.U.D.S.) and at various times managed the Royalty, Criterion, Garrick, and His Majesty's.]

My dear Alec.

What a bore for you—more rehearsals at the Lane!

Very well; I look forward to seeing you next week, or whenever you care for the trip.

Were I you, I should look out for some little lady other than Miss Hawkins—"a wise-looking" child (so described in the play) with serious eyes. Bourchier speaks fair—but his telegraphic address is discouraging. / Yours always / AWP.

198. TO GEORGE ALEXANDER

[Cx/16; Pe/32] Stillands, / North Chapel, / Sussex. 22nd Sep: 1905.
[Pinero again discusses *His House in Order*.]

My dear Alec,

Yes, the character is that of a boy—"a serious, wise-looking child of delicate physique." He is eight years old. I doubt whether you could find a real boy to look it and do it, a girl is, as a rule, so much the more graceful, charming, and receptive. A comic boy is to be got, but hardly the other sort. However, if you can put your hand upon the prodigy Barkis "is willing."

The dates you give me in your letter are most attractive. But can it be managed? You ask me if I have finished. Cruel! Heartless! Have I ever finished till about ten minutes before the first rehearsal? The position of affairs is this. Acts I and II go to the printers on Monday. Act III I am now engaged upon; and then there is Act IV to follow. I can't *hurry*; that paralyses me. But the piece *may get itself done* by the date you mention—or earlier—and I will spare no natural effort to that end.

I have taken enormous pains over the thing, as I know you will believe; and when it is complete, it will appear—I hope—as if it were a week's work. Which is what I understand by technique.

It would indeed, be delightful if we could get the earlier production you propose and, once more, I assure [you] I will do all in my power to aid your altered plans. / Yours ever, / Arthur W. Pinero.

P.S. I do hope you won't be disappointed at the, apparent, simplicity of the play.

199. TO DANIEL FROHMAN

[Ax/8(ii)] Stillands, / North Chapel, / Sussex.   2nd. Oct. 1905.
[Irene Vanbrugh played Nina Jesson in *His House in Order*. Charles Frohman (1860–1915) was an American manager who leased the Duke of York's in 1897. He was drowned when the *Lusitania* sank in 1915.]

Dear Frohman.

It is the best of good news that there is a chance of your running over in January. The piece is, I think, coming out rather well and I should much like you to see it.

I have had Miss Irene Vanbrugh engaged for the principal female part—a fine one. She is clever and sympathetic and has done me good service always; and I see no fresher actress in the market. Of course, I could not have obtained her but for the kindness of your brother Charles in releasing her; and so he adds to the obligations I am already under to him. When you meet him, please shake hands with him for me.

Begging to be favourably remembered by Mrs. Frohman, I am, with warm regard for yourself, / Yours always truly / Arthur W. Pinero.

200. TO GEORGE ALEXANDER

[Cx/16; P/32] Stillands.   12th Oct. 1905.
My dear Alec,

Here is the proof of the print of acts I and II [of *His House in Order*]. I wish I could have sent you Act III—which is progressing famously—at the same time, so that you could have seen at the first glance how every hint and every clue contained in the earlier acts are followed up and rounded off. However, I shall not, I think, keep you long without the concluding portions of the piece.

I hope you won't allow yourself, at this stage, to be very seriously disappointed with the character of Hilary Jesson—who, necessarily, has to play somewhat of a waiting game. / Yours always, / Arthur W. Pinero.

201. TO GEORGE ALEXANDER

[Cex/16; P/32] [Stillands, / North Chapel, / Sussex.]

14th October 1905.

[Charles Macready Lowne (1863–1941) played several parts for Pinero, including Pryce Ridgeley in *His House in Order* and Peter Mottram in *Mid-Channel* (St. James's, 2 September 1909). Nigel Ross Playfair (1875–1934; knighted 1928) was an actor-manager who took several roles in Pinero's plays including Dr. Dilnott in *His House*. He was notable later for his management of the Lyric, Hammersmith (1918–1933).]

I need not tell you how pleased I am that you are satisfied with the work so far as it is in your hands.

I think there is no doubt that we shall be able to begin rehearsing on Dec. 1st. Even if the last act is not by that time through the press, the three other acts will fully occupy us till it is.

. . . . .

You have seen, of course, with your keen eye, the importance of the *child*—an importance which does not lessen as the play proceeds. Iris Hawkins would, I suppose, be the *best*; but if she is not available, and you know of no one in particular, Boucicault might help us. If we could find a child *as clever as little Hawkins*, the novelty might be better for us.

I have asked Lowne to write you again.

Would Nigel Playfair do for Dilnott? . . .

. . . . .

A handsome, *real* French lady would be the ticket for Mlle. Thomé, don't you agree with me. It would [put] just the right touch to the thing.

202. TO GEORGE ALEXANDER

[Cex/16; Pe/32] [14 Hanover Square, / W.]   20th Jan. 1906.

[Percy Macquoid (1852–1925) was a dress and scenic designer.]

I am glad to receive your kind note because it gives me the opportunity of saying, more expressly than I have been able to say hitherto, that I have *every* confidence in your ability to deal successfully, and brilliantly, with your very difficult task. My anxiety that you

should do yourself the fullest justice in a part which is a little foreign
to your usual methods may show itself too strongly; but you will not
blame me in your heart for this. Once more, Alec—I look to you to pull
us through, and I feel sure that I shall not be disappointed.

No, it is not you but one or two other things that worry me—
unnecessarily, you may think. The tone of our library, in particular,
mocks at me in my sleepless hours. This scene was to have been our
touch of the picturesque—"the old part of the building"—and Mr.
Macquoid has given us a bit of brand-new Shoolbred. It is this apart-
ment that was to have conveyed the idea that Annabel's boudoir was
also an old room. How else could the dry-rotten boards of the
cupboard have been so easily removable? But perhaps you will tell
me I fret about trifles. Do, if you can—for my consolation.

The drawing-room is perfect—just what I imagined. And the hall
will be good when finished off. Get an important bit of furniture to
face the fireplace, if you can put your hand readily on such a thing. /
Again, God bless you and send you luck, / Yours always, / P.

203. TO R. H. DAVIS

[Ax/17] 14 Hanover Square, / W.   17th. Dec. 1906.
[Richard Harding Davis (1864–1916) was an American journalist, novelist, and dramatist who edited *Harper's Weekly* beginning in 1890.
His *Farces: The Dictator, The Galloper and "Miss Civilisation"* was
published in New York in 1906.]

My dear Davis.

Nothing is so pleasant as the unexpected—when it comes in a
pleasant shape. I was delighted, on languidly opening a parcel the
other day, to find that it contained your *Farces*. Thank you a thousand
times for the book—ultimately to join others on my shelf which I
prize greatly, by the same writer.

I am a bit of an invalid, suffering from an illness following an
attack of influenza. Tomorrow I go into the country, with your plays
in my bag. I know I shall enjoy them. / Mention my name kindly to
Mrs. Davis and / believe me / Yours always / Arthur W. Pinero.

204. TO GEORGE ALEXANDER

[Ax/9] Hotel Vendome, / Place Vendome, / Paris.

12th. March 1907.

[Alexander's new production was *John Glayde's Honour* (St. James's, 8 March 1907) by Alfred Sutro.]

My dear Alec.

Thank you for your line. It was a keen pleasure to me to hear from my wife, and from others, of the triumph of your new production. I am glad for your sake, and for Sutro's—and for the sake of the theatre which seems to me to be for the moment the only home of the British Drama.

Here there is enough, perhaps, to amuse, little to edify and instruct. I return on Saturday and shall then be ready for our talk at any time allowed you by your multifarious duties—I believe that is the correct expression.

Again, warm congratulations—and kindest messages to Mrs. Alexander. / Believe me / Yours always / Arthur W. Pinero.

205. TO GEORGE ALEXANDER

[Ax/9] Stillands, / North Chapel, / Sussex.   27th. June 1907.

[In letters 205, 207, and 215, Pinero discusses the casting of *The Thunderbolt* (St. James's, 9 May 1908). Mabel Lucy Hackney (Mrs. Laurence Irving; d. 1914) made her debut at the St. James's as part of the crowd in H. A. Jones's *The Masqueraders*. Pinero cast her in the role of Phyllis Mortimore in *The Thunderbolt*. Nancy Price (1880–1970) played Hilda Gunning in *Letty* and Sophy in Hare's revival of *The Gay Lord Quex* (Garrick, 30 April 1908). She married Charles Raymond Maude (1882–1943) in 1907. Eugène Brieux's (1858–1932) *Les Hannetons* was produced at the Imperial on 24 March 1907. Alexander represented South St. Pancras on the London County Council from 1907 to 1913. On 25 June 1907 the council passed an amendment prohibiting exhibitions of "living statuary" (see *Times*, 26 June 1907, p. 12).]

My dear Alec.

Thanks for your note. I have had my eye on Miss Hackney for some time, and think I've made a fair estimate of her abilities. It is not unlikely that she will be engaged by Hare to play "Sophy" in *The Gay Lord Quex* on his forthcoming tour—to replace the recently wedded Miss Price who, with admirable promptitude, is in an "interesting" condition. Hare's tour finishes in December. It might be possible—and, if so, I think it would be a wise step—for you, without definitely pledging yourself, to establish some sort of a claim upon Miss Hackney in regard to my new play.

I know Brieux's piece, which is of the startling order and rather deceptive. I saw the rottenest actress in the world play the woman's part in it with considerable effect. But it is probable that I shall be rehearsing Miss Hackney in September, and this would give me a still more intimate notion of her powers.

So they carried their amendment against you at the L.C.C. meeting on Tuesday. I believe that, in this instance, the purity Brigade is right in principle, however inoffensive the particular entertainment may be which you witnessed. Frankly, I see no relation to art in this living statuary. And, if it isn't artistic, what is it? Besides, there's no knowing where these young ladies will stop. Give them an inch—! An inch is a great deal where nudity is concerned. / Yours always / P.

206. TO W. S. GILBERT

[A/3(iii)] Stillands, / North Chapel, / Sussex.   28th. June 1907.
[William Schwenck Gilbert (1836–1911) was knighted in 1907.]

My dear Gilbert.

Let me offer you hearty congratulations on the new honour that has come to you. It will please all those who are acquainted with your work; but it gives especial satisfaction to your brother dramatists, who are able to recognise more clearly how just and fitting the honour is. It has been, officially, too long delayed; but they had already conferred it on you.

With many kind messages to Lady Gilbert, I am / Yours sincerely / Arthur W. Pinero.

207. TO GEORGE ALEXANDER

[Ax/9] Stillands, / North Chapel, / Sussex.   31st. July 1907.
[Pinero discusses several possibilities for the cast of *The Thunderbolt*.
Stella Patrick Campbell (Mrs. M. H. Beech; b. 1886) made her London
debut in February 1907, and subsequently played Ellean in *The Second
Mrs. Tanqueray* and Nella in *The Notorious Mrs. Ebbsmith* when her
mother revived these plays in New York in November 1907. She was
cast as Helen Thornhill in *The Thunderbolt*. Edmund Maurice (Edmund Fitzmaurice Lenon; 1863–1928) had previously played Tong in
The Rector and Sir Tristram Mardon in *Dandy Dick*. Louis Calvert
(1859–1923) was an actor-manager who spent much of his early career
touring the English provinces with his own company. He played James
Mortimore in *The Thunderbolt*. Esmé Beringer (b. 1875) made her
debut in *The Real Little Lord Fauntleroy* (Terry's, 14 May 1888) and
played Justina Emptage in *The Benefit of the Doubt*. May Lever Pal-
frey (Mrs. Weedon Grossmith; 1867–1929) was cast as Rose Pointing.
Kate Bishop (1847–1923) was an actress and the mother of Marie Löhr
(b. 1890). One of Kate Bishop's early roles was Zaida Dalrymple in
Imprudence and she played Ann Mortimore in *The Thunderbolt*.
Maud Milton (1859–1945) spent her early career (1882–1887) with Wilson Barrett before joining Irving at the Lyceum. Frances Ivor made
her debut in 1888, understudying Ellen Terry for a time, and later
played in Shakespearean productions. Alice Mansfield (1858–1938)
played extensively in the provinces. Alice Beet (d. 1931) made her
debut in a provincial production of *The Schoolmistress*. She was cast
as Louise Mortimore in *The Thunderbolt* and as Lady Ridgeley in
His House in Order (revived, St. James's, 15 October 1914). Florence
Haydon (1838–1918) began her career at the Haymarket and Olympic.
Henrietta Cowen played Miss Tesman in the original production of
Hedda Gabler. Cyril Harcourt (Cyril Wotsley Perkins; 1872–1924) was
an actor and dramatist; his best known play was *A Pair of Silk Stockings* (Criterion, 23 February 1914). E. Vivian Reynolds (1866–1952), an
actor and stage manager for Alexander from 1901 to 1917, often took
small roles, such as Forshaw in *His House*, Jayne in *Mrs. Tanqueray*
(revived, St. James's, 4 June 1913), and Dunning in *The Big Drum* (St.
James's, 1 September 1915). Robert Horton (b. 1876) made his debut at
the St. James's in 1904 and was a member of Alexander's Company for
a few years. He played Harding in *His House*. Alice Crawford (b.

1882) was an Australian actress who, after performing with Wilson Barrett in Australia, came to England with him in 1902. Subsequently she played many Shakespearean roles.]

My dear Alec.

It may be that the author Mrs. Campbell alludes to is myself. I had a letter from her a short time ago begging me urgently to do something for her and her daughter. The only reply I could make was to tell her that the play upon which I am engaged *might* enable me to serve her girl, and I asked her not to dispose of Miss Stella without first consulting me. Perhaps it would be possible—and worth Mrs. Campbell's while—either to leave the daughter in England or to send her back at the beginning of the year. You might go a little further in the matter. The part will not be a great one, but it will be one that would exhibit a young lady to advantage.

Thanks for yours of the 29th.—characteristically prompt and helpful.

Maurice is not the man I see in Ponting, (for which Harry [?] is the ideal) good actor as he is. He could play James, but whereas his James would be a bit of acting, fat Mr. Calvert's James would, probably, be a bit of nature.

I am wondering whether Miss Esmé Beringer would not be better for Rose than Mrs. Grossmith. The latter might prove incapable, which Miss Beringer couldn't do. Leave it for a time, till I see how things progress.

Playfair we could *try* as Ponting. The audience liked his little mayor.

Miss Kate Bishop strikes me as having more the appearance of the stolid Ann than Miss Milton. She is, or was, quite bulky and has a fat face with small features. Character ready made! There are also Miss Ivor and Miss Alice Mansfield—but Miss Bishop seems to me most like it.

Miss Alice Beet I have seen but fail to remember. I trust to you, only we must be sure to avoid caricature. I had made a note of Miss Florence Haydon and Miss Henrietta Cowen in this connection. Miss Beet is doubtless the superior.

Mr. Harcourt, if he can act an elderly man—and he is clever

enough, I should say, for anything—would serve well as Elkin. Reynolds hasn't sufficient presence for Vallance. I suggest your Mr. Horton for this.

If we should slip up, or modify our impressions of the lady, in the matter of Miss Hackney—what about Miss Alice Crawford? She is clever and interesting, is she not?

I think I have covered the ground—and now I promise not to trouble you again for months. / Yours ever / Arthur W. Pinero.

208. TO WILLIAM ARCHER

[A/3(i)] 14 Hanover Square, / W.   13th. Novr. 1907.
This is to certify that, notwithstanding that he is, and has been for many years, a dramatic critic, William Archer has more virtues than are possessed by any other individual of my acquaintance. Eloquent with his pen, and logical in mind, he does not hesitate, even at the cost of much personal comfort and profit, to devote that eloquence and that logic to advancing the interests, and striving for the welfare, of those who stand in need of assistance. He is invariably prompt and dependable in his undertakings, courteous and forbearing in contro- versy, and ever ready to yield, at the dictates of reason and conscience, to the arguments of lesser intellects than his own. He is also strictly sober and clean in his habits and person.

He may make whatever use he chooses of this testimonial. / Arthur W. Pinero.

209. TO LEWIS MELVILLE

[Tx/12] 14 Hanover Square, / W.   14th Nov. 1907.
["Lewis Melville" (Lewis Saul Benjamin; 1874–1932) was the author of many books on Thackeray and honorary secretary of the Titmarsh Club. The club was founded to honor Thackeray in the summer of 1906 by W. L. Courtney (who was also chairman) and the original members included Pinero, Alexander, Barrie, Belloc, F. S. Boas, Ches- terton, Gosse, H. B. Irving, George Saintsbury, Tree, and Wells.]

My dear Mr. Melville,

I am a most unworthy member of the Titmarsh Club. I cannot accept the invitation you and the Committee honour me with. I am seriously behindhand with my work, which I cannot hope to finish before February or March next, and dare not allow myself to be distracted by having to make speeches at any gathering, however informal it may be. I shall make an effort to come to the dinner, if you will allow me to fill my proper *rôle* on the occasion—that of a silent, modest, obscure person. / With repeated acknowledgements, I am / Yours most truly / Arthur W. Pinero.

210. TO WILLIAM ARCHER

[T/3(i)] 14 Hanover Square, / W.   27th Nov. 1907.
[Granville-Barker's *Waste* was produced at the Imperial on 24 November 1907 by the Stage Society. On the deputation to Downing Street (to protest theatrical censorship) see letters 212–214.]

My dear Archer,

Yes, some day—one of those rare days when you have a sick headache and I have'nt one—do come up here and let us thresh the matter out. In the meantime (as you would, and do, say) I have the honour to inform you that I am not in the least unmindful of the fact that the Younger Generation is knocking at the door. What I am concerned about is that the youngsters are knocking at the wrong door—the side-door which admits to a narrow, dim passage, and not the front-door, opening into a lofty, spacious, sunlit hall. (There's langwidge!) I should like to see you encouraging the young dramatists to come into the "regular" theatre and fight there, accommodating themselves to the condition—after all, not so very irksome—imposed by the "regular" theatre. It is from the "regular" theatre that reforms must spring; it is in the "regular" theatre we want help; it is from the "regular" theatre that we have to kick out your intruding foreigner.

I am ready to accept responsibility for the ancient epigram you fasten upon me; and I would remind you that the Empire Theatre, and kindred establishments, are still paying dividends of say, twenty per cent; while as for Ibsen, so far as the English stage is concerned, where is "dat barty now"?

At any rate, I am consistent in my pigheadedness. In the early part of the year 1893, when I was trying to persuade a manager to produce *The Second Mrs .Tanqueray*, you advised me to let the Stage Society, or whatever the side-show of that period was, do the piece. I replied that I would rather throw the manuscript on the fire. I was'nt an old fogey in those days, however you may regard me now; but what I thought then I still hold to—that the only victory worth gaining in the theatre is a victory, by high aim and artistic means, over the great public.

I agree with you that it is a mistake to call Barker a follower of Mr. Shaw. The great difference between the two, I take it, is that the one means every, and the other not a single, word that he says. Barker, I fear, has wasted (I don't mean to pun on his title) a fine play by lugging in what is really not essential to his scheme—namely, the abortion business. And, oh! why could'nt somebody have sat on his head and prevented him from producing his piece until after we had gone to Downing Street? A week ago we had the Press pretty well with us; to-day it is thanking God for His mercy in bestowing a Censor upon us.

Pray don't think of acknowledging this even by a single line. / Yours always / AWP.

P.S. In case anything I have said should convey to you the impression that I am among the "anti-Ibsenites," if any such foolish people remain, let me tell you that in the long ago I went down on my knees to Irving, begging him to do *Hedda Gabler* at the Lyceum with himself and Ellen Terry as Lövborg and Hedda. That would have been a fight in the open, and no mistake; but unfortunately it was not to be.

211. TO WILLIAM ARCHER

[T/3(i)] 14 Hanover Square, / W.   2nd Dec. 1907.
[Pinero refers to his two plays *The Thunderbolt* and *Mid-Channel.*]

My dear Archer,
I can't see you to-night, greatly as I should enjoy doing so. I must sit down at my bench at 4 o'clock and work till 9 or thereabouts without interruption. My present job refuses to get itself forward at anything like a decent pace. The fact is, I have grown tired of my story, through long dwelling on it, and my head is buzzing with a scheme for its successor. A distracting state of affairs; but you know these moods, which have to be overcome, and will understand. / Yours always / AWP.

212. TO WILLIAM ARCHER

[T/3(i)] 14 Hanover Square, / W.   1st February 1908.

[The deputation to Gladstone was to reiterate the terms of the letter of protest to the *Times* (29 October 1907, p. 15). There, the leading theatrical men protested that the censorship had changed from being a political to a moral instrument, that there was no appeal against the decision of one man, that the drama was consequently debased, and that dramatists should receive the same legal treatment as any other citizen.

Gilbert Cannan (1884–1955) was a dramatist and drama critic of the *Star* for a short time (1909–1910). He married Mrs. Mary Barrie after her divorce from J. M. Barrie (1860–1937). Barrie lived at Leinster Corner.]

My dear Archer,

I received a pamphlet yesterday about a Society which has been formed to bring about the "Abolition of the Censor." Unfortunately it, and a circular letter which accompanied it, fell into the waste-paper basket, but I remember that the latter gave particulars of a Committee—which includes our Mr. Cannan—and other formidable details. This looks as if there is to be a decided split in the camp of the dramatists, and I am wondering whether a certain proportion, perhaps a considerable proportion, of the dramatists will consider themselves "sold" if the speakers at the deputation get up and propose the compromise which was settled upon at the meeting at Leinster Corner. It seems to me that, unless the deputation can claim to represent a decided majority, the idea of the visit to the Premier had better be dropped altogether. I confess, however, that the pamphlet and circular letter did not at the moment strike me as being worth much consideration; but I think I ought to refer the point to you. / Yours always / Arthur W. Pinero.

213. TO HARLEY GRANVILLE-BARKER

[Tx/16] 14 Hanover Square, / W.   10th Feb. 1908.

Dear Mr. Barker,

Thank you for your letter in which you tell me that the deputation of dramatic authors is to go before the Prime Minister, at 10,

Downing Street, on Friday, the 21st inst., at mid-day. I take it that it is not necessary for me to attend the preliminary meeting of the signatories on the 17th. I should be glad to be excused from doing so, as I am rather busy; but, of course, I will come if it is necessary. / Yours very truly / Arthur W. Pinero.

214. TO WILLIAM ARCHER

[T/3(i)] 14 Hanover Square, / W.   26th Feb. 1908.
[The deputation, postponed from 21 to 25 February 1908 because Sir Henry Campbell-Bannermann (1836–1908) was ill (he died in April 1908), was received at the Home Office by Herbert John Gladstone, First Viscount Gladstone (1854–1930), Home Secretary from 1905 to 1910. The deputation proposed that there be a court of appeal to arbitrate the case of any play refused a license by the Lord Chamberlain. The court would have three arbitrators, one appointed by the dramatist, one by the Lord Chamberlain, and one agreed upon by the dramatist, the Lord Chamberlain, and the Lord Chancellor (see *Times*, 26 February 1908, p. 18). Murray revealed that this arbitration plan was a compromise and that many dramatists wanted the complete abolition of the censorship.]

My dear Archer,
    We tumbled through, yesterday, somehow or other. Barrie opened the entertainment with a reading from the works of the late Charles Dickens. I followed. Any doubts as to my qualifications for playing Mark Antony in the next revival of *Antony and Cleopatra* were at once removed. It was a tear-compelling performance. Then came Gilbert with an anecdote about his own dealings with the Censor, almost Georgian in their remoteness from the present day. Mr. Gladstone replied, giving me the idea that he found in our visit matter that would cheer and amuse the sick Premier.
    Anyhow, the thing does'nt look badly in the papers; and, apart from my personal indebtedness to you, the dramatists owe you much for your invaluable counsel and guidance.
    Please don't trouble to acknowledge this, but believe me / Always yours sincerely and gratefully / Arthur W. Pinero.
P.S. I ave forgot to say as our Mister Gilbert Murray e gave the ole

show away at the hend by reveeling the fack that we was a disunited boddy.

215. TO GEORGE ALEXANDER

[Tx/9] 14 Hanover Square, / W.   10th March 1908.
[It appears that the success of *The Thief* (St. James's, 12 November 1907) by Cosmo Charles Gordon-Lennox (1869–1921) was holding up the production of *The Thunderbolt. The Thief* eventually ran for 186 nights, and this lengthy run undoubtedly prompted the suggestion Pinero makes here, but which was never followed up.

Frederick Harrison (1854–1926) was an actor and lessee of the Haymarket from 1896, first with Cyril Maude (until 1905) and then alone (until 1926).]

My dear Alec,

I have another proposal to make to you. How would you like to do the play at the Haymarket Theatre with somebody else as Thaddeus? Harrison would be content to make a very reasonable arrangement with you for the sake of having my play in his theatre; so that, if *The Thief* ran you through the season in King Street, you would be making money in both places. This scheme would have the additional advantage that, supposing the play were successful, it would run through the summer at the Haymarket without the drawback of a substitute appearing in your part. I think I could carry this plan through very easily.

I make this suggestion without prejudice, as the lawyers say, to our existing agreement. / Yours always / Arthur W. Pinero.

216. TO WILLIAM ARCHER

[A/3(i)] 14 Hanover Square, / W.   10th. June 1908.
[Pinero, in his speech (preserved in the British Museum, Add. MS. 45294) at a meeting held at the Lyceum on 19 May 1908 to establish a national theatre as a memorial to Shakespeare, argued against those who thought a national theatre was needed because little Shakespeare was being produced and because modern drama was not developing strongly. Those reasons, he thought, were not only false but good grounds for *not* establishing a national theatre. He wanted the theatre

to be a permanent showcase for the best in British drama, especially because prevailing economic trends often prevented the revival of good plays.]

My dear Archer.

Which I hope this will find you safely returned from your holiday, and greatly refreshed in body and spirit by the same.

Much has been going on in your absence. Particulars will reach you, I've no doubt, from Barker and others, and you shall be troubled with no description from my humble pen. But I should like you to glance at the enclosed, and then destroy it. It brought me into some disfavour, I believe, in certain quarters. That I don't care a rap about, but I should be sorry if you thought I had done anything, of malice prepense, to injure the cause. / With warm regard, I am, as always / Yours sincerely / Arthur W. Pinero.

217. TO WILLIAM ARCHER

[A/3(i)] 14 Hanover Square, / W.   17th. June 1908.
[*The Thunderbolt*, despite Pinero's pessimism here, did not finish its run until 3 July 1908.]

My dear Archer.

I am sincerely grateful to you for your letter. As to *The Thunderbolt*, I cannot flatter myself that it has failed from any other cause than that it is composed of material for which the public has no fancy. The drab in literature and drama is not for our climate. I don't let myself think of these things while I am working; but, in the case of *The Thunderbolt*, I realised its deficiencies fully when the job was finished. If I remember rightly, I confided my misgivings to you when I saw you just before you left England. At the same time, the play perhaps scarcely deserved the sneers which I understand it received at the hands of many of the gentlemen of the press. That I sadly missed your public pronouncement I need hardly tell you; for I have never failed to get much encouragement from you, even when you have given me a good "blowing up." Walkley, however, was kind to me; and by kindness I don't mean praise, but consideration.

I have now snapped my fingers, and am at work again.

It is a relief to me that you approve of the speech. / Yours ever /
Arthur W. Pinero.

218. TO WILLIAM ARCHER

[T/3(i)] 14 Hanover Square, / W.   1. July, 1908.
[The recent amalgamation of the Dramatic Authors' Society (founded
1833) with the Society of Authors (founded 1884) was not entirely a
successful one. A number of dramatists were unhappy with the Dramatic Sub-Committee of the Society of Authors and proposed a new society for dramatists, with Pinero as head of the organizing committee.
This action led to a reorganization of the Dramatic Sub-Committee (see
letter 221) and also to the inauguration on 17 March 1909 of the
Dramatists' Club, of which Pinero was the first president. (See Bernard
Shaw, *Collected Letters 1890–1910*, ed. Dan H. Lawrence, London
1972, pp. 799–801 and 832–834.)

The Society of Authors was located in Old Queen Street. George
Herbert Thring (1859–1941) was secretary of the Society of Authors
from 1890 until 1930. Robert George Windsor-Clive, First Earl of
Plymouth (1857–1923), Reginald Baliol Brett, Second Viscount Esher
(1852–1930), and Victor Alexander George Robert Bulwer-Lytton, Second Earl of Lytton (1876–1947), all held minor government posts at
various times.]

My dear Archer,
Many thanks for your kind letter. I think it quite proper that
you should be on the Dramatic Sub-Committee of the Authors' Society,
and I was heartily glad to see you there.
I have no objection to a union between the Dramatic Authors'
Society and the Society of Authors—at least, I had not until Monday
last, when I felt really indignant at the doings of the people in Old
Queen Street. Monday's meeting was simply an attempt to cut the
ground from under the proposed Dramatic Authors' Society—to burke
the movement, in fact—and though I have no great personal interest
in the matter, I will not allow myself to be mixed up in such tricks.
There are a great many dramatic authors who do not like the establishment in Old Queen Street, who have no special fondness for Mr.
Thring and for the gentlemen who help him pull the strings, and I
confess I am now almost inclined to be one of them. What we are likely

to do is to let Thring and Company play their own game, while we form a little, exclusive society for our amusement and, perhaps, benefit.

Hare, Shaw and I were nearly two hours with Lord Plymouth yesterday. Lord Esher also turned up. After having assisted in the discussion of the formation of committees, Lord Lytton rose and said he had to go down to the House of Lords. As he was leaving, he asked Shaw, Hare and me, in a whisper, to bring before Plymouth the points of dispute between the original Shakespeare Memorial Committee and the National Theatre Committee! I thought this distinctly amusing, but we did as we were told, and gave Plymouth to understand that our committee is firm upon the use of the word "national," and upon the giving up of the "world-wide" appeal. So there it stands at present, and I hope Plymouth will be as outspoken with his lot as we were with him. I rather fancy that Lytton is frightened of Plymouth.

I am just off into the country with my work. Mrs. Pinero is going to write to Mrs. Archer by-and-by. It would be a great delight to us both if we could get you down in our simple country for a while. / Yours always, / AWP.

219. TO WILLIAM ARCHER

[A/3(i)] Stillands, / North Chapel, / Sussex.   1st. Octr. 1908.
[Archer sent Pinero his "Blue Book" on the National Theatre.]

My dear Archer.

The Blue Book and your memorandum reached me this morning. I will apply myself to them in my spare moments.

Hare is touring, as well as Barker—which is the deuce. *I* shall be in town, I think, in about a fortnight's time; and at your service.

Warm regards from both of us to you and to Mrs. Archer. The weather here is extraordinary. In the day a scorching sun, and at night a sea of mist. / Yours always / Arthur W. Pinero.
What a grip you have of this National Theatre business! If ever the thing comes into being, I know you will be found carrying bricks up a ladder.

220. TO IRENE VANBRUGH

[Ax/19(i)] 14 Hanover Square, / W.   18th. Dec. 1908.
[Irene Vanbrugh played Zoe Blundell in *Mid-Channel*.]

Thank you for your kind letter, dear Irene. I look forward gladly to working with you again. You and I will do our best, as we have done so often before. The rest is in the lap of the gods. / Love to Dot. / Yours / Arthur W. Pinero.

221. TO G. B. SHAW

[A/3(iv)] 115A Harley Street, / W.   11th. Feb: 1909.
[The list for the new Dramatic Sub-Committee of the Society of Authors comprised Barrie, Carton, Cicely Hamilton, Granville-Barker, Jerome, Jones, Locke, Marshall, Pinero, Raleigh, Shaw, and Sutro. Shaw's letter to Pinero, discussing this matter and dated 3 February 1909, is printed in *Collected Letters 1898–1910*, pp. 832–834.]

My dear Shaw.
    Please note that I have removed to this address, where I hope to merit and receive a continuance of that patronage and support which have hitherto been accorded me. The gentry waited on at their own residences. Plumbing in all its branches.
    I have written to Mr. Thring, telling him that "my" Provisional Committee assent to the list of names proposed for the Dramatic Sub-Committee of the Authors' Society.
    Let me offer you my hearty thanks for your good offices in this matter, without which, I am sure, the present *rapprochement* could never have been brought about.
    I hope you have fully recovered your strength. Your recent utterances give no evidence of weakened energies. / Believe me / Yours always truly / Arthur W. Pinero.

222. TO G. H. THRING

[T/3(vi)] 115A Harley Street, / W.   5th March 1909.
Dear Mr. Thring,
    Mr. Charles Frohman writes me that he has secured in the Supreme Court of Illinois—the highest State Court, equal to the New York Court of Appeals—a reversal of the decision of the Appelate Court of Illinois with regard to the copyright and play-right of the work of English dramatists. By this decision, Mr. Frohman says, we are all protected. He adds: "it is a great victory from the fact that the

216

leading solicitor from Chicago refused to take the case, feeling that he could not get a reversal decision, but I went on and we have won."

Perhaps you will, when you have the opportunity, convey this good news to those belonging to the Society whom it may concern, and I suggest that mention should be made of Mr. Frohman's spirited action in the matter. / Yours very truly, / Arthur W. Pinero.

223. TO G. H. THRING

[T/3(vi)] 115A Harley Street, / W.   16th March 1909.
[Cecil Raleigh (1856–1914) was a dramatist who wrote several plays in collaboration with R. C. Carton and also with G. R. Sims and Sir Augustus Henry Glossop Harris (1852–1896).]

Dear Mr. Thring,

All being well, I will attend a meeting, if you will call it, on Tuesday the 30th. instant.

I note all you say about matters generally.

When the occasion arises, I shall venture to make some suggestions as to what should be done to attract to the Society of Authors the rank-and-file playwrights. I agree with you that it would be advantageous to the Society—especially to the dramatic side of it— were it fully representative of all classes of writers for the stage. I have no reason to suppose that Mr. Carton or Mr. Raleigh would oppose any sane measure which might be taken to induce those who are now outside the Society to join it. Pray don't allow yourself to be too distrustful of Messrs. Carton and Raleigh. Their grievance the other day is a perfectly understandable one, however alarming their method of expressing it. It is that, having been summoned to serve "for the ensuing year," they were told that they were not yet qualified to discharge the first and obvious duty of a new committee. Had these gentlemen been informed that they had been elected for the ensuing year *and for so much of the current working year as remains unexpired,* the unfortunate incident would not, I think, have arisen. / Yours very truly, / Arthur W. Pinero.

224. TO G. B. SHAW

[T/3(iv)] 115A Harley Street, / W.   6th. May 1909.

[In his letter of 4 May 1909 (*Collected Letters 1898–1910*, pp. 841–842) Shaw urged Pinero to contribute something to the repertory Charles Frohman was planning for the Duke of York's. Shaw also dubbed this new movement as intellectual, in opposition to the fashionable long-running play, such as *Charley's Aunt* (see letter 49). Pinero was eventually the most successful author in Frohman's venture, but with an old play, *Trelawny of the "Wells"* (revived, Duke of York's, 5 April 1910); it was performed forty-two times. Other contributions were Galsworthy's *Justice* (twenty-six performances), Housman and Granville-Barker's *Prunella* (seventeen), Elizabeth Baker's *Chains* (fourteen), Shaw's *Misalliance* (eleven), and Granville-Barker's *Madras House* (ten). Barrie, with George Meredith, contributed a triple bill of one-act plays. On Frohman's unsuccessful attempts see P. P. Howe, *The Repertory Theatre: A Record and a Criticism* (London, 1910) and William Archer, "The Theatrical Situation," *Fortnightly Review*, n.s. LXXXVIII (1910), 736–750. *When Knights Were Bold* (Wyndham's, 29 January 1907) by "Charles Marlowe" (Harriett Jay; 1863–1932) ran for 579 performances. The Duke of York's is in St. Martin's Lane.]

My dear Shaw.

Thank you for your letter. Nothing but the very kindest intention is behind it—which disposes of the dreadful charge you bring against yourself of impertinence.

When Barrie spoke to me about the proposed Repertory Theatre, his first condition was that I should have a new play ready for Frohman in the early part of next year. I was obliged to tell him that this is impossible; and any further talk we had upon the subject was, on my part, purely in the way of conversation.

As to your suggestion that, unless I cling desperately to the coat-tails of the Intellectuals, my work will be for ever classed with *Charley's Aunt* and *When Knights were Bold*—well, I must resign myself, if needs be, to that fate. But somehow, I have at the back of my mind a notion that in the long—or the short—run it is only the quality of work that tells; and that when a man does his best, his best will be no better in St. Martin's Lane, and no worse, let us say, in King Street.

On the point of mere temporary policy, however, I have no doubt that your arguments, wicked and Jesuitical though they may be, are

sound. / With repeated acknowledgements and warm regard, I am /
Yours always / Arthur W. Pinero.

225. TO G. B. SHAW

[T/3(iv)] 115A Harley Street, / W.   7th July 1909.
[Robert Vernon Harcourt (1878–1962), Liberal M.P. for Montrose
(1908–1918) had asked for a Committee of Enquiry into Theatrical
Censorship (see *Hansard*, 22 June 1909, vol. VI, 1909, col. 1545). A
committee was established, held sittings from July to November 1909,
and gave its report in *Report from the Joint Select Committee of the
House of Lords and the House of Commons on the Stage Plays (Censorship)* (London, 1909). When Shaw heard of the committee, he began
lobbying fellow dramatists and others to take some constructive action
in the matter. Although Pinero here did not wish to be troubled, he
later gave evidence to the committee (see *Report*, pp. 335–341, and letters 227 and 228).
    Mid-Channel actually opened on 2 September 1909 at the St.
James's, and not the first as Pinero mentions here.]

My dear Shaw,
    No ordinary inconvenience to myself would prevent me from
responding to your call; but I am in such a backward state with my
work, and in such a serious position of responsibility with regard to
the St. James's Theatre—which I have to open on September 1st., that
I must put my foot down firmly and say that I cannot allow myself
to be disturbed on any account whatever. I ask you to believe that I
say this very reluctantly, and that I do not lightly estimate what is due
from me to the Authors' Society and to my brethren generally. To
spring this sort of thing upon one at this time of year, when one is
entitled to look for a little freedom, is a bit too bad of them! As to
evidence of the fact that our Dramatic Sub-Committee passed a
resolution approving Harcourt's bill, that evidence can be given by
the Vice-Chairman, Mr. Henry Arthur Jones.
    I share your feeling of sorrow for poor Barker, and agree with
you that he ought to be working at his play, and recovering health in
the country. I begin to think that the preservation of the drama is
engaging so much of the dramatists' time that soon there will be no

drama to preserve. / In great haste and with warm regard, / Yours
always / Arthur Pinero.

226. TO GEORGE ALEXANDER

[Tx/9] 115A Harley Street, / W.   15th July 1909.
My dear Alec.

I think you are very wise to relax the tension somewhat for the
moment. I only hope my work as a whole will justify your good
opinion of it in part, and that its production may give you the little
bit of rest which you have so well earned. I shall be delighted to work
the piece with you in the country if we get any sort of success. /
Love. / Yours / P.

227. TO G. H. THRING

[T/3(vi)] 115A Harley Street, / W.   29th July 1909.
[Alfred Sutro gave evidence to the Parliamentary Committee on Censorship.]

My dear Mr. Thring,

Many thanks for your letter. Mr. Sutro is worried on the point
of his evidence not being in accord with the feelings of the total
abolitionists. I have told him that, in my opinion, he is entitled, if he
gives evidence at all, to present his own individual view. If you agree
with me, as I gather you do, will you reassure him?

A lot of material from Mr. Shaw reached me last night. I am
writing him saying that I hope you will be able to arrange with the
Joint Committee for me to appear before them later on. I am inexor-
able in my determination not to be disturbed just now. / With kind
regards, I am / Yours always truly, / Arthur Pinero.

228. TO WILLIAM ARCHER

[A/3(i)] 115A Harley Street, / W.   25th. Sept. 1909.
[Pinero appeared before the Parliamentary Committee on Censorship
the previous day. The Dramatic Sub-Committee of the Society of
Authors did meet and drafted a letter (*Times*, 29 November 1909, p.
10) commenting on the *Report* of the parliamentary committee. The

letter urged the adoption of the *Report's* recommendation of an optional censorship, with some modification, whereby a dramatist would be protected from prosecution if he submitted a play to the Lord Chamberlain and gained a license; alternatively he could trust his work to the normal law of the land. The letter further demanded "as complete freedom of conscience and speech as our fellow subjects enjoy."

The N.L.C. was the National Liberal Club of which Archer was a member. The memorandum (on Barrie) was sent as a private letter to the editors of leading newspapers in an endeavor to keep the publicity of Barrie's divorce proceedings to a minimum. It was signed by several eminent people. The text of the memorandum is printed in Janet Dunbar, *J. M. Barrie: The Man behind the Image* (Boston, 1970), p. 226 (see also Denis MacKail's account of the incident in *The Story of J. M. B.*, London, 1941, pp. 414–417). Alfred Charles William Harmsworth, Viscount Northcliffe (1865–1922), was a journalist and newspaper proprietor. He founded the *Daily Mail*, the *Daily Mirror*, and was chief proprietor of the *Times*.]

My dear Archer.

I'm glad you are pleased with the way things went yesterday. If I may say so, I really think my performance of the *rôle* of The Reasonable Man did the comedy no disservice.

I shall keep myself free for you on Monday. Let me know as early as you can when and where you will want me. Perhaps you would like to bring Barker up here; I should be delighted to see you both.

I am strongly against summoning a meeting of the dramatic sub-committee of the Authors' Society. Even if I could get the fellows together, it would mean discussion, dissension, and—G. B. S.!

I shall ring up this evening at the N.L.C.; but I've small hope of finding you there, for I have to leave my house soon after seven.

Your memorandum about poor J. M. B. is excellent. The only suggestion I can make is that, in a word or two, after "a writer of genius," you should bring in a reference to his old association with journalism.

Esher was in town yesterday—cos I sore him. I will write to him willingly, asking him to approach Northcliffe. Send me a copy of the Memorandum as settled to enclose in my letter. / Yours ever / Arthur Pinero.

229. TO EDMUND GOSSE

[Tx/10] 115A Harley Street, / W.   29th Sept. 1909.
[Gosse was invited to sign the memorandum on Barrie's divorce.]

Dear Gosse.

   The enclosed memorandum—to be sent to the editors of news-papers—speaks for itself. It is suggested that the names of not more than a dozen leading men should be attached to it. Will you let your name be of the number? As time presses, I beg for an early reply. / Believe me / Always yours truly / Arthur Pinero.

230. TO G. H. THRING

[T/3(vi)] 115A Harley Street, / W.   5th. Oct. 1909.
[Pinero was working on *Preserving Mr. Panmure* (Comedy, 19 January 1911); consequently, he suggests here that H. A. Jones be asked to organize the letter on censorship to the *Times* (see headnote to letter 228).]

My dear Mr. Thring,

   I have been expecting such a letter as you now write me for some time, and have been trying to summon up courage to tell you that I am going into the country, to shut myself up with my work, and that I shall not be able to give attention to any business away from my own desk for the remainder of the present year at least. I am very sorry, but there it is. I am wondering whether the Vice-Chairman will come to our assistance. If, in the circumstances, you think my resig-nation of the Chairmanship would ease matters, you have only to give me a hint to that effect. My earnest wishes are for the success and usefulness of the Dramatic Sub-Committee, and I have no feeling beyond that. / Believe me, my dear Mr. Thring, / Always yours truly, / Arthur Pinero.

231. TO G. B. SHAW

[A/3(iv)] 115A Harley Street, / W.   26th. Nov. 1909.
[In his letter of 24 November 1909 [A/14], Shaw gave Pinero details of a meeting of the Dramatic Sub-Committee of the Society of Authors

that was convened to draft a manifesto on theatrical censorship which appeared as a letter in the *Times* (29 November 1909, p. 10). Shaw also reported that H. A. Jones and Raleigh were reproached by the meeting for revealing committee secrets to the press.

Shaw's *The Philanderer* (1907) was produced in Stockholm on 14 September 1909, running for only five performances.]

My dear Shaw.

I came back to town to-day.

Your letter gave me a chuckle, which is good for me just now. I've signed the manifesto. In its reconstruction, the primary tenses had got a little mixed, so I made a few alterations; but they are too slight to demand a calling together of the sub-committee. The thing has therefore now gone through. As it stands, it is, as you anticipated it would be, a *dull* letter; but it will serve us as a formal declaration of our views and as something to refer to when the business goes a step further—if ever it does go a step further.

All being well, I shall attend, with my cough, the next luncheon of the Dramatists' Club and the meeting, on Dec. 7th., of the Authors' Society—(Dramatic Sub-Committee).

What do you say to the Dramatists' Club making a rule that the Club should, on occasions, authorise the publication of its proceedings and that any individual member shall be at liberty to apply for such authorisation, and that in no other circumstances shall the doings of the Club be published? I don't express myself clearly—haven't I had influenza?—but you will dig out my meaning.

I'm sorry you and Barrie have had such dreadful reverses—he at home, you at Stockholm. / Yours ever / Arthur Pinero.

232. TO G. B. SHAW

[T/3(iv)] 115A Harley Street, / W.   1st. December 1909.
[In his letter of 29 November 1909 (*Collected Letters 1898–1910*, pp. 884–887), Shaw wrote about the suggestion he made, at a "scratch" luncheon, that Hall Caine be a member of the Dramatists' Club. He also discussed the eligibility of Gilbert Murray for membership, and reported that George Alexander and Arthur Bourchier were about to denounce the national theatre scheme because there were no actors on the organizing committee. Shaw offered his "brotherly criticism"

on *Mid-Channel* and *The Thunderbolt*, especially in relation to the audience which habitually frequented the St. James's.]

My dear Shaw,

I agree with you, our manners at table are not always Vere de Vere. We must try to mend them. There are so many matters in your busy brain, however, that you have got mixed up as to our course of procedure in electing a member. The meeting at which you brought forward the name of Hall Caine was not qualified to invite him to become a member, let alone to elect him. The rule is, that a man shall be proposed at one meeting and that his claims shall be discussed and voted upon at the following meeting, and that in the meantime every member of the Club shall be notified that such-and-such a person has been nominated—the object of this rule being to remove the possibility of any man being elected without the consent, tacit or expressed, of the whole body of members. Such a contingency, therefore, as an undesirable person being sneaked in at a "scratch" lunch cannot occur; and I think you will see that, in the present instance, no decision has been gone back upon. The only decision arrived at on the occasion of which you speak—was that the claims of Mr. Caine should be discussed. That discussion took place, and it appears that the vote was against his being invited. It would perhaps be wise, as you suggest, to frame a rule forbidding the members to mention the matter of a nomination outside the Club while it is in the air.

My own view of Gilbert Murray is that he has claims upon us which are hardly assailable. The words "established reputation," which figure in the rules, were my own, but I cannot help thinking that a man who has done what Murray has done is a dramatist of that character. Anyhow, I shall certainly support him.

I thought the statement about the National Theatre scheme which appeared in the *Daily Mail* a treacherous business. I am not surprised, though, that the gentlemen you mention have forgotten that Hare and Robertson are on the Committee, for I never knew an actor who was not capable of forgetting everybody but himself.

I thank you warmly for your wise and brotherly criticism. I would make fuller acknowledgement of it, but that my wife is waiting impatiently to take me to a shop to buy Christmas toys for some children. I grieve to hear that Mrs. Shaw has the influenza. If I felt myself privileged to do so, I would beg to be allowed to send a sympathetic message to her. / Yours ever, / Arthur Pinero.

[In his reply, dated 2 December 1909 (*Collected Letters 1898–1910*, pp. 887–888) Shaw defended the principle of sounding out the membership's attitude toward a prospective member before a formal nomination was put forward. He also maintained that perhaps not all the members of the Dramatists' Club knew what the rules of the game were.]

233. TO G. B. SHAW

[A/3(iv)] Knowle Hotel, / Sidmouth.   16th. March 1910.
[See headnote to letter 224 for more details of Charles Frohman's repertory at the Duke of York's. The various plays joined the repertory in the following order: *Justice* (21 February 1910), *Misalliance* (23 February), triple bill (*Old Friends, The Twelve-Pound Look, The Sentimentalists*, 1 March), *The Madras House* (9 March), *Trelawny of the "Wells"* (5 April), *Prunella* (13 April), and *Chains* (17 May). Shaw, in his letter of 14 March 1910 (*Collected Letters 1898–1910*, pp. 905–906), advised Pinero to hold back the production of *Trelawny* until *Justice* proved less popular.]

My dear Shaw,
      I came down here last Thursday with my wife. She has been, and still is more or less, ill. A bad cold, neglected, and then pleurisy. This place is only half a success—plenty of sun but a keen wind from the east—and I shall return on Saturday. My invalid will do as well, perhaps better, at her own little home in the country; and Boucicault is bothering me to go to work in St. Martin's Lane. He says we must get on with *Trelawny* because they've two other plays to produce in quick succession—*Chains* and *Prunella!*
      Dear Shaw, this Repertory Theatre, at any rate in the making, is a cut-throat business; I don't see what good there is in it for anybody concerned. The public will make one play its favourite, and then to hell with the rest of the pieces. *Justice* would have prospered just as much if it had been given in the ordinary way, and *Misalliance* and *The Madras House* far more. The poor things are choking one another.
      Thank you for your information and kind hint. But I fear I am

too far gone to draw back now; and my little piece is an old one, and not of great consequence anyhow. Were it a new one I should be dancing about like a cat on hot bricks. However, I shall see how the wind blows when I get back. / Forgive this scribble, and believe me / Yours ever / Arthur Pinero.

234. TO G. B. SHAW

[A/3(iv)] Knowle Hotel, / Sidmouth.   18th. March 1910.

[After telling Pinero he thought *Trelawny* would probably do very well, Shaw, in a letter dated 17 March 1910 (*Collected Letters 1898–1910*, pp. 909–911), related an incident at the Dramatists' Club during which he had protested that his nominees for membership were always blackballed. He cited the cases of Hankin, Caine, and Murray to prove his point.

St. John Emile Clavering Hankin (1869–1909) wrote realistic, cynical plays; his best known works are *The Return of the Prodigal* (1905), *The Charity That Began at Home* (1906), and *The Cassilis Engagement* (1907). Anders Ryman was a Swedish doctor who specialized in massage and whom Shaw had recommended for Lady Pinero's cold.]

My dear Shaw.

Only one word, and that refers to the statement in your letter—no, not your letter, your Despatch—of yesterday that members of the Dramatists' Club should reflect that by blackballing your nominees they are "placing" a personal affront and "outrage" upon yourself. Don't think this. No member of the club is more beloved than you are—indeed is so much beloved; but the fellows like to attack you, because they know you are clever, don't mind really, and can defend yourself. And two thirds of your candidates are, you will yourself admit (in the privacy of your chamber) rotten. Poor Mr. Hankin! It is a cowardly objection to wage against him that he is dead; but, when he was alive, he used consistently to attack men who were more successful than himself, and that was not considered quite good form— men, I mean, practising the same calling as himself. The big 'uns never do this; not the nice little ones. As to Caine—that able, preposterous creature—you cannot, and do not I am sure, wonder that he is regarded as unclubable. He is, from a reasonable point of view, uneverythingable. Murray is, however, in my opinion, entirely eligible. I told the members so months ago, in your absence, said all I could for him, and was, like yourself, crushed. We shall get him in, in time.

My wife thanks you warmly for your very kind interest in her care. I hope to persuade her to consult Ryman. / Yours always / Arthur Pinero.

[In his reply of 21 March 1910 (*Collected Letters 1898–1910*, pp. 911–913), Shaw elaborated on the reasons why some nominees were blackballed. These people represented the younger generation of dramatists, whom Shaw and Pinero had often championed, but whom other club members saw as unsociable, "unclubbable," and a threat to their own position.]

235. TO MISS MARIE LÖHR

[T/18] 115A Harley Street, / W.   20th. April 1910.
[Marie Löhr played Josepha Quarendon in *Preserving Mr. Panmure*.]

My dear Miss Löhr,

Many thanks for your kind letter. The play is a light one—as you may guess from the fact that, all being well, it is to be done at the Comedy Theatre—but the part will, I hope, turn out to be at least up to the level of parts generally found in pieces of that character. It will be, I think you will find, pretty, varied and sympathetic. Neither the piece nor the part, however, is quite what I wanted to be associated with you over. I should have liked to try to carry your talents further than they have yet been allowed to travel, and I shall not be satisfied until I have had an opportunity of doing this. In the meantime, we must take things as they come—must we not?—and you may feel assured that the Comedy Theatre piece will not show you at the smallest disadvantage. I look forward to meeting you on the stage with great delight. / Give my warm regard to your mother, and believe me / Yours most truly, / Arthur Pinero.

236. TO THE EDITOR, THE *TIMES*

[Pp/37] 115A Harley Street, / W.   June 27 1910.

[Pinero's letter (published 28 June 1910, p. 13) was in response to Granville-Barker's letter published 27 June 1910, p. 10.]

Sir,

In *The Times* of to-day there is a letter from my friend Mr. Granville Barker defending his methods of playwriting and complimenting the elder brethren of his craft by telling us that the development of our native drama is an event quite of recent date. On the same page of your journal appears the announcement that an English syndicate, with Mr. J. E. Vedrenne, Mr. Barker's partner at the Court Theatre and elsewhere, as one of its directors, has been formed for the purpose of importing on a large scale the plays of French dramatists. This announcement provides a significant commentary upon Mr. Barker's letter. I believe I am as warm an admirer of the modern French drama as anybody; but I, and I fancy a great many other people, would prefer that playgoers should be put to the expense of travelling to Paris to see it.

The fact is, however, that Mr. Barker and those of his school are, in a measure, undoing the work of the despised older playwrights, who for a considerable time succeeded in keeping the importation of foreign goods more or less in check. By leaving Aristotle out the "new" dramatist is helping to let the Frenchman in. Evidently Mr. Vedrenne, profiting, it is to be assumed, by his experience at the Court and Savoy Theatres, has taken this lesson to heart. / I am, Sir, your obedient servant, / ARTHUR PINERO.

237. TO THE EDITOR, THE *TIMES*

[Pp/37] 115A Harley Street, / W.   June 30 1910.
[In a letter published 29 June 1910, p. 3, Vedrenne maintained that there should be "reciprocity in the world's intellectual and artistic output," and that his own aim was to produce the best drama of whatever nationality. Granville-Barker (*Times*, 30 June 1910, p. 13) believed the drama was developing then because apprentice playwrights realized the true nature of writing plays instead of merely attempting to copy French models, still the dominant influence on British drama. Pinero's letter was published 2 July 1910, p. 13.]

Sir,

If Mr. Vedrenne will forgive me for saying so, he is just a little wide of the mark. Not being a "new" dramatist, I find difficulty in talking about myself; but it is hardly immodest to remind Mr. Vedrenne that it is not a matter of importance that *Trelawny of the "Wells"* should be acted in California or that *The Second Mrs. Tanqueray* should be presented in Berlin. What is of importance is that every country should develop a native drama upon its own lines. This is exactly, Mr. Granville Barker assures us, what has been happening in England during a period coincident with his own activities; and he claims that there is growing up amongst us a lay opinion upon dramatic subjects quite at variance with the doctrines of experts. I fancy, however, that if Mr. Frohman were to publish figures in connexion with his recent spirited enterprise in St. Martin's-lane they would be an eye-opener as to the precise value of that lay support when confronted with the go-as-you-please drama in its latest aspect.

Mr. Barker, for whose talent and high ideals I have the deepest respect, says that much of our modern popular drama is already more French than English, and that it is better to have the real than the spurious article. This is an argument in favour of the operations of Mr. Vedrenne's syndicate; and I am so far in agreement with Mr. Barker that, desirous as I am that our stage should not be swamped by adaptations from, or imitations of, French drama, it is a question in my mind whether French influences are not likely to be more serviceable to Mr. Barker's "playwright in embryo" than those of Scandinavia, *minus* the great Norwegian's fine and strict sense of dramatic form. / I am, Sir, your obedient servant, / ARTHUR PINERO.

238. TO L. E. SHIPMAN

[Ax/19(i)] Stillands, / North Chapel, / Sussex.   19th. Sept. 1910.
[Louis Evan Shipman (1869–1933) was an American novelist, dramatist, and editor of *Life* (1922–1924). From 1910 until his death, he was one of Pinero's close friends. His *D'Arcy of the Guards* was produced at the St. James's on 27 September 1910.]

My dear Mr. Shipman.

The announcement, by Alexander, of the forthcoming production of your play—*D'Arcy of the Guards*—stirred pleasant recollections of our meeting a few months ago. Why, of course I shall see it—though it must be after I have come back from a holiday which I hope to be able to take shortly.

May your piece meet with great success, enjoy a long run, and encourage you to give us more! And—most important—may you be inclined to superintend your productions here in the future, and so let us see you often on this side!

Amen!

Again, and again—Good luck to you, and warm regard! / Believe me / Always yours truly / Arthur Pinero.

239. TO MRS. PATRICK CAMPBELL

[A/3(ii)] Stillands, / North Chapel, / Sussex.   21st. Sep: 1910.
[Mrs. Campbell was currently touring the United States and presumably wrote to Pinero to see if he had a new play she could use, or act in, on her return to England. Pinero's "little light play" was *Preserving Mr. Panmure*.]

My dear Mrs. Campbell.

Why do you write to me to the Garrick Club, where I very seldom go, and make me appear discourteous and ungrateful? Your letter of the 8th. did not reach me till this morning.

I don't know what I shall turn to after I've finished a little light play upon which I am now engaged; but should I become possessed of an idea leading in your direction I should be delighted. By-and-by, when I come back to town, I will ask you to let me have a talk with you.

You are now docile, you say. Well, I have never found you anything but a good comrade; and as for wrinkles, the only wrinkles I can associate with you are those which, through your great intent, you are bounteous enough to give to others.

Pray mention my name favourably to Miss Stella, and believe me, my dear Mrs. Campbell, / Yours always truly / Arthur Pinero.

240. TO L. E. SHIPMAN

[Ax/19(i); P/33] Stillands, / North Chapel, / Sussex.   8th. Oct. 1910.
My dear Mr. Shipman.

Sir John Hare was down here the other day and talked about your play. He had seen it on its first night in King Street and was delighted with the charming writing, delicate characterization, and pleasant fancy contained in your work. He had much praise, too, for the acting and mounting.

I scribble this line because Hare is a man of great taste and one whose opinion is, to my thinking, well worth having.

I am just now out of the way of things theatrical and don't know, therefore, how *D'Arcy* is "going," but I hope that Alexander is able to send you excellent news. / Hurriedly but sincerely yours / Arthur Pinero.

241. TO WILLIAM ARCHER

[A/3(i); P/20] 115A Harley Street, / W.   29th. April 1911.
[Archer's *The Life, Trial and Death of Francisco Ferrer* was published in 1911.]

My dear Archer.

I have just finished reading your *Life, &c., of Francisco Ferrer*. I must tell you, to satisfy my own feelings, how much I have been moved and impressed by it. You have told the terrible story finely and moderately, with a clearness of style which, I honestly think, is all your own to-day in literature. Most heartily I congratulate you on your valuable work.

If there is ever to be a Day of Judgment your work will lie on the Judge's table!

Begging that I may be kindly remembered by Mrs. Archer, I am, my dear Archer, / Yours sincerely / Arthur Pinero.

242. TO H. A. JONES

[Ax/10; P/28] 115A Harley Street, / W.   8th. May 1911.
My dear Jones.

It grieved me to read in yesterday's paper that you have been ill and in a nursing-home. The statement may be untrue but, as you

were complaining when we last met of sleeplessness, and of being generally run down, there appears to be some likelihood in it. At any rate, I hope you are now fully recovered. We have been fellow-workers for so many years—side by side, as it were—that any mishap to you comes to me with a sense of personal shock. Please therefore send me just one line of good news of yourself, and believe me to be, with affectionate regard, / Yours always / Arthur Pinero.
I beg to be remembered kindly by Mrs. Jones.

243. TO GEORGE ALEXANDER

[Tx/9] 115A Harley Street, / W.   31st. May 1911.
[Ethel Irving (Mrs. Gilbert Porteus; 1869–1963) played in a successful production of A. E. W. Mason's (1865–1948) *The Witness for the Defence* (St. James's, 1 February 1911). Pinero was beginning work on *The "Mind the Paint" Girl* (Duke of York's, 17 February 1912). W. S. Gilbert died on 29 May 1911. Alexander played Alfred Evelyn in Bulwer Lytton's *Money* revived at Drury Lane on 17 May 1911 as a command performance for King George V.]

My dear Alec.

As I think I told you when we last had a talk together, I have failed, for the moment, to hit upon a scheme for a play which would give opportunity to you and Miss Ethel Irving in combination; so there is nothing for it but for me to work at the play which I had in my head when we lunched at the New Gallery Restaurant, to place it where I can, and meanwhile to let my brain evolve naturally something which I hope will shape in the direction of King Street. This is a much better plan, in my opinion, than to go on squeezing my powers of invention and producing, perhaps, something which is in the result dry and mechanical. Of course, I am disappointed at this state of affairs but you may rely upon my missing no opportunity of getting back to your theatre, where I have always received so much courtesy and sympathetic treatment. You shall hear from me again on this point as soon as an idea strikes me which, in my view, would justify me in suggesting such a happy consummation.

I am full of sorrow about poor Gilbert, though he passed away gallantly. With all his aggressive intolerance, he had a big heart. He and I have been frequently together of late and I can hardly realise that I am to see the grim old fellow no more.

Your acting at the Command performance is spoken of as a triumph. It is said generally that you carried the whole thing through, in spite of many opposing circumstances, by your talent, grit and determination. / Yours always / Arthur Pinero.

244. TO GEORGE ALEXANDER

[Ax/9] Stillands, / Chiddingfold, / Godalming.   21st. June 1911.
[Alexander was knighted in 1911.]

My dear Alec.

I must write just a word of congratulation to supplement the telegram my wife sent you yesterday in her name and my own. No announcement in the coronation honours' list, or in any list of honours that has appeared for a long time, has given me keener pleasure than the one which concerns you and Lady Alec. I am genuinely delighted. Bless you both! / Yours ever / Arthur Pinero.

245. TO L. E. SHIPMAN

[Tx/19(i)] 115A Harley Street, / W.   25th. October 1911.
[Shipman's play was *The Grain of Dust* (1911). *Preserving Mr. Panmure* was produced at the Lyceum, New York, from 27 February 1912 to 23 March 1912.]

My dear Shipman.

The precious parcel has arrived safely; and here am I dictating this poor acknowledgement of your goodness, instead of sitting down to my table and writing you an ample letter with my own hand. But I dare say you will have no difficulty in understanding why I avail myself of this medium, and, understanding, will forgive. I am working very hard just now and the pen is so hateful a thing to me that I shun it on all possible occasions.

Anyhow I should find it difficult adequately to thank you for your beautiful and valuable gift—additionally valuable because it comes to me from one for whom, brief as our meeting was I have formed a great personal liking. The catalogue and portfolios will take a place among my most cherished possessions. I can say no more.

I rejoice to hear of the success of your new play. The public! well, we are always abusing it, but even in the lowest and least intelligent class of playgoer there is an instinctive perception which often has in it something finer than the cool reasoning of the scientific critic.

Between ourselves, *Preserving Mr. Panmure* is not likely to do much good in America in the conditions in which it is to be presented; nor would it succeed, I believe, were those conditions more favourable. It is a grimy little satire at best. And I have made alterations in it, to please Frohman, and robbed it even of artistic cohesiveness. But there it is, and I must hope that I shall be able to send my kind American friends something worthier and more pleasing on another occasion.

I grasp your hand warmly and again tell you how kind I think you are. God bless you, my dear friend! / Believe me / Yours always / Arthur Pinero.

246. TO G. B. SHAW

[T/3(iv)] 115A Harley Street, / W.   27th. Nov. 1911.
[Charles Hallam Elton Brookfield (1857–1913), actor and dramatist, succeeded G. A. Redford as Examiner of Plays for the Lord Chamberlain.]

My dear Shaw,

As I hope to be able to come to the meeting of the Dramatists' Club on Wednesday when, as I understand, it is proposed to thresh out the matter of the Brookfield appointment, I won't trouble you with my views on the subject by letter—except to say that, while I am as much opposed to the principle of Censorship as you are, I don't think Brookfield is at all a bad man for the post which has been offered him. His trivial plays and his stupid utterances in the magazines become things of the past when he enters upon his official position. A government, or Court, official has no politics, and I believe, from what I have seen of Brookfield, that he is a sufficiently shrewd man not to be betrayed into personal bias in the discharge of his duties as reader. At any rate it will be time enough to attack him—will it not?—when he really does misbehave himself.

But I am doing just what I said I wouldn't do—troubling you with a long letter.

Begging that I may be kindly remembered by Mrs. Shaw, I am, my dear Shaw, with warm regard to yourself, / Yours always truly / Arthur Pinero.

Oh, but it has just struck me—you are out of town till Thursday! What a bore!

247. TO G. B. SHAW

[T/3(iv)] 115A Harley Street, / W.　　19th. Dec. 1911.
[In a letter (16 December 1911, [T/14]), Shaw argued that individual negotiations over royalties gave managers the opportunity to give less reasonable terms to unknown or weak-minded dramatists. Thus there was a need for a common agreement or treaty over terms between all dramatists and managers. Harry Major Paull (1854–1934) was a civil servant, dramatist, and honorary secretary of the Dramatists' Club.]

My dear Shaw,

This is the first opportunity I have had of acknowledging your kind, violent, friendly, abusive letter, and, as it is, so pressed am I by work with which I am seriously in arrear, I can send you only a scrappy line.

I can't charge my mind with ever having dealt, while I was Chairman of the Dramatic Sub-Committee of the Authors' Society, with the question of a Managerial Treaty, though on this point your recollection may be more accurate than mine. What I do remember is that we devoted some time, during my term of office, to framing a model agreement which, when finished, was to lie at the Office of the Society for the use of young dramatists and others. As to the Treaty, to put it no higher, the Managers, if it were submitted to them, would fling it back into our faces. Of this I feel perfectly sure. If they accepted it, however, they could bind only themselves as individuals; they could not bind the new man who starts management next week or the week after. Nor can we, on our side, bind the young author who, desiring to get his play produced, will make any sacrifice to that end. There is no body of men more liquid, as you know, than those who make up what is called the Theatrical World, and the only method, I believe, of holding Dramatist and Manager to a settled form of agreement is to pass an Act of Parliament for that purpose. Even then, I fancy, it would be necessary, occasionally, for you and me—with the assistance, say, of Paull—to do a little bit of peaceful picketing.

By the way your argument as to the cutting down of authors' fees by Managers will not do anyhow. Your Treaty does not touch the question of royalties at all.

Redford is going! He resigned yesterday! ! ! ! ! ! ! ! ! ! ! ! ! ! ! ! !
Yours ever / AP.

248. TO WILLIAM ARCHER

[T/3(i)] 115A Harley Street, / W.   20th Dec. 1911.
Private.

My dear Archer,

I meant to write to you yesterday, but could not find time to do so, to tell you that Mr. Redford has resigned his appointment, being unable to comply with the conditions imposed upon him for next year. His position, he says, has been made intolerable for some time past, and his hope now is that he will receive an adequate pension in consideration of his past services.

The news of Redford's resignation is public property; his reasons for it, as expressed to me, are strictly between ourselves. / Yours ever. / AP.

P.S. I have told Shaw just the bare fact, but not the rest.

249. TO G. B. SHAW

[T/3(iv)] 115A Harley Street, / W.   27th Dec. 1911.

[A conference at the Society of Arts was held on 31 March 1911 and passed a resolution instructing the Dramatic Sub-Committee of the Society of Authors to "take into early consideration the possibility of negotiating a general treaty with the West-end Managers' Association embodying the clauses common to all dramatic authors' agreements, with a view to simplifying dramatic contracts." Pinero commented at that time that the objective was to protect young dramatists and not to encourage them to be extravagant in their demands (*Times*, 1 April 1911, p. 6). Shaw, in his lengthy letter of 20 December 1911 [T/14], argued the many necessary reasons for such a treaty, although he readily admitted no one would be bound by it. See also letters 256 and 257.]

My dear Shaw,

I have not had a moment till now in which to reply to your voluminous letter of the 20th.

On page 18 of it you say, "All we want is to get a treaty concluded between some ostensibly representative body of Managers like the Association and an ostensibly representative body of Authors like our Society." Now, the Dramatic Sub-Committee of the Society of Authors is certainly a representative body of Dramatists, and, what is more, an official body. Don't you think it will be enough for your purpose, therefore, if you chaps in Old Queen Street submit your treaty to the Association of West End Managers and leave the Dramatists' Club, in this matter, to their eating and drinking and facetious table-talk? You will never get an agreement among the members of the Club on the question, while you have, it appears, a complete agreement among the members of the Dramatic Sub-Committee.

Perhaps this plan is really what you are proposing, for I observe that in your letter (p. 23) you mix up the Authors' Society and the Dramatists' Club.

With regard to your charge against me (p. 30) that I gave a practical assent to the treaty by my attitude at the Conference held at the Society of Arts, I must remind you that I was in the Chair—a mere judicial dummy—and, as became my position, took no side, one way or the other.

Your assertion that I no longer come to the Dramatists' Club or to the Dramatic Sub-Committee (p. 42) is a shameless one. I served for two years on the Dramatic Sub-Committee, was constant in my attendance, and then resigned to make room for somebody of fresher intelligence—a course which I have always thought you favoured. It is true that I have been only once to the Burlington Hotel this session—on which occasion you were absent—but this default has been owing, as I have explained, to pressure of work and it is understood that, as soon as my new play is out, and has met with well-deserved condemnation, my attendance will be resumed with all its previous regularity. Your tweaking of my Wellingtonian nose over this is the one cowardly act I have ever known you commit.

And now, let your Dramatic Sub-Committee submit its treaty,

and we shall see what happens.

I should never think of wishing you a happy Christmas, and didn't; but I see no reason why I should not express the hope that you and Mrs. Shaw will have a prosperous and healthful New Year. / Yours always, / Arthur Pinero.

250. TO EDMUND GOSSE

[Ax/10] 115A Harley Street, / W.   28th Jan: 1912.
[Pinero was rehearsing *The "Mind the Paint" Girl*. He gave a talk, "Browning as a Dramatist," on 7 May 1912 in Caxton Hall as part of the Royal Society of Literature's Browning Centenary celebrations. He became a F.R.S.L. in 1910 and at various times served on the society's Council and Academic Committee. The Browning talk was published in *Transactions of the Royal Society of Literature*, 2nd series, XXXI (1932), 255–268.]

My dear Gosse.

A restful Sunday gives me the first opportunity I have had of writing to you. I am at work in a theatre every week-day, on my legs and with strained nerves, from eleven till four, sometimes later, preparing for the production of what *you* would mischievously call "another masterpiece." My general correspondence has, therefore to be disposed of with the aid of a type-writing machine; and, as I couldn't employ that medium with you, for fear of jeopardizing a valued friendship, I have been delayed in offering you a proper acknowledgement of your kind, though unwelcome, request of the 23rd.

Even now I write merely to say that I am *going* to write you in a little while to ask you whether you will be so very good as to give me an evening on which you have nothing better to do—as if that were likely to happen!—so that we may dine together quietly, as the phrase goes, and afterwards, over a cigar, that I may have the privilege of hearing you talk about Browning. How delightful and profitable this would be to me I need hardly assure you, and I hope you will find it in your heart to agree to the suggestion.

Pray don't trouble to answer this, but keep your reply for my further letter. / With warm regard, I am / Yours always sincerely / Arthur Pinero.

251. TO EDEN PHILLPOTTS

[T/16] 115A Harley Street, / W.   17th Feb. 1912.
[Eden Phillpotts (1862–1960) was a novelist and dramatist. His play *The Secret Woman* was banned by the Lord Chamberlain and a letter protesting this action was published in the *Times* (14 February 1912, p. 10). The signatories, including Pinero, also supported six private productions of the play given by Granville-Barker at the Kingsway in February 1912.]

My dear Mr. Phillpotts,
        Forgive me for employing this medium; I use it, at a time of great pressure, to avoid delay in answering your kind letter.
        In my opinion, you have been treated abominably, and I have said so, and am saying so, pretty freely. I hope that the agitation that is being raised in your behalf will result in bringing about a reversal of the ban upon your play and that we may yet see it presented under ordinary conditions.
        Yes, dear Barrie is a splendid fellow. / Believe me, / Yours always truly, / Arthur Pinero.

252. TO WILLIAM ARCHER

[A/3(i)] 115A Harley Street, / W.   21st. Feb: 1912.
[Miss Löhr played Lily Parradell in *The "Mind the Paint" Girl*, and in an interview with me indicated that in fact several people were planted in the first-night audience by George Edwardes (1853–1915), a manager, who thought the play an attack upon one of his artistes, Lily Elsie (1886–1962). The *Times* report (19 February 1912, p. 11) that "the gallery were unable to hear some of the players" is therefore inaccurate.]

My dear Archer.
        Accept my most grateful thanks for your letter. We hear now that the opposition on Saturday night, which manifested itself before the rising of the curtain, was inspired by some gentlemen in the City who are "protecting"—an odd word in such a connection—certain ladies of the musical-comedy world!
        Miss Löhr is hardly woman enough for her character but she is

everything else—or was till her courage was shaken. The bullies treated her brutally, evidently being under orders to "go" for the heroine of the play.

Again, thanks, my dear Archer, from my heart. / Yours ever / Arthur Pinero.

253. TO P. W. AMES

[T/14] 115A Harley Street, / W.   25th March 1912.
[Percy W. Ames (1853–1919), LL.D., F.S.A., was secretary of the Royal Society of Literature from 1890 to 1917. The (Royal) Academy of Dramatic Art held a public performance at the Duke of York's on 29 March 1912, at which several works were performed, including Act I of *Trelawny of the "Wells."* Pinero was a member of the Council of the Academy from 1906 to 1926.]

Dear Dr. Ames,
Academic Committee
I fear I shall not be able to attend the meeting on Friday. The public exhibition by the students of the Academy of Dramatic Art, in which I am interested, takes place on the afternoon of that day, and I have to be present.

Will you be so very kind as to give me five minutes of your time one morning when you are in town? I want to talk to you, if you will let me do so, about the Browning Celebration. / Yours most truly, / Arthur Pinero.

254. TO G. B. SHAW

[A/3(iv)] 115A Harley Street, / W.   29th. March 1912.
[In a letter (28 March 1912, [T/14]) Shaw reported that his wife, speaking of Browning's poetry, thought Browning a great dramatist but said she knew nothing of his plays. He also invited Pinero to write a review of Archer's *Play-making: A Manual of Craftsmanship* (published in 1912) for the *Nation*.]

My dear Shaw.
Please thank Mrs. Shaw on my behalf very warmly for her kind hint. I quite agree with her, and shall say something resembling what

is in her mind in my little paper.

With regard to Archer's book, I really don't feel inclined to write about it in the press. I have read it with interest and pleasure, as I do everything that Archer writes, but I fail in this instance to see clearly what he is driving at. If he is merely reviewing the dramatic work of the past five-and-twenty years, his review is sketchy and incomplete. If, on the other hand, he is attempting to teach the craft of playwriting to the would-be dramatist, it is not enough to point out only the faults of Shaw and Pinero. Have they no virtues? The special attraction of the book, to me, is that it is written by one of the few honest critics I have known; and, by Jove, I've known *precious* few! But, as I say, I am not inspired to write anything in the journals on the subject.

You yourself, Shaw, are an Enigma—not to me, unless I misread you, but to many others; only you are a voluble one. Shakespeare, too, was an Enigma, and he made a jolly good thing of it. So I am in excellent company. / Your attached / A. P.

255. TO IRENE VANBRUGH

[Ax/19(i)] 115A Harley Street, / W.   Munday mourning.
dere ireen i hoap you got mi tellyfoan messidge on satday ingoplaning wy i coodden dyne with you and dott larse nite it wos eggstreamly sweat of you too arst me and i truss to be moar forchnit on annother akashun with bess luv to you boath yoars affeckshunitly / A. Penroe.
too ireen boosko
for windam plaice
bryanstoane squair.

256. TO G. B. SHAW

[A/3(iv)] 15 Brock Street, / Bath.   18th. May 1912.
[Shaw, in a letter dated 15 May 1912 [A/14], threatened to approach the theatre managers alone and assert a treaty in the name of all the other dramatists (see letter 249). Shaw termed *The "Mind the Paint" Girl* "an awful play." George Augustus Moore (1852–1933) was a novelist and dramatist.]

My dear Shaw.

Your letter finds me here, whither I have flown to escape the disturbing pleasures of the town and, incidentally, for a light "cure."

How *can* I back you up in a step that I believe to be unnecessary and, it seems to me, wilfully provocative! I did take it upon myself, at the last meeting I attended of the Dramatists' Club, to advise Raleigh—Carton standing aloof—as to the way in which, according to my notions, the managers should be approached. I suggested that in the first instance they should be invited to assent to the *principle* of a settled treaty, as a matter of convenience to themselves as well as to authors, and that then, their assent being obtained, the authors should offer to draw up and submit to them such a treaty for discussion. Why, surely, these are the common methods of diplomacy; and the only objection raised, on the occasion I mention, was that more delay would be caused by adopting them. I ventured to point out that, as the proposed treaty had already been a business of years, a further delay—not really a delay at all, since the affair would actually be progressing—of a few weeks was of little consequence. Raleigh seemed to listen with agreement; and the next thing that happened was that I met a manager a'walking in the street, and he pulled me up and told me that this treaty had been abruptly flung at him and his brother-managers, and that they are all most indignant about it and are in a "see you damned first" mood, from the first to the last of them.

Of all the specimens of "how not to do it" I've ever seen—well, there!

And now you're in for a pretty considerable rebuff, which I've said all along you'd get, and may the Lord have mercy upon your soul!

Sir, I thank you for your criticism of The *"Mind the Paint" Girl*. Yes, I know it's unpleasant, in parts; but not in others. And I thought the others would make amends. And so they would, with stronger, more human and less theatrical, handling. And isn't *Othello* unpleasant; and some of the plays of Isben—as George Moore used to call him; and a few of those of Shaw? As to what impels me to write such things, if it isn't a desire to speak the truth I dun'no what it is. Yet I read only yesterday that I've depicted a phase of life which a serious dramatist should disdain to handle. Pouah! That's rot, at any rate; and while I preserve *your* letter, I kick *that* stuff into the grate. / Yours ever / Arthur Pinero.

257. TO G. B. SHAW

[T/3(iv)] 115A Harley Street, / W.   29th June 1912.
[Shaw wrote to Pinero 25 June 1912 [T/14] about the royalties and terms he was negotiating for the trilogy of one-act plays, consisting of his *Overruled*, Barrie's *Rosalind*, and Pinero's *The Widow of Wasdale Head*, to be produced by Charles Frohman at the Duke of York's on 14 October 1912. Shaw also reported on the latest developments in the treaty negotiations with the theatre managers.]

My dear Shaw,

I am settled for the summer in my little place in the country, but I am passing through London today on my way to paying a week-end visit; so I take this opportunity of dictating a few words in reply to your letter of the 25th.

You are a regular Shylock, but I shall have no hesitation in taking my share of any sum you may wring from Frohman over and above what he has himself proposed. As a matter of fact, I did not treat the matter of terms in connection with the forthcoming trilogy very seriously, regarding the affair rather as a spree; but though I despise a usurious character, I am inclined to agree with you that Frohman should not begin by practising his novel spirit of economy upon the dramatists. I assume this question of terms is now quite settled and that all can go ahead with composed minds. I give you my word that I have not written a line of my stuff yet. I have a paltry little scheme in my head, and that is all.

I derive great entertainment from the accounts you are good enough to give me from time to time of the progress of the negotiations with the managers. Of course, though I stand apart from these negotiations, I shall be very glad if you can bring to a successful issue a scheme which I feel is very near to your heart. / Greetings and regards. / Yours always, / A. P.

258. TO G. B. SHAW

[A/3(iv)] Stillands, / Chiddingfold, / Godalming.   23rd. July 1912.
[This, and letters 259 and 261, deal with various aspects of the production of the triple bill for Frohman, particularly royalties and the nature of each play.]

My dear Shaw.

No, I don't want Dot [Dion Boucicault]; but I shall be glad, for all our sakes, if you can employ him. For then we can be sure that there will be somebody of authority to look after the show when we have left the building.

What you tell me of your scheme and Barrie's naturally interests me very much. Both ideas sound first chop. For my part, I have tried to get away as far as possible from you and J. M. B.—which is prudent of me, for I could ill afford to risk direct competition with either of you. I concluded too, in less selfish moments, that as you were likely to be purely—or impurely—Shavian and immoral, and Barrie to be whimsical and tender, it would be better for the programme if I contributed something rather romantic and picturesque. So I am doing a little "costume" drama wherein the men say "Egad" and "Zounds" and the lady is continually dropping courtesies.

As to the method of announcing the pieces, &c., I will share in any feat you may devise; and, though I also have given up taking calls—don't always get 'em to take—I will be the Nijinsky to you and Barrie's Karsavina and Pavlova with the greatest pleasure.

A pleasant and healthful holiday to you and Mrs. Shaw! / Yours always / AP.

259. TO G. B. SHAW

[A/3(iv)] Stillands, / Chiddingfold, / Godalming.   8th. Aug: 1912.
[William Lestocq (1851–1920) was a dramatist, actor, manager, and Charles Frohman's London representative; as such he was involved in negotiating terms for the trilogy.]

My dear Shaw.

When the terms I proposed at our conference in Barrie's rooms were upset, I left the matter to him and to you; and I understood that *you* had settled the figures. So that the only point of dissent I raised on receiving Lestocq's letter was as to the five years. I told Lestocq that it is not my custom to let the control of my property go out of my own hands; and I have heard nothing from him since. Possibly he has taken to his bed.

Although I shall, of course, support you and Barrie in any reasonable demands you may make jointly, I am willing for my part

244

to accept the terms set out in Lestocq's letter. We should have stuck
to the arrangement I proposed to you, Barrie, and Boucicault. The
moment we wavered on that, we weakened our position.

As to the date of production, I am in your hands and Barrie's;
but I am inclined to think that the sooner we chuck the thing off our
chests the better. As you have a lot of rehearsing to do in September,
and as rehearsals disable one for regular work, you may as well rehearse
all day as three-quarters.

I send this to Adelphi Terrace not knowing whether you are
making anything like a stay at Kissingen. / Yours ever / AP.

260. TO L. E. SHIPMAN

[Ax/19(i)] Stillands, / Chiddingfold, / Godalming.   9th. Sep: 1912.
[George Pierce Baker (1866–1935) did much to encourage little theatres
in America and in 1905 established "47 Workshop" at Harvard University, a laboratory for the staging of plays by students (such as O'Neill,
Dos Passos, and Behrman). He moved to Yale in 1925. *The "Mind the
Paint" Girl* was produced at the Lyceum, New York, on 9 September
1912.]

My dear Shipman.
No sign of your friend—and, being your friend, my friend—Mr.
George Baker. Perhaps it's as well, however, that he has delayed
presenting your letter, for I am still in the country. But I go back
to town within the next few days, and then I hope he will turn up.

I *ought* to have gone to America to help over the rehearsals of
The "Mind the Paint" Girl, but August in New York was a bit too
much to ask me to face. I shall run over some day when there is no
business to be done, and I can see my good American friends with
undisturbed enjoyment. In the meanwhile it is high time you took
another trip to this young and promising country, and I should like
to think that you are looking at your travelling-trunks with serious
intent. / Warm regards and a hearty hand-shake! / Yours always /
Arthur Pinero.

261. TO G. B. SHAW

[T/3(iv)] 115A Harley Street, / W.   12th Sept. 1912.
[*Trespassers* was the original title of *Overruled*, which Shaw sent Pinero to read. Pinero reciprocated by sending Shaw a copy of *The Widow of Wasdale Head*, which Shaw read to his wife with "immense success" (letter dated 13 September 1912 [A/14]). Frohman apparently practiced some duplicity over the royalty business. Pinero wrote to Shaw on 14 August 1912 [A/3(iv)]: "We have been played off one against the other. *You* were told that Barrie and I had agreed to so and so; *Barrie* was told that you and I had settled to terms; *I* was told that Barrie and you had arranged matters."]

My dear Shaw,
   Your kind letter, and its enclosures, did not reach me till this morning. I returned to town on Tuesday.
   I have read *Trespassers* with keen enjoyment, and congratulate you upon it. I hope to be able to send you a "pull" of my simple stuff in the course of to-morrow. The only criticism I would venture to offer upon *Trespassers* is that a short Act of Parliament should be passed making it a criminal offence to include such work in a programme not composed wholly by yourself, or at any rate by yourself and others of your school and style. Your piece is disillusionizing to the furthest degree, and destructive of any item of ordinary character that may precede or follow it.
   As to those wretched "terms," let us arrange a meeting with Dot, and in five minutes we shall settle the whole business. Barrie can please himself as to whether he will be present. If he remains away, he may be sure that we will guard his interests. In the meantime I am, without prejudice, calling a rehearsal of my little play for Monday. / Yours ever, / AP.

262. TO GEORGE ALEXANDER

[Ax/9] 115A Harley Street, / W.   2nd. Octr. 1912.
[*The Turning Point* by Peter Le Marchant was produced at the St. James's on 1 October 1912; it ran 111 nights. Godfrey Seymour Tearle (1884–1953) was the son of G. O. Tearle and a fairly regular member of Alexander's Company (particularly from 1909). He was later

the first president of the actors' union, Equity, and was knighted in 1951.]

My dear Alec.

Only a line, to supplement my talk on the telephone last night. A very interesting play; you perhaps showing a power and virility you have never shown before; Miss Irving—the best English actress to-day— too lovely for words; Reynolds and Tearle admirable. Result, a fine success. / Bless you! / Yours / P.

263. TO G. B. SHAW

[A/3(iv)] 115A Harley Street, / W.   15th. Oct. 1912.
[The trilogy for Frohman as a whole was not successful; *Overruled* and *The Widow of Wasdale Head* were withdrawn after three weeks, *Rosalind* was kept on as a curtain raiser. The "one artist" was Irene Vanbrugh who played Mrs. Page in *Rosalind*. Margery Maude (1889–1967) played Mrs. Jesmond in *Wasdale Head*. J. M. Barrie's *Peter Pan* was first produced at the Duke of York's on 27 December 1904 and revived there every subsequent December until 1914.]

My dear Shaw.

I can send you only the merest scratch of the pen. I am throwing things into a trunk furiously. Early tomorrow morning I leave for Paris. In fact, I am flying the country.

The truth is we didn't do the right sort of stuff for *that* audience. Just think for a moment what the successes at the Duke of York's Theatre have been and then you can gauge our folly in attempting to play a different game. Not that we should have succeeded, in the circumstances, anyhow. It is a Barrie audience—more power to him. The Duke of York's is his dunghill, much as the Kingsway, or the Little Theatre is yours; and we were idiots to raise our crow there in his company.

Besides, there is but one artist in the present bill upon whom the eye of the public rests with interest and expectation; and she appears in *Rosalind*. The rest of the lydies and gents are nobodies. If I had known—suspected even—! But there, the whole affair has been one of muddle and miscalculation.

My piece wasn't acted. Poor little Miss Maude crumbled completely from nervousness. (It wouldn't have made much difference, perhaps, if she hadn't.) I fancy your crew didn't do great things for you.

I've suggested to Boucicault that he should advance his preparation for *Peter Pan* and in the meantime release the Libraries from their obligation. We oughtn't to let *them* in; we shall need 'em again. / Yours ever / Arthur Pinero.

264. TO MRS. PATRICK CAMPBELL

[A/3(ii); P/22] 115A Harley Street, / W.   6th. June 1913.
[*The Second Mrs. Tanqueray* was revived at the St. James's on 4 June 1913 with Mrs. Campbell and Alexander in their original roles.]

You are indeed bountiful to me. I take the books into the country, where they will give me many pleasant hours. I can't thank you formally.

As to Wednesday, people are saying that you are acting *Paula* better than ever. The revival, therefore, I am glad to think, won't hurt your reputation. But I know it irks you—as it does me—to retread these old paths, and I am grateful to you for this subduing of your spirit. Bless you!

If you need a testimonial at any time to your sweet reasonableness and pretty behaviour at rehearsals, don't fail to apply to / Yours faithfully and affectionately / A. P.

265. TO GEORGE ALEXANDER

[Ax/9] Stillands, / Chiddingfold, / Godalming.   17th. June 1913.
[Pinero was already thinking of the cast for *The Big Drum* (St. James's, 1 September 1915), although he had not written very much of it at this time. Phyllis Neilson-Terry (b. 1892) had appeared in a revival of *The Amazons* (Duke of York's, 14 June 1912), but did not play in *The Big Drum*.]

My dear Alec.

Your letter did not reach me till this morning owing to its having gone to Northchapel. The authorities have altered my postal address as above. Telegrams only should be sent to Northchapel. It is very confusing.

As to Miss Neilson-Terry, I will not say a word to urge you to carry your expenses beyond a reasonable and proper limit. The necessities of my play demand a handsome and very charming woman of about three-and-thirty; but I am content, if you are, to risk being able to pick up such an article later on. Or I will, if you prefer it, abandon my present scheme and try to frame another which would perhaps offer less difficulty—with regard to the principal female *rôle*—in casting. In fact, I will, as of old, do anything that is within my power to *help*. Let me know what you decide.

My wishes and hope is to get my piece finished by the end of the year. / Yours always / P.

266. TO GEORGE ALEXANDER

[Ax/9] Stillands, / Chiddingfold, / Godalming.　　21st. June 1913.
[Maldonado and St. Olpherts are roles in *Iris* and *The Notorious Mrs. Ebbsmith* respectively, but neither was revived by Alexander.]

My dear Alec.

Should I be coming to town, I won't fail to advise you in advance of my intention. Yes, there's a lot of stuff we might do at odd times, when opportunity offers. Maldonado and the Duke of St. Olpherts would furnish you with two good parts. I always "saw" you in the latter, even before I produced the play. I remember telling you so while I was writing it, one morning in Hyde Park. / God bless you. / Yours ever / P.

267. TO GEORGE ALEXANDER

[Ax/9] Stillands, / Chiddingfold, / Godalming.　　22nd. April 1914.
[Wilde's *An Ideal Husband* was revived at the St. James's on 14 May 1915.]

My dear Alec.

I had intended coming to town to see you within the next few days; but your letter, which I was glad to get this morning, prompts me to put what I want to say in writing. I am, I think, after many set-

backs, now getting on well [with *The Big Drum*]. My invalid is
stronger, and I am freer from anxiety than I have been for several
months past; but I have still much to do to my job—one of the most
difficult and delicate I have ever undertaken—and I should like you,
if you can possibly manage it, to make my new play the second
production, instead of the first, of your next season. Let me know
if you *can* contrive this rearrangement, which would be, I believe to
the advantage of all parties.

I have heard rumours of your plan of reviving *The Ideal Husband*.
It is, in my opinion, a happy idea on your part. As poor dear Irving
used to say, "it has never been done." / Love to you and Lady Alec
from us both. / Yours ever / P.

268. TO GEORGE ALEXANDER

[Ax/9] Stillands, / Chiddingfold, / Godalming.   2nd. June 1914.
[Alexander did not produce any of W. S. Gilbert's plays at this time.
Laurence Irving and his wife (Mabel Hackney) were drowned in the
sinking of the *Empress of Ireland* on 29 May 1914. The *Titanic* sank
on 14–15 April 1912.]

My dear Alec.

I "begged off" from Hall Barn, thinking I should be better
employed in getting on with my work. I go back to town tomorrow—
Wednesday.

As to the Gilbert fairy play—all right, if you consider it a wise
proceeding.

———————————

I had seen the placards before we met on Friday, but I couldn't
believe that another such appalling disaster could happen so soon
after the loss of the Titanic, and wouldn't buy a paper. Poor Laurence!
I had known him since he was ten, or less. His wife too—a good soul!
My heart is very heavy. / Yours ever / P.

269. TO IRENE VANBRUGH

[Ax/19(i)] 115A Harley Street, / W.   18th June 1914.
[Irene Vanbrugh played Nina Jesson in a revival of *His House in Or-
der* at the St. James's on 15 October 1914 and Ottoline in *The Big
Drum*. Pinero could be referring equally to either role.]

Dear Irene.

Yes, let us have a walk and a talk before I go away. I will tell you then the history of the girl up to the time of the opening of the story, so that you may live that part of her life in your imagination. You shall hear from me soon, asking you to name a day.

It *is* jolly, our walking together once more.

My poor dear invalid is better, but is not yet allowed to leave her bed. / Thank you for writing to me. Love to you both. / Yours / AP

270. TO G. B. SHAW

[T/3(iv)] 115A Harley Street, / W.   14th July 1914.
[Shaw's *Pygmalion* was produced at His Majesty's on 11 April 1914 with Tree as Professor Higgins. Since the play closed on 24 July 1914 Bernard Merefield, who had played Vincent Bland in The *"Mind the Paint" Girl*, did not play Tree's role there (although Shaw may have had him in mind for a provincial tour). Pinero sent Shaw a picture of Merefield to help him cast the role.]

My dear Shaw,

The enclosed, as the saying goes, explains itself. What it doesn't explain is whether Mr. Merefield is capable of playing Sir Herbert Tree's part in your play. Not having seen *Pygmalion*, I am hardly qualified to express an opinion of that point; but I am able to assure you that if, at any time, you engage Mr. Merefield you will find in him a very earnest, painstaking actor who will work for you loyally.

I send this to Adelphi Terrace, but I suspect you are at the sea-side with your spade and pail.

We seem to have given serious offence to certain members of the Council of the Academy of Dramatic Art by suggesting that they should do their duty!

Begging that I may be kindly remembered by Mrs. Shaw, I am / Yours always, / Arthur Pinero.

271. TO GEORGE ALEXANDER

[Ax/9] Stillands, / Chiddingfold, / Godalming.   9th. Aug: 1914.
[Alexander's "forthcoming production" was *Those Who Sit in Judge-*

ment (St. James's, 19 September 1914) by "Michael Orme" (Alice Auguste Greveen; 1874–1944), a dramatist and wife of J. T. Grein. The play ran for only twenty-one performances. Alexander did not adopt Pinero's suggestion to revive T. W. Robertson's *Ours*.]

My dear Alec.

I have finished the first part of Act III [of *The Big Drum*]—it is in two parts—and am trying to work at the remainder just as if things were normal. You may rely upon my pushing on as quickly as I can; I can do no more. I can't help feeling that the stroke of circumstance has thrown the piece thoroughly out of touch and tone with the times, and that I might as well fling the manuscript into a drawer and endeavour to forget its existence and all the thought and labour it has given me; which doesn't help to inspire my pen, as you may imagine. Anyhow I must antedate the play and describe its period as "1913."

I hope fervently that your forthcoming production will coincide with the success of our arms and induce the public to rally to the theatre. Is there anything in the idea of a revival of *Ours*—for the sake of its moving second act—with yourself as Hugh Chalcot? It has become a costume play, of course, but the cost of a revival would be comparatively small. / Yours ever / P.

272. TO GEORGE ALEXANDER

[Ax/9] Stillands, / Chiddingfold, / Godalming.   21st. Sep: 1914.
[Pinero was considering either Winifred Emery or Pollie Emery (1875–1958) for a role in *The Big Drum*; however, neither actress appeared in the play.]

My dear Alec.

I congratulate you heartily on your success [*Those Who Sit in Judgement*].

I cannot let you have my third act until it is finished and in print, and that will not be for some weeks. I will be perfectly plain with you. To work at such times is a difficult matter; and if the play had been designed for anybody but you, I should have put it aside promptly. As it is, I am sticking to my task with resolution and devotion. Should you, however, feel dissatisfied, I am quite willing to abandon it and to release you from any agreement you may consider yourself under to me.

I can send you Acts I and II, revised and complete, within the next few days, if you would like them.

For the moment perhaps it is hardly worth while to say anything about Miss Emery. / Yours ever / Arthur Pinero.

273. TO GEORGE ALEXANDER

[Ax/9] Stillands, / Chiddingfold, / Godalming.　　24th. Sep: 1914.
[See headnote to letter 269.]

My dear Alec.

Of course you shall have the third and fourth acts when they are finished—the third before long, I hope. After I've done the third—which *is* the play—my great difficulties are overcome.

Should you have to do anything—though I trust it will not be necessary—between your present piece and my new one, do you think a revival of *His House in Order* would serve? It might do well at the cheaper prices. Don't answer. / Yours / P.

274. TO GEORGE ALEXANDER

[Ax/9] 115A Harley Street, / W.　　19th Oct. 1914.
My dear Alec.

I write even these few lines with an effort. The cold I was fighting against during our rehearsals [of *His House in Order*] ended by laying me low. I have been much in bed; and though I am now struggling to get about a little, I am still very weak and unsteady. I hope to be right again in a few days.

I shall go on with my work as soon as I feel fit to face it. I have the latter portion of Act III [of *The Big Drum*] to do, and the whole of the Fourth Act; but, as I said in a previous letter, my difficulties end with Act III. As to a date of production, it would be simply throwing the play away, in my opinion, to produce it in such times as we are now going through. If the fortunes of war favour our country, things may brighten with the new year; but even then I fear my new piece is not of the kind that scales mountains. However, it shall be at your service when it's finished, and as strong and as good as I can make it.

I am under the depression of my illness, as you see. / Yours ever / P.

275. TO L. E. SHIPMAN

[Ax/19(i)] 115A Harley Street, / W.   6th Dec. 1914.
[Samuel Harden Church lived from 1858 to 1943. Percy Wallace Mac-Kaye (1875–1956) was an American poet and dramatist. From 1939 to 1944 he was librarian of Congress and from 1949 to 1952 Boylston Professor at Harvard University.]

My dear Shipman.

On re-reading your kind letter of Oct. 20th., I am surprised, and not a little ashamed, to find how long I have allowed it to remain unacknowledged. Do forgive me.

I circulated your newspaper cuttings. They were much appreciated. What a splendid reply to the German appeal is that of Mr. Church, the President of the Carnegie Institute at Pittsburgh!

All the news that comes to us from the "front"—I don't mean only press news—is encouraging. We—the Allies—are doing well, and shall do still better when our forces are augmented. The mobilization in France is barely completed, and our own new army is yet in the making. In another month or two things will move at a quicker rate.

As for work, I am pegging away at my job; but the deuce of it is that, having done two thirds of it, I can't recollect what I've written! With me it is as if an iron door had suddenly banged and shut out the operations of one's brain before the war. But these are small matters.

Various volunteer corps are being formed in this country for Home Defence. One of them is called the United Arts Force and I am its Chairman. This interests me more for the moment than play-writing. We are about 1,700 strong—art workers of all grades. There are more than a million of such volunteers in England, drilling hard and ready to shoulder a rifle if need be.

Do you keep Christmas in America in the English fashion? I forget. Anyhow you can't avoid a New Year, and I wish very heartily

that it may bring you increase of happiness and prosperity. / Yours ever / Arthur Pinero.
P.S. Mr. Percy MacKay's poems are fine.

276. TO THE EDITOR, THE *TIMES*

[Pp/37] 115A Harley Street, / W.   10 May 1915.
[Pinero's letter was published on 11 May 1915, p. 9. The *Lusitania* was sunk by enemy action on 7 May 1915. More than 200 naturalized Germans responded to Pinero's idea (see *Times*, 12 May, p. 9; 13 May, p. 9; 14 May, p. 10; 15 May, p. 10).]

Sir,
        The sinking of the *Lusitania*, involving the cruel murder of hundreds of helpless and innocent non-combatants, affords those Germans who are naturalized British citizens holding prominent positions in this country an opportunity of performing an act which, even in the opinion of many who bear them no particular ill-will, is long overdue. We are in the tenth month of a war which has from the beginning been carried on by Germany with almost unspeakable treachery and vileness; but up to the present time not a single one of the distinguished Germans in our midst has thought fit to make a public avowal of his disagreement with the deliberate policy of barbarism pursued by the German Powers or to utter a word of indignation and disclaimer. Surely the moment has arrived when these gentlemen, in their own interests, if for no higher reason, should break silence and individually or collectively raise their voices against the infamous deeds which are being perpetrated by Germany. I venture to suggest that they might with propriety band together and present a loyal address to the King embracing an expression of their detestation of Germany's methods of warfare; but perhaps this may be better left to their own discretion and good feeling. What I would emphasize, however, is that continued silence on their part lays them open to the supposition that, thinking that the fate of England is hanging in the balance, they are—to use the common phrase—sitting on the gate. A word of warning, therefore, is neither gratuitous or unfriendly. The temper of this country, slow to rouse, is becoming an ugly one. The gate may fall from its hinges. / Your obedient servant, / ARTHUR PINERO.

277. TO GEORGE ALEXANDER

[Ax/9] Stillands, / Chiddingfold, / Godalming.   21st. May 1915.
[The "blood-curdles" was a spy drama, *The Day before the Day* (St. James's, 19 May 1915) by Chester Bailey Fernald (1869–1938), an American writer and dramatist. It ran nineteen nights.]

My dear Alec.

Try as I may, I fear I cannot wring the third act [of *The Big Drum*] from the printers in time for you to read it before Thursday. I have only just received proofs of the earlier pages which I supplied them with on the 10th.! They have got all my stuff, but I suppose they are working shorthanded, and now the Whitsun holidays intervene.

In these circumstances, shall we postpone our meeting arranged for Thursday, or not? The delay will not be more than a few days. I leave it to you. In any event I return to town on Wednesday morning.

I hope the blood-curdles is doing well. Of course the critics—kind, helpful souls!—complain of its not being a "St. James's play." But as you have produced every form of drama in King Street from Shakespeare to farce, it is difficult to understand what a "St. James's play" really is. / Yours ever / P.

278. TO GEORGE ALEXANDER

[Ax/9] Stillands, / Chiddingfold, / Godalming.   25th. May 1915.
[The Society of Authors had relocated in Gower Street.]

My dear Alec.

It is impossible for me to come to you on Thursday, I am sorry to say. I have engagements—I am not speaking of Gower Street—from which I cannot extricate myself. Let our meeting stand over for a few days, when you will have read Act III and will be less in the dark. I will run down to Chorleywood then with pleasure.

No, I have not written Act IV; I am now engaged upon it.

If you feel you would rather not do the piece in the autumn, or at any other time, don't hesitate to say so.

Please thank Lady Alec for her kind postscript, and believe me / Yours ever / P.

279. TO GEORGE ALEXANDER

[Ax/9] Stillands, / Chiddingfold, / Godalming.   18th. July 1915.
[Irene Vanbrugh played Ottoline and Alexander played Philip Mackworth in *The Big Drum*.]

My dear Alec.

I shall be prepared, if I am alive, to rehearse at the St. James's on Wednesday, August 4th., at 11 o'clock. But please don't ask me to read the play. I haven't done such a thing for years; and when I did do it, never found it of the smallest help. Apart from the fact that my printed books are exhaustively—and perhaps exhaustingly—descriptive, the custom dates, as you know, from the time when the author didn't rehearse with the actors; when, after reading his piece in the Green-room, he handed his manuscript to the stage-manager and vanished, so far as that particular play was concerned, for evermore. *Autre temps, autres moeurs*—which is my best French.

I am glad you have managed to meet the modest demands of the self-denying I[rene] V[anbrugh].

The Fourth Act progresses. It will be short and, I think, effective.

When you are visualizing Philip, remember that some of his moral and physical attributes are:—

> *Robustness.*
> *Virility.*
> *Straight legs.*
> *A stiff back.*
> *Shoulders squared and chest out, and*
> *a bit of a defiant swagger.*

Don't give them too much of "the polished Sir George Alexander," or "the elegant Sir George Alexander," we have read a great deal about. Let them have the *human* Sir George Alexander.

My duty to Lady Alec. / Yours ever / P.

280. TO DANIEL FROHMAN

[Tx/9] 115A Harley Street, / W.   August 9th., 1915.
[Charles Frohman was drowned in the sinking of the *Lusitania*.]

Dear Frohman,

Sir George Alexander has shewn me your reply to his cable in which you tell him that you have already made contracts for Mr. John Drew to appear in my new play [*The Big Drum*]—that, in effect, the whole matter is settled and disposed of.

May I ask, by whose authority?

What has happened is this. At the end of last May I received a letter from you telling me that you were going to assist your late brother's management to carry out his Star contracts for the approaching season, and that your brother had expressed the hope that he would have my new piece for America. In answer to this, I informed you that the piece was to be produced in London at the beginning of September, that I would send you a book of it when it was through the press, and that in the meantime I should be glad to receive a definite proposal from you. This proposal I have never had. All I *have* had is a further letter from you, dated June 8th., saying:—"Regarding the new play, I should be very happy to have you consider us in connection with this proposed American production later on, when you are quite ready. We are carrying on the Charles Frohman management here. We have, of course, John Drew and Otis Skinner, and there are others who if better adapted to the part we could secure. A hint from you as to the man and the woman you desire, would meet with our ready co-operation."

Now, I have come to the conclusion—and I should have told your brother so—that the leading character in my new play does not exactly suit Mr. Drew. It is a fine part, and Mr. Drew is a fine actor; but he has not the touch of romance in figure or method for the hero of my piece.

I suggested to Sir George Alexander that he should cable you his wish to present the play himself in America because I wanted you to be associated with it in the event of my accepting Sir George's proposal. Your message to him, therefore, has quite taken my breath away. I have no contract with you, no arrangement as to terms, or as to the cast generally, or as to the "producer" (a point I intend to be very firm about in all my productions or revivals in America in the future)—nothing!

I think that on reflection you will see that, to put it mildly, you have acted rather precipitately. / Yours sincerely, / ARTHUR PINERO.

281. TO THE EDITOR, THE *TIMES*

[Pp/37] 115A Harley Street, / W.   Sept. 23 1915.
[Laurence Hardy (1854–1933) was Conservative M.P. for Ashford, Kent.
For his proposals see *Hansard*, 5th. series, LXXIV (1915), 399. Pinero's
letter was published on 24 September 1915, p. 9.]

Sir,

The limits of inventiveness in finding new sources of revenue
are not very broad. Even the idea of imposing a duty upon ladies'
hats—it is plain that it is ladies' head-wear which is chiefly aimed at—
is over a hundred years old. On April 12, 1797, my grandfather, writing
to Pitt from Charles-street, Cavendish-square (Letters of Mark Pinero,
Attorney-at-law, to the Rt. Hon. William Pitt, Record Office, Chatham
MSS.), after repeating a former suggestion as to "the propriety of
laying a tax on plated articles, as also on carriages (not used in
husbandry) to be collected at the Toll Gates," says:—

"I now beg to submit to your consideration the propriety of having
a similar duty layd on Hats and Bonnets worn by Ladies to that layd
on hats worn by Gentlemen, and an exception may be made in regard
to those under the value of five shillings. The very great number of
Hats and Bonnets of every denomination rendered unserviceable after
being worn but a few days induces me to hope this proposition may
be adopted."

The adoption of the proposition, though in a less drastic form,
has been reserved for the present Chancellor [Lloyd George]. More
fortunate was my grandfather in his proposal of a carriage tax, for a
fortnight afterwards he again writes to Pitt, saying:—"Having taken
the freedom on several occasions to submit to your consideration
certain articles for taxation, I am happy in finding one proposed
by me is about to be adopted—namely, that on Carriages." One
wonders whether the collection "at the Toll Gates" was found feasible!
The taxation of those who attend places of amusement, which gained
a fresh advocate on Tuesday in Mr. Hardy, the member for Ashford,
was also urged by my grandfather. In a further communication to
Pitt, dated June 30 of the same year, he says:—

"I have another tax to submit to your consideration; and although
the proprietors of the theatres in London may make great efforts to
prevent its being passed into law, I really think it less liable to

objection than many now payable. This is, that the proprietors or other persons in the receipt of the admission money at the theatres do ask and receive of each and every person going to the boxes of the respective theatres, or to such part of the house which pays five shillings for the use of the Government one shilling, or sixpence, and this sum to be paid whether the person goes to the theatre to see the whole play or what is termed half-price. Whether the pit should pay likewise I shall not venture to offer an opinion. The proprietors thought proper some time since to add to the price of admission, merely because the theatres had been repaired; to which the public submitted. It is but reasonable to suppose therefore that the most opulent part of the public who only frequent the boxes will cheerfully, in taking their amusement, subscribe towards the exigency of the State."

I may perhaps be pardoned for expressing the hope that Mr. Hardy's advocacy in this connexion will prove no more successful than my grandfather's. / I am, Sir, your obedient servant, / ARTHUR PINERO.

282. TO G. B. SHAW

[T/3(iv)] 115A Harley Street, / W.   September 25th. 1915.
[Henry Hyde Champion (1859–1928) was a social reformer and journalist who had published Shaw's *Cashel Byron's Profession* in serial form in 1885–1886. He settled in Melbourne in 1893 and was founder of the Australasian Authors' Society. On R. B. Brough and Boucicault in Australia see headnote to letter 29. James Cassius Williamson (1845–1913) was an American actor-manager who moved to Australia in 1879 and eventually formed the leading Australian theatrical firm. His organization became a company (J. C. Williamson Ltd.) in 1911; Pinero was apparently unaware of his death.]

My Dear Shaw,

About the film business, I don't think your offers from America are at all bad. Five plays of mine are now in process of being "pictured." I get a bit of money down and a further bit within 30 days after the "release" of the film, and then I receive a percentage of sales and rentals. When the whole thing is totalled I don't suppose I shall get more per play than is offered you from America, while you would have the advantage of getting your money in a lump, without having to wait for it and without running the risk of being cheated by fraudulent "returns." I should not hesitate myself between the two systems.

I now return you Mr. Champion's letter. What is wanted in Melbourne is not a side-show—i.e., a Repertory theatre which opens with *Justice* and shuts with *Chains*—but a bold-spirited manager who will give the Public—with a big P—good work of all kinds artistically decorated and soundly acted. When Messrs. Brough and Boucicault were in partnership in Australia the drama flourished there. Since then it has fallen into the hands of men like Mr. Williamson and the poor Public—again with a big P—is given nothing but melodrama and musical comedy. Let the right sort of manager crop up and there will be no need for the conversion of the Snowdon Picture Hall.

I don't think my "war profits" will amount to much. Alexander has my play on war terms and the "business," though fair, is distinctly war business. Where I am going to be stuck is over the year 1913. That year, as it happened, was a very good one for me, and, while my income dropped to next to nothing when the war broke out, they are able, by using it to force up the average, to make me pay on that rich year for three years in succession. / Mention me kindly, please, to Mrs. Shaw, and believe me, / Yours always, / Arthur Pinero.

283. TO L. E. SHIPMAN

[Ax/9] 115A Harley Street, / W.   12th. Decr. 1915.
[The United States did not declare war on Germany until 6 April 1917.]

My dear Shipman.

Some days before receiving your letter of Novr. 26th. I had—just as a token of remembrance—posted you a copy of *The Big Drum*. So you see, my good friend, you are in my thoughts as, I am happy in knowing, I am in yours.

The parcel you are sending me will, I have no doubt, under the improved conditions at sea, come safely to hand, and I will acknowledge it on its arrival. But it is very wrong of you to break into your treasures on my account, and you must never do such a wicked thing again. I thank you heartily—affectionately—for your kindness, nevertheless.

Yes, we are a little puzzled here occasionally by the attitude of America towards the mighty struggle for Freedom that is going on; but what nation ever did, or ever will, quite understand another? Of this, however, we are certain—that the *real* American is with us.

You shall hear from me again shortly. In the meantime, and at all times, believe me / Yours most faithfully / Arthur Pinero.

284. TO HENRY JAMES

[Tx/8(i)] 115A Harley Street, / W.   3rd. January, 1916.
My dear Mr. Henry James,

As President of the Dramatists' Club, it is my pleasant duty to offer you the warm congratulations of the members upon the Honour which has just been conferred upon you; and I am further instructed to say that it is our earnest hope that you will soon be able to come amongst us again, to receive our plaudits in person.

You must on no account think it necessary, when you are well, to acknowledge this simple message formally. Perhaps it shews a little want of consideration on our part that you should be troubled by us at all at such a moment. Pray forgive us. / With profound admiration and regard, I am, my dear Mr. James, / Yours most truly, / Arthur Pinero.

285. TO GEORGE ALEXANDER

[Ax/9] 115A Harley Street, / W.   14th. March 1916.
My dear Alec.

Many thanks for your kind note. I am sure you will agree with me that, in the case of serious work, these Cinema pictures will never be quite satisfactory till actor, author, and film "producer" are brought into closer relation. There is a lot of good effect, however, in the *Tanqueray* film; your own performance particularly—as I tried to convey on the telephone—being full of grace, tenderness, and, where it is called for, power.

The last paragraph in your letter would surprise me were it not, as you say, that one oughtn't to be surprised at anything in these days. But you must forgive me for not going into the subject of my wretched experience in King Street in September. I wish to forget it. In fact, I have forgotten it. *The Big Drum* is now as remote to me as the tragedies of Aeschylus, and the St. James's Theatre as the Pass of of Thermopylae. / Yours ever / Arthur Pinero.

286. TO G. H. THRING

[T/3(vi)] 115A Harley Street, / W.   24th. March, 1916.
[From 1914 to 1916 Pinero was involved in litigation in the United States over the illegal filming of *The Second Mrs. Tanqueray*. The case was badly handled by the Society of Authors' lawyer in New York, Hugh Aiken Bayne (1870–1954), who later had a distinguished career connected with various legal problems arising out of World War I.]

Dear Mr. Thring,
    I am much obliged to you for your letter informing me that the Society's lawyer in New York has now collected the 250 dollars due to me on account of the *Tanqueray* litigation, and asking me whether I will agree to accept the sum of £52.10.0. as representing that amount. In ordinary circumstances my answer would be Yes; but, although in my opinion these legal proceedings have been muddled and mismanaged, I am most anxious that the Society should not be out of pocket through having acted on my behalf. Perhaps you will therefore be kind enough to tell me what has been the cost to the Society in the matter. / Yours very truly, / Arthur Pinero.

287. TO EDMUND GOSSE

[Ax/10] 115A Harley Street, / W.   15th. May 1916
My dear Gosse.
    The members of the Athenaeum were in a lenient mood this afternoon, and elected me. I confess I am a little surprised. Accept my very grateful thanks for the interest you have felt in my fortunes. / Always warmly yours / Arthur Pinero.

288. TO ARTHUR MACQUARIE

[T/14] 115A Harley Street, / W.   31st. October, 1916.
[Arthur Macquarie was sometime honorary foreign secretary of the

Royal Society of Literature. Christopher Sandeman (1882–1951) was a writer, dramatist, and traveler. José Echegaray (1832–1916) was a Spanish dramatist and statesman who won a Nobel Prize in 1904. As a result of Sandeman's suggestion, Echegaray's *The Cleansing Stain* was produced at the Queen's on 4 February 1917 by the Pioneer Players, with William Archer giving an address on Echegaray before the performance.]

My dear Mr. Maquarie,

What I was going to tell you the other day is that, at the suggestion of Captain Sandeman of the War Office, I am trying to bring about a memorial performance of one of the late Señor Echegaray's plays. In this I am having the kind assistance of Mr. William Archer. Whether we shall succeed in our efforts I don't know, for Echegaray's dramas have become as old-fashioned in form as they are rhetorical in style; but we shall do our best. I understand that the Spaniards are very impressionable to acts of this kind. At the time of Señor Echegaray's death I sent a personal message of sympathy to his family, and another from the Dramatists' Club of which I am President. Several other writers with whom I am associated did the same thing, and I believe these messages were much appreciated by Echegaray's relatives and by the Press and public. / Believe me, / Yours most truly, / Arthur Pinero.

289. TO P. W. AMES

[T/14] 115A Harley Street, / W.   5th. February, 1917.
[The report of Echegaray's play was in the *Times*, 5 February 1917, p. 5.]

Dear Dr. Ames,

I am sorry to say that I shall not be able to attend the meeting of the Entente Committee on Monday, the 12th. I already have an engagement for the afternoon of that day.

You will see in to-day's *Times* a report of a performance which took place yesterday of one of Echegaray's plays. This is the performance about which I had some correspondence a little while ago with Mr. Maquarie. It doesn't look as if the thing made much impression, but I hope it will serve. I suppose some measures are being taken to communicate an account of the affair to the Spanish press.

Mr. William Archer, who has interested himself in the matter most
warmly, and who gave an address yesterday on Echegaray's works, will,
I dare say, attend to that. / Yours most truly, / Arthur Pinero.

290. TO L. E. SHIPMAN

[Tx/19(i)] 115A Harley Street, / W.   17th. May, 1917.
[The "War Economy sketch" was *Mr. Livermore's Dream* (Coliseum,
15 January 1917). Walter Hines Page (1855–1918), an American jour-
nalist, was United States ambassador to Britain from 1913 to 1918 and
sympathized strongly with Britain in World War I. Admiral William
Sowden Sims (1858–1936) commanded American naval operations in
European waters from April 1917 to March 1919. Joseph Hodges
Choate (1832–1917) was an eminent American lawyer and United
States ambassador to Britain from 1899 to 1905. *Robert Louis Stevenson: The Dramatist* was published in 1903.]

My dear friend.

For many weeks your letter dated April 3rd. has been staring me
in the face reproachfully. I ought, of course, to have answered it
promptly. Even now, this is not a proper acknowledgment—only an
apology for one. The fact is I have been very much upset of late, and
thrown out of my stride. Lady Pinero has been seriously unwell and I
have had no spirit for work or correspondence.

Yes, some of our documentary exchanges are undoubtedly lying at
the bottom of the sea. Two or three months ago I sent you, accompanied by a note, a copy of a little War Economy sketch I had written
for our National War Savings Committee. This I am pretty sure didn't
reach you. The thing is of no consequence; I dispatched it only as a
sign of my constant remembrance of you.

I wore a small flag in my coat on "America Day." I am glad your
country is coming into the job, but I am not going to spread myself
on this subject. All I will say is that I hope to God you are not too late.

I see Dr. Page pretty frequently—he dined here not long ago—and
I have had the pleasure too of meeting Admiral Sims, a charming
and interesting man. I proposed his health the other night at a
gathering of "The Kinsmen," an Anglo-American club of which I am a
member. At the same meeting we cabled an affectionate message to Mr.

Choate. Alas! we shall never send another. In him England has lost a true friend.

I have been searching high and low for a copy of the Stevenson lecture; up to the present with no success. It was printed in two forms—a small print and a large one. The former I know are exhausted, but I am still under the impression that a few of the larger prints are stored away here somewhere. I shall not give up the quest, for I very much want you to have one.

I will write to you with my own hand shortly. In any case, never think that silence on my part means forgetfulness. / Yours ever / Arthur Pinero.

291. TO "S," THE *TIMES LITERARY SUPPLEMENT*

[Pp/38] [115A Harley Street, / W.   20 October 1917.]
[Pinero's letter was published on 25 October 1917, p. 517. The letter was in response to a question on Pinero's methods of preparing his texts and his opinion on Shakespeare's methods. H. A. Jones and Shaw received similar enquiries from "S."]

The best answer I can make to your main question is to send you the accompanying privately-printed book of one of my plays. This book is a copy of my manuscript—exact, save for a few revisions made in correcting the proofs—and it is the book of the play as performed by the actors, and also the text, as regards both business and action, of the book as published later by Mr. Heinemann. It has been the same with all my pieces for many years past. Beyond this, I may tell you that it is my practice to have my plays "set up" by the printer, act by act—that is, when I have finished my first act it is put into type before I begin my second. I follow the same course with the second, and so on. Very rarely do I make any alteration in these acts once they are in print.

In answer to your particular inquiry as to whether I ever in a second, or any subsequent, edition make alterations in my text, I have on two or three occasions done so: but the alterations have been very slight—the change of a word here or there—and it is certainly not usual with me to do this.

Although I don't profess to know much of other men's methods, I am under the impression that mine is not one generally followed. I

266

fear, therefore, that I am not contributing anything of much value to your argument.

As to Shakespeare, the first state of his plays—the state in which they were first hurriedly presented to the public—was, it is reasonable to suppose, a very rough one. His principal consideration must have been to keep his theatre supplied, and he can have had precious little time to smooth and polish. It is equally reasonable to suppose that later he *did* subject his work to a process of reconsideration, revision, and, in some instances, elaboration. This, I fancy, is the point you want to make; if so, I agree with you. / Yours always truly / ARTHUR PINERO.

292. TO JOHN DRINKWATER

[Ax/19(i)] 115A Harley Street, / W.   13th. Nov. 1917.
[John Drinkwater (1882–1937), an actor, dramatist, and poet, was a founding member of Sir Barry Jackson's Pilgrim Players which developed into the Birmingham Repertory Theatre. Drinkwater was producer and general manager of the Birmingham Repertory until 1919. *Trelawny of the "Wells"* was produced at Birmingham on 10 November 1917 and ran for thirty-eight performances.]

My dear Mr. Drinkwater.

The news of your successful production of *Trelawny of the "Wells"* at the Birmingham Repertory Theatre is pleasant reading. Accept my hearty congratulations.

Alas! I cannot come to you as you are good enough to propose. I am very busy—not always over work connected with the theatre—and every day brings its engagements and responsibilities. Pray offer Mrs. Drinkwater my warm thanks for her share in your most kind invitation, and believe me / Yours sincerely / Arthur Pinero.

293. TO L. E. SHIPMAN

[Ax/19(i)] 115A Harley Street, / W.   19th. Nov. 1917.
[Clayton Meeker Hamilton (1881–1946), a dramatist and critic, edited *The Social Plays of Arthur Wing Pinero* (New York, 1917–1922). His *Problems of the Playwright* was published in New York in 1917.]

My dear Shipman.

Your letter of Oct. 24th., which got to me a few days ago, is more than an interesting one—yours are always *that*— and I have read it, and talked of it, again and again. Thank you for writing me so fully, and so openheartedly. It is indeed good to hear of the big efforts that are being made on your side, for *we shall need them.* My poor old country has her hands full. Money, men, and material—all her allies are clamouring at her skirts. The strain, naturally, is beginning to tell, and every minute seems a month. (Up to Sep: 29th. last we had advanced to our allies the sum of one thousand one hundred millions of pounds sterling; that gives you an idea of part of our responsibilities.) At the moment we are fearing for the safety of Venice—for the safety of the city's structure, I mean. I think there is little doubt that the enemy will get there. But mere occupation would be the least of possible evils.

Our friend Clayton Hamilton has sent me a new book of his— *Problems of the Playwright.* Opening it at random, I have come across some utterances he has placed in my mouth. From failure of recollection, as I suppose, he has made me say things I never did say, and never could have said or thought. The sight of the wretched words has spoilt my day; and yet what trivial matters these are to be distressed about at such times!

I hope your daughter has received comforting news of her husband, and that all your other belongings are well. / A hearty hand-shake! / Yours ever / Arthur Pinero.

294. TO L. E. SHIPMAN

[Ax/19(i)] 115A Harley Street, / W. 7th. Jan: 1918.
[The "new little play" was *The Freaks* (New, 14 February 1918).]

My dear Shipman,

The snuff-box followed your letter of Dec. 7th. within a few days, so the Germans are not sinking everything—not even our spirits. I am very proud of your gift—its significance at such a moment doesn't escape me—and I shall carry it with me at the next meeting of *The Kinsmen* (the Anglo-American club I have told you about), where I shall flourish it and boast of my good friend at Cornish in New

Hampshire. My heartiest thanks are yours for this and many other kindnesses.

The character you, far from spitefully, give that well-intentioned fellow C[layton] H[amilton] disturbs me. I wonder what further foolish utterances he will put into my mouth in his Introductions. Ugh!

I am busy rehearsing my new little play. It is indeed a little play, in every respect, and I have not been able, I grieve to say, to secure a strong cast for it. But, with luck, it may serve for a while; one can't do more than mark time in these exciting days. *I* can't, anyhow.

God bless you, my dear Shipman—you and yours. Most fervently I respond to your greetings, and am / Always your affectionate / Arthur Pinero.

295. TO UNKNOWN CORRESPONDENT

[A/3(v)] 115A Harley Street, / W.   25th. Jan: 1918.
My dear Sir,

I am very much obliged to you for your kind letter; but I am a poor hand at talking about my work. I don't think I can add much to what has already appeared in the papers concerning *The Freaks*. The little piece is simple in subject and treatment, and has no higher aim than to amuse—which I take to be the function of the theatre at the present moment. There are more ways than one of trying to be amusing, you will say. I must hope *The Freaks* will not be judged as falling into the lowest category. / Yours most truly / Arthur Pinero.

296. TO L. E. SHIPMAN

[Tx/19(i)] 115A Harley Street, / W.   19th. March, 1918.
[*The Freaks* was withdrawn on 30 March 1918.]

My dear Shipman,

A hurried line to acknowledge and thank you for your kind cablegram. I have replied to "Hyrellim" as follows:—"*Freaks* please communicate Daniel Frohman. Pinero."

I wrote to Frohman, who acts more or less as my agent in America, two or three weeks ago and sent him a copy of the little play, telling him at the same time the fate that had befallen it. It had an enthusiastic reception at its first performance and full houses up to its fourth. Then came an air-raid and the "business" immediately went to pieces. There were signs of a rally, but another air-raid took place and the thing is now practically done.

I mail you a book of the ill-fated work with this. You will see at a glance the difficulties of presentation, and I cannot think that anyway this is a favourable time for production in America. I have said this to Frohman and I repeat it to you. However, it would interest me to hear your views. / With affectionate regard, I am / Yours always / Arthur Pinero.

297. TO L. E. SHIPMAN

[Ax/19(i)] Stillands, / Chiddingfold, / Godalming.   24th. Dec. 1918. [The "wretched little play" was *Quick Work* (the first performance of this play is variously recorded as Stamford Theatre, Stamford, Conn., 14 November 1919, and Court Square Theatre, Springfield, Mass., 17 November 1919).]

My dear Shipman,

You overwhelm me with your goodness. Your very handsome and useful gift has reached me. How can I thank you? Believe me I am greatly touched by the kind thought which prompts the tokens of remembrance I am continually receiving from you.

And I owe you a reply to two letters! What a poor sort of a friend I am! But I have been very busy lately, trying to finish my wretched little play, and working under a burden of grave anxiety. Lady Pinero, who suffers from a weak heart, was terribly frightened the other day by an aeroplane which came down in a meadow adjoining my garden. After nearly removing my chimney pots, it hovered over her and her dogs for some time, and she thought she would never escape from it. She has been seriously ill ever since, as a consequence of this upset.

Your President [Woodrow Wilson] arrives in London on "Boxing day"—as we call the day after Christmas-day—much to the inconvenience of our royal people who had managed, according to their custom, to spend Christmas at Sandringham, their country home. It is to be a hurried visit which will not, he markedly states, permit of his seeing our "Grand Fleet." I hope to God, Shipman, that Mr. Wilson will not end by selling your country and mine by the ears. In this connection it is reassuring to read your letter of Nov. 29th.

God gless you and those who are dear to you. A Happy New Year to us all! And, again and again, my earnest thanks. / Yours ever / Arthur Pinero.

298. TO WILLIAM ARCHER

[A/3(i)] 115A Harley Street, / W.   26th. March, 1919.
[Archer's play was *War Is War; or, The Germans in Belgium: A Drama of 1914*; it was published in 1919 and appears to be unperformed.]

My dear Archer,
   It is indeed a pleasure—and a relief, for I thought I had lost you— to see once again on a flyleaf the valued inscription, "A. W. P. from W. A."

   I shall read your play before I go to bed to-night. Thank you for sending it to me. / Yours ever / Arthur Pinero.

299. TO WILLIAM ARCHER

[A/3(i)] 115A Harley Street, / W.   31st. March, 1919.
My dear Archer,
   I have read and re-read your play. Accept my congratulations on a fine, solid bit of work. The form is admirable, and I envy the *ease* of the whole thing—though I know what pains have gone to the making of it.

   Some day, when we come together again, let us talk over—if we do nothing else—an idea of a one-act piece you and I might write in partnership. I've been trying to hit upon a notion ever since we last met, without success. Now your play has suggested one!

   I hope sincerely that *War is War* will be acted by-and-by, but the Theatre will have to right itself first. / Yours ever / Arthur Pinero.

300. TO L. E. SHIPMAN

[Ax/19(i)] Stillands, / Chiddingfold, / Godalming.   9th. June, 1919.
[Pinero refers possibly to *A Seat in the Park* (Winter Garden, 21 February 1922); Irene Vanbrugh, *To Tell My Story*, pp. 120–121, hints that

this play was written for her to perform for a charitable organization. Ethel Barrymore (1879–1959) was a leading American actress and a niece of John Drew. She also appeared in London under Irving and Charles Frohman, as well as playing Rose in *Trelawny of the "Wells"* (Empire, New York, 2 January 1911) and Paula in *The Second Mrs. Tanqueray* (Cort, New York, 27 October 1924). Pinero contributed three letters to the perennial debate on Dickens's *The Mystery of Edwin Drood*, arguing that Bazzard was Datchery (see *Times Literary Supplement*, 10 April 1919, p. 200; 1 May, p. 237; and 15 May, p. 265). The Versailles Peace Conference was being held at this time.]

My dear Shipman,

I was glad to get your bright, cheery letter. I need cheering, for my poor wife is very, very ill, and I am borne down by trouble and anxiety. I can't write about it.

The *Referee* is read only by cabmen, and, apparently—and much to my surprise—by American gentlemen of the highest refinement and intelligence. Let me give you some news of the little play, for tidings of which you have vainly searched its columns. It was finished long ago, and then Boucicault, under whose management it was to be produced, discovered that he hadn't a theatre and, at present rates, couldn't afford to rent one. So—the principal female character having been shaped for Miss Vanbrugh, and there being no other lady to whom I care to offer it—the thing is on the shelf.

It may be done first on your side, by Miss Barrymore. This is between ourselves, for I have signed no definite contract.

Forgive my troubling you with these rubbishing details. You have brought it on yourself by your kind inquiry.

Your explanation of the recent correspondence in the *Times Literary Supplement* may be the right one, as a general reason. My idea, however, is that, in times of stress and worry, some of us take to *Edwin Drood* as others take to drink. It is a form of "doping." It is so with me, at any rate.

I have given up ever wondering what the devil they are doing in Paris. But of one thing I am sure, and that is that Mrs. Wilson is enjoying herself. Thank God somebody is happy! / Bless you, my dear friend. You are indeed good to me. / Yours always / Arthur Pinero.

Quite half-a-dozen business people are at me to go to America to lecture, but I can consider no proposal which involves leaving my poor invalid as a condition.

301. TO MRS. H. A. JONES

[Ax/10] Stillands, / Chiddingfold, / Godalming.   4th. July, 1919.
[Lady Pinero died on 30 June 1919.]

My dear Mrs. Jones,

I am very grateful to you and your good, kind husband for your sympathy. The blow has been hanging over me for many years, but it is none the less severe now that it has fallen.

Your flowers lie on her grave in the pretty churchyard at Northchapel. I saw them there this morning, still fresh and pretty. / God bless you both. / Yours most sincerely / Arthur Pinero.

302. TO WILLIAM ARCHER

[A/3(i)] 115A Harley Street, / W.   3rd. May, 1920.
[Archer's *The Green Goddess* was produced at the Booth, New York, on 18 January 1921 (440 performances) and the St. James's on 6 September 1923 (416 performances). Pinero's "little fantastic thing" was *The Enchanted Cottage* (Duke of York's, 1 March 1922). Percy Anstey (1878–1920) acted from 1898 to 1906 before becoming an economics lecturer. In 1914 he became principal of the Sydenham College of Commerce and Economics in Bombay. Henry Byron Warner (1876–1958) was an English actor who had played extensively in America since 1905. Sir Alfred Butt (1878–1962) was associated at various times with the Gaiety, Globe, Victoria Palace, and Drury Lane. Sir Charles Blake Cochran (1872–1951), as well as being a manager of various London theatres, was a former actor. Gilbert Heron Miller (1884–1969) took over the St. James's after George Alexander's death in 1918 and controlled the theatre until it closed in 1957. Miller was, therefore, responsible for the London production of *The Green Goddess*.]

My dear Archer,

The news that your play has been accepted for production in American gladdens me more than I can say. I pray it won't be muddled over there by bad, unintelligent stage-management. Keep your eye on this, I beg, and take every possible precaution.

I have resumed work upon a little fantastic thing I started upon many months ago, but which the break in my life obliged me to lay aside. Though I write slowly in these days, it should not hold me long; and when I am through with it I will at once turn my thoughts to the idea of our collaborating over something really good and solid. In the meantime, if any likely scheme stirs in me spontaneously, you shall hear of it.

Anstey is *the* man for your Raja, in my opinion, now that poor H. B. Irving has passed away; but Warner has qualities for the part that are worth considering. It is a shocking suggestion to make, but why not let some of these commercial gents read your drama—the Butts, the Cochrans, the Gilbert Millers? / Yours ever / Arthur Pinero.

303. TO L . E. SHIPMAN

[Ax/19(i)] 115A Harley Street, / W.   26th. Dec. 1920.
[Shipman's play was probably *Fool's Errant* (1921).]

Once more, my dear Shipman, I have to send you affectionate thanks for a kind thought and a pretty gift. The pencil will be as useful as it is handsome—if I ever dare to sully its beautiful polish by handling it. You are far too good to me, as I have often told you.

How are you, I wonder? And when is your new play to be produced—or *has* it been produced? I hear no news from America now, save from you.

I am forcing myself to work, and I suppose something will come of the effort. But the theatres are in a parlous state here, and most of the managers people one would not touch with the end of a twenty-foot scaffold pole.

I hope you will tumble against William Archer while he is on your side. A splendid fellow when you get to know him; as honest as he is able. But perhaps you do know him.

God bless you—you and yours. May the New Year hold a plenitude of happiness for you. / Again, warm thanks. / Arthur Pinero.

304. TO W. CLARKSON

[Tux/2] Theatre Royal, Drury Lane, / WC.   10th. January 1921.
[Pinero was chairman of the general committee organizing "Warriors' Day" (held on 31 March 1921), the aim of which was to raise money for Lord Haig's fund by means of entertainment as a way of repaying "one-millionth part of the debt due to those who served us in the Great War" (*Times*, 10 January 1921, p. 10). The effort raised £115,140, and, although the idea was repeated in subsequent years, Pinero did not serve as chairman, being succeeded by Squire Bancroft.
    W. Clarkson (1865–1934) was a leading London costumier and *perruquier*. David Beatty, First Earl Beatty (1871–1936), was an admiral; he became commander in chief of the Grand Fleet in 1916 and first sea-lord in 1919. Douglas Haig, First Earl Haig of Bemersyde (1861–1928), a field marshal, became commander in chief of the British forces in December 1915. Hugh Montague Trenchard, First Viscount Trenchard (1873–1956), was the "father" of the Royal Air Force. Captain W. G. Willcock was honorary secretary of the Warriors' Day Committee.]

Dear Mr. Clarkson,
    May I hope that you will be one of those who join in receiving the Prince of Wales, Lord Beatty, Lord Haig and Sir Hugh Trenchard at the Meeting to inaugurate Warriors' Day at Drury Lane Theatre on Tuesday morning, January 18th. at 11.15? / Yours sincerely, / ARTHUR PINERO / (Chairman) / R. S. V. P. / Captain W. G. Willcock, / Theatre Royal Drury Lane, / London, W.C.2.

305. TO JOHN DRINKWATER

[Tx/19(i)] 115A Harley Street, / W.   22nd. June, 1921.
[Hackett played Macbeth at the Aldwych (2 November 1920) and the Odéon, Paris (June 1921).]

Dear Drinkwater,
    I am asking a few men to lunch with me at the Garrick Club on Wednesday, July 6th., at 1.15, to meet Mr. James K. Hackett and to congratulate him on his recent success here and in Paris. Will you be one of them? If you will, it will be a delight to me, and a great compliment to Mr. Hackett. / Yours most truly / Arthur Pinero.

306. TO JOHN DRINKWATER

[Ax/19(i)] 115A Harley Street, / W.   26th. June, 1921.
[Drinkwater's *Abraham Lincoln* was revived at the Lyceum on 6 July 1921.]

Dear Drinkwater,

It would be nothing less than a shame to disturb you still further on July 6th., and I couldn't hear of it. It was stupid of me not to have pondered the date, with regard to yourself, more closely. I hope for another and a better opportunity of getting hold of you.

Let me tell you what a pleasure it is to an old Lyceum man that your *Lincoln* is to be acted within its ancient walls. There should be some noble ghosts behind the curtain to welcome you. / Yours always / Arthur Pinero.

307. TO L. E. SHIPMAN

[Ax/19(i)] 115A Harley Street, / W.   29th. Dec. 1921.
[Pinero probably refers to *The Enchanted Cottage* rather than *A Seat in the Park*.]

My dear Shipman,

Your beautiful gift reached me yesterday. Your constant remembrance of me is one of the good things left me. But you shouldn't send me presents. My place in your memory is all I want, and need. Nevertheless the note-case will come in handy as a receptacle for my rapidly diminishing means. The income tax here is reducing us all to beggary.

I wish I knew what you are doing—whether you have a new play on the stocks. I start rehearsing in about a fortnight's time—a fanciful thing which may amuse or (more likely) fail miserably. You shall have a book of it by-and-by. But, oh, the altered feeling with which one enters a theatre nowadays! With rare exceptions, nothing but commercialism of the vulgarest kind!

God bless you. May the year we are just entering upon be bountiful to you and yours. / Ever affectionately / Arthur Pinero.

308. TO H. A. JONES

[Ax/10; Pe/40] 115A Harley Street, / W.   6th. June, 1922.
Dear Henry Arthur,

Affectionate thanks for your kind letter and for the pamphlets—which I shall read with great interest.

I hope Mrs. Jones is better. It was a sorrow to me to hear the other day that she was unwell. Give her an old friend's love. / Yours always / Arthur Pinero.

309. TO WILLIAM ARCHER

[A/3(i)] 115A Harley Street, / W.   20th. May 1923.
[Archer's *The Old Drama and the New: An Essay in Re-valuation* was published in 1923.]

My dear Archer,

Thank you for sending me your book—*The Old Drama and the New*. It has the same clearness of thought and directness of expression which have always distinguished your work, and which stir me to the warmest admiration.

I am much touched by the numerous references to myself. You are the only critic—I don't include among the critics the writers who merely "do" the theatres for the papers—who has unvaryingly treated me with common fairness, and your appreciation is in itself no small reward for the labour and the striving of so many years. But for you, I honestly believe I couldn't have managed to keep my end up. I think I have told you this before, and I am glad of the opportunity of repeating it. / Thank you again for the book. / Yours ever / Arthur Pinero.

310. TO DION BOUCICAULT

[Tx/19(i)] 115A Harley Street, / W.   12th. November, 1923.
[In 1923 and 1924 Boucicault toured South Africa, Australia, and New Zealand, including *His House in Order*, *The Second Mrs. Tanqueray*, and *The Notorious Mrs. Ebbsmith* in his repertory. The "Old Bailey piece" was *Dr. Harmer's Holidays* which was not performed until 16 March 1931 (at the Shubert-Belasco, Washington, D.C.).]

My dear Dottridge,

Thank you for your letter of October 2nd., and for writing to me so fully. I quite understand your reason for withdrawing *His House in Order* while it was doing so well. You must take every care of yourself. With rehearsing all day and acting at night, you are having a terrible time of it. Perhaps when you have got through your entire repertory, things will be easier for you. Truly I hope so.

I await with great interest the news of your production of *Tanqueray*. I remember sitting in the stalls at the Court Theatre years ago watching Irene rehearse Rose Trelawny, and saying to myself, "why, I believe this girl could do Paula!" How I wish I could see her do it!

The Old Bailey piece makes fair progress; but, as you say, the times are not favourable for concentration. However, if one didn't work one would go cranky. / My best love, as always, to you both. / Your affectionate old friend / Pin.

311. TO L. E. SHIPMAN

[Tx/11(iii)] 115A Harley Street, / W.   9th. March, 1925.
[*Iris* was revived at the Adelphi on 21 March 1925 with Dame Gladys Cooper (1888–1971) as Iris.]

Good man! Let me know your whereabouts when you arrive in London, so that we may fix up a meeting.

I got back a fortnight ago, having to look after an ancient play of mine which is being revived here. I hate the old thing for taking me away from the glorious sunshine I enjoyed in the Riviera—if for no other reason.

Snow was falling when I passed through Paris. I am glad you have found a suitable villa in Normandy. / Yours. / AP.

312. TO L. E. SHIPMAN

[Ax/11(iii)] 115A Harley Street, / W.   16th. March, 1925.
My dear Shipman,

You are right: a muddled revival of *Iris* is bothering me greatly this week. And, through the recent cold "snap," and a draughty theatre, I have a return of my—my very own—bronchitis. And the consequent catarrh has made me almost stone deaf. And because of all this I want to see you.

Will you dine with me here—just ourselves—on Wednesday next, the 18th., at a quarter past eight?

To save you trouble, let me explain that this little house, though nominally in Harley Street, is actually in Devonshire Street—that part of Devonshire Street which is on the left of Harley Street, going northward. We do these things in England. / Yours ever / Arthur Pinero.

313. TO L. E. SHIPMAN

[Tx/11(iii)] 115A Harley Street, / W.   15th. May, 1925.
[*Trelawny of the "Wells"* was revived at both the Old Vic and the Knickerbocker, New York, on 1 June 1925. Pinero was made an honorary member of the Players Club, New York.]

My dear Shipman,

You are, as always, very good; but, alas! I am fixed here till at least the beginning of next month. As a contribution to the movement for acquiring Sadler's Wells Theatre—to be run on the same lines as the "Old Vic"—I am letting the management of the Old Vic perform *Trelawny of the "Wells"* (which is, as you know, a history in miniature of Sadler's Wells Theatre in its decaying days), and I have promised to superintend the production myself. So I can't be with you just now, except in spirit and affection.

Yes, I have heard that the Board of Directors of The Players has done me the honour of electing me as an Honorary Member. I think I can detect your kind hand in this. Anyhow, few things could give me greater pleasure.

The news about *Trelawny* in America stirs me deeply. It is not my custom to see my own plays acted; but I truly believe that if I were in New York, when the ancient piece is presented, it would be a struggle for me to resist sitting it out. / Bless you. / Yours ever / Arthur Pinero.

314. TO C. M. HAMILTON

[Tx/7] 115A Harley Street, / W.   16th. May, 1925.
[Laurette Taylor (1884–1946) was an American actress distinguished
for her roles of Peg in *Peg o' My Heart* by her husband (J. H. Manners)
and the Mother in *The Glass Menagerie* (1945) by Tennessee Williams
(b. 1914).]

My dear Clayton Hamilton,

   I am much touched by the news that the Board of Directors of
The Players has paid me the compliment of making me an Honorary
Member of their distinguished Club, and I beg that you will convey
to the Board my most grateful acknowledgements. There are few
things that could happen to me at this stage of my life that could move
me more deeply than has this generous and spontaneous action. In
spirit I grasp the hands of every member of the Club, and from the
bottom of my heart I declare that I am proud and happy to be one
of them.

   Please thank Mr. McKinlay, too, for his kindness in sending me
the Catalogue and the Book of Rules. I am engaged in studying both,
with a comfortable feeling of part proprietorship.

   By the same post which brought your letter I heard from Louis
Evan Shipman—in Paris just now—that Miss Laurette Taylor is to play
Rose, and my dear old friend and comrade John Drew the part of
the Vice-Chancellor, in your approaching performance of *Trelawny of
the "Wells."* I am indeed lucky to be so interpreted. I hope that
by-and-by I may be told the complete cast, in order that I may fully
realize the extent of my good fortune. It will interest you to know that
I am at this moment rehearsing *Trelawny* at the "Old Vic" here,
where it is to be done as my contribution to the Fund which is being
raised to acquire and reconstruct Sadlers Wells Theatre—the "Wells"
of the play—and to conduct it on the same lines as the "Vic." / With
the warmest regard, I am, my dear Clayton Hamilton, / Your very
faithful Fellow Player / Arthur Pinero.

315. TO G. P. BAKER

[Tx/19(iii)] 115A Harley Street, / W.   14th. November, 1925.
My dear Mr. Baker,

   It is kind of you to keep me informed of the progress of your

University Theatre. I am most interested in your work and follow
it with wonder and admiration. By giving me further news from time
to time you will add to the obligations I am already under to you. /
With a hearty handshake, I am / Yours always / Arthur Pinero.
I wish I had seen more of you when you were here.

316. TO G. H. THRING

[T/3(vi)] 115A Harley Street, / W.   23rd. February, 1926.
[Captain William Babington Maxwell (d. 1938), chairman of the Society of Authors, added this note to Pinero's letter: "I wrote in reply—
to effect French not necessary—it is Sir A. Pinero they want whether he
speaks French or not. I asked him to leave it open, & we would write
to him again when we had the exact date & knew who was going."
Pinero eventually went (see letter 317).]

My dear Mr. Thring,

I am greatly complimented by the request that I should represent
the English Dramatists at the approaching International Congress
to be held in Paris. But it seems to me that an essential qualification—
if not the chief qualification—of such a representative is that he
should have a quick understanding of the French language as spoken
by a native, and the ability to take a ready part in that language in
the discussions which arise. Unfortunately I am not so qualified.

May I suggest that Mr. Sutro would be an excellent man for
the job? / Always yours truly / Arthur Pinero.

317. TO DION BOUCICAULT

[Tx/19(i)] 115A Harley Street, / W.   24th. June, 1926.
[Robert de Flers (1871–1927) and Francis de Croiset (1883–1937) were
French dramatists. Aristide Briand (1862–1932) was a French socialist
and eleven times French Premier; he was awarded a Nobel Prize in
1926 for his advocacy of a United States of Europe. Gaston Doumergue
(1863–1937) was the first Protestant President of France (1924–1931).
Squire Bancroft died on 19 April 1926. Pinero's *A Private Room* was
eventually produced at the Little on 14 May 1928.]

My dear Dottridge,

I am much cheered by your letter of May 17th. I found it lying
on my table on my return from Paris the day before yesterday. I have
been over there attending an International Congress of Dramatic
Authors, and have had a very interesting time. I took Myra with me,
and after the Congress had ended its sittings we enjoyed ourselves for
a few days quietly—in spite of the atrocious weather, which seems
general all over Europe. I made several acquaintances in Paris among
men whom you know very well—Robert de Flers, de Croiset, and
others. We were received on different days at the Hôtel de Ville, at the
Quai d'Orsay—by the Premier, M. Briand—and at the Elysée by the
President, M. Dumergue. It is surprising that these eminent gentlemen
could have put themselves out over a body of dramatic authors at a
time of political crisis, when their country, too, is on the verge of
bankruptcy. The government resigned, in fact, within three or four
hours after our interview with M. Dumergue. An amazing people!

Yes, there will be no "B" [Bancroft] to welcome you on your
return. You will guess what the loss of him means to me. Although
your friendship with him began earlier than mine, I had known
him for over fifty years, and for the greater part of that time we had
been cronies. I was with him during the last week of his life. The
coffee-room at the Garrick, however crowded it may be, seems
strangely empty to me now.

I rejoice to hear of the success of your present venture. Irene
also is doing finely; so all is well with you. May your good fortune
never cease.

Warm thanks for your kind observations concerning *Dr. Harmer's
Holidays* and *A Private Room*. I am not trying to do anything with
these pieces; you are likely, therefore, to find them still unacted when
you return. I am nearly halfway through another play, of a lighter
sort, which you shall read when it is finished.

I will give your message to Myra, who will be glad to get it, and to
Laura when I next see her. The latter has been out of England for
a long while—at Biarritz and at Vichy. At the present moment she
is at a place called St. Briac, near Dinard.

God bless you, dear old friend. Our little group is dwindling;
which draws us closer together. / Yours ever / Pin.
Do try to direct your rehearsals from a chair, as much as possible.

318. TO G. P. BAKER

[Pp/30] 115A Harley Street, / W.   7th December 1926.
My dear Mr. Baker.

I rejoice to know that by the time this reaches you the University Theatre at Yale will have opened its doors. My best wishes go out to the fortunate students. It would be difficult to conceive more favourable conditions than those under which they will henceforth pursue their work, and I predict that the result will be permanently ennobling to the American stage. / With cordial greetings to yourself, I am / Always yours most truly, / ARTHUR PINERO.

319. TO G. C. TYLER

[Ax/13] 115A Harley Street, / W.   1st. Aug: 1927.
[George Crouse Tyler (1867–1946) was an American manager.]

My dear Mr. Tyler,

Thank you for your very kind letter. I quite agree with what you say about *Dr. Harmer's Holidays.* As you suggest, an opportunity might present itself for an experimental performance; and I should have no objection to such a production provided it were given under circumstances as favourable as possible.

I am glad you like the little play [*A Private Room*]. I know the difficulty of placing short pieces.

It was a great pleasure to me to see you and to have a talk with you yesterday. When you next come to London I hope I sha'n't be on the point of running away. / Believe me / Always yours truly / Arthur Pinero.

I wrote *A Private Room* with the idea that it should be billed with *Harmer*, to enable the actor of Dr. Harmer to give a *tour de force.*

320. TO THE EDITOR, THE *TIMES*

[Pp/37] 115A Harley Street, / W.   Jan. 7, 1928.
[The Memorial Theatre at Stratford burned down on 6 March 1926; the new theatre, designed by Elizabeth Scott, was opened on 23 April 1932. Pinero's letter was published on 10 January 1928, p. 15.]

Sir,

May I be allowed to suggest that when the approved design for
The Shakespeare Memorial Theatre at Stratford-on-Avon is completed,
but before it is proceeded with, the detailed plans should be publicly
exhibited, in order that those who have a considerable knowledge
of theatres on both sides of the curtain, though not members of the
advisory council, should be afforded an opportunity of offering their
criticisms before it is too late to do so? It may be that such a step
is already contemplated. The necessity for it cannot, in my opinion, be
too strongly urged. / Yours faithfully, / ARTHUR PINERO.

321. TO J. H. McCARTHY

[Ax/12] 115A Harley Street, / W.   1st. April, 1928.
[R. C. Carton died on 1 April 1928.]

My dear McCarthy,

Thank you for ringing me up. Your news is a great shock to me.
We had been friends since 1877. You had seen more of him, I think,
than I had lately; but the events of the past crowd upon me, and I
am sorrow-stricken. / Yours always / Arthur Pinero.

322. TO MRS. PATRICK CAMPBELL

[A/3(ii)] 115A Harley Street, / W.   12th May 1928.
My dear Mrs. Pat,

How kind of you to write to me! Yes, though the play [*A Private
Room*] I am rehearsing is—like the baby in the old story—"only a
little one," I am better; very well, in fact. But I don't care much for
the theatre in these days, knowing that I shall meet upon the stage
no troublesome Mrs. Campbell (who was never troublesome when
she and I worked together), nor anybody else with a tithe of her
charm and power. / God bless you. A thousand affectionate thanks. /
Yours / Arthur Pinero.

323. TO MRS. THORNE

[Ax/19(i)] Hotel Régina, / Dieppe.   24th. July, 1929.
[Mrs. Thorne (Doris Arthur Jones; b. 1888) was the daughter of H. A.

Jones; she wrote *The Life and Letters of Henry Arthur Jones* which was published in 1930.]

My dear Mrs. Thorne,

Your letter finds me here, where I am with Myra. I sha'n't be in London again for some time, but you shall hear from me when I return.

I grieve to hear about the operation. I hope you will soon be restored to complete health. Congratulations on the progress you are making with the work. / Yours ever / Arthur Pinero.

324. TO MRS. THORNE

[Pp/29] [115A Harley Street, / W.   May, 1930.]
Dear Doris Arthur Jones,

Let me send you a word of warm congratulation on your book. You have done your job splendidly—courageously—*man*fully. Your father's references to me recorded in your work touch me deeply. I grieve that he and I met so seldom of late years. But I never ceased to hold him in high regard—and regrets are useless now. How often one has to reproach oneself in this way when one loses a friend! With admiration and affection, / I am / Yours always / ARTHUR PINERO.

325. TO H. H. FYFE

[Pp/25] 115A Harley Street, / W.   13th. May, 1930.
[H. Hamilton Fyfe (1869–1951) was a drama critic who worked variously for the *Times, Morning Advertiser, World,* and *Daily Herald.* He published two books on Pinero, *Arthur Wing Pinero, Playwright: A Study* (London, 1902) and *Sir Arthur Pinero's Plays and Players* (London, 1930), to which Pinero here refers.]

Dear Hamilton Fyfe,

Reading the opening chapter of your book last night, I almost had a fit. Who on earth has been imposing on you those stories of my Lyceum days? Utterly false, every one of them. I had too great a regard for Irving—to say nothing of the awe in which I held him—to treat him with pertness and familiarity. And as for the sticking of an impudent notice on the call-board by a member of the company, such an outrageous proceeding would have brought disgrace upon the offender, and perhaps summary dismissal. The theatre was strictly conducted and its rules reverently obeyed. In that respect I may have been influenced by my association with Irving; in no other way, I think.

I was not present at the first performance of *The Bells*, nor have I ever acted Sir Peter Teazle at the Haymarket or elsewhere.

My father practised in South Square, Gray's Inn, in Prince's Street (since renamed), Bedford Row, and in Great James Street, never in Lincoln's Inn Fields.

I was born at No. 21 Dalby Terrace, Islington, then a pleasant enough Locality—not in the Old Kent road or the Seven Dials.

I am wondering whether, for the sake of my peace of mind, I dare read any further. / Forgive this outbreak, and believe me, / Yours always / ARTHUR PINERO

326. TO H. H. FYFE

[Pp/25] 115A Harley Street, / W.   17th May, 1930.
[In his defense, published in Dunkel, *Sir Arthur Pinero*, pp. 120–121, Fyfe was not greatly concerned about his inaccuracies ("But what does it matter?") and claimed he got his information from various sources, including the theatre historian Percy Hetherington Fitzgerald (1834–1925).]

Dear Hamilton Fyfe,

Thank you for your light-hearted letter. I have no recollection of your asking me to give you particulars of my life, I understand that your book was to be a critical survey of my work; that and nothing more. This is clearly suggested by your title—*Sir A. P.'s Plays and Players*. If I had thought you had intended to go further I should either have begged you to abandon the idea or have put myself to the pains of supplying you with details. You must forgive me for saying that my refusal to furnish you with facts, if I ever did so, is no justification for raking together, and accepting without question, the stuff written by other people.

What does it matter? I have always acted on the principle that everything matters; but, then, I am much your senior, and was brought up in a stupid, old-fashioned school. / Please don't bother to acknowledge this. / Sincerely yours, / ARTHUR PINERO.

Percy Fitzgerald! Good heavens! Fancy regarding that writer as an authority on any subject! He was notoriously inaccurate.

327. TO WILLIAM ROTHENSTEIN

[Ax/8(i)] 115A Harley Street, / W.   2nd. March, 1931.
[Rothenstein's *Men and Memories* was published in 1931. (Henry) Max(imillian) Beerbohm (1872–1956) was a writer and caricaturist. He succeeded Shaw as drama critic of the *Saturday Review* and was knighted in 1939.]

My dear Rothenstein,

I have just finished reading your *Men and Memories*—a fascinating book upon which I congratulate you with all my heart. My only regret in connexion with it was in watching the unread pages gradually diminish.

Well, perhaps not my only regret, for I was pained to see, on the top of page 301, my extremely uncivil reference to your friend Mr. Max Beerbohm. Though I have, I hope, a fairly modest estimate of my abilities, I have never been able to understand the rancour with which Mr. Beerbohm has pursued me; but to-day I would not speak of him in those terms. It gives me some little satisfaction therefore, as between you and me, to withdraw the implication I allowed myself to indulge in at that time.

This is purely a personal matter and one, you may think, hardly worth mentioning. Certainly my admiration for your fine book is not affected by it. Eagerly I look forward, as so many others must be doing, to your next volume. / With repeated congratulations, and very warm regard, I am / Yours ever / Arthur Pinero.

328. TO THE EDITOR, THE *TIMES*

[Pp/37; P/25] 115A Harley Street, / W.   July 25 1931.
[Pinero's letter was published on 27 July 1931, p. 11.]

Sir,

With reference to the varying statements made by eminent people as to their place of birth, I may perhaps be pardoned for calling attention to another side of the picture—the departure from truth which is sometimes indulged in by self-appointed biographers in dealing, even in the lifetime of their subjects, not only with eminent persons, but, as in the instance I am now citing, with persons of no eminence whatever.

Not long ago a well-known author who thought it worth while to write a book about myself gave my birthplace as the Old Kent-road, and proceeded to enhance his statement by a description of the house in which that unimportant event took place. Upon my remonstrating with him on this inaccuracy and informing him that I was born at Islington, he cheerfully replied, "What does it matter?" I agree; in my case it matters little, except in so far as the Old Kent-road is concerned. The credit of the Old Kent-road should be maintained at all costs. / I am, Sir, yours faithfully, / ARTHUR PINERO.

329. TO JOHN DRINKWATER

[Gx/19(i)]   15 February 1932.
[Drinkwater's *Abraham Lincoln* was revived at the Old Vic on 15 February 1932.]

John Drinkwater   9 Grove   Highgate.
Warm wishes dear Drinkwater for the renewed success tonight of your fine work. I hope you are better. / Arthur Pinero.

330. TO H. H. KÜTHER

[Pp/31] 115A Harley Street, / W.   10th. May, 1932.
My Dear Sir,

When I wrote *The Profligate* I had no knowledge of Ibsen, nor have I, I believe, been influenced in the smallest degree by his works. But it is the critical fashion here to ascribe any new movement in English art, no matter of what kind, to foreign influence, & this encourages other countries to take the same view.

I have nothing more to say on the subject. / Yours most truly, / ARTHUR PINERO.

288

331. TO JOHN DRINKWATER

[Ax/19(i)] 115A Harley Street, / W.   24th. May, 1932.

Thank you, dear Drinkwater and dear Mrs. Drinkwater, for
your kind thought of my withered old birthday. I am so glad and
relieved that the one of you who has been ill has fully recovered and
is again as active as ever. Bless you both. / AP.

332. TO A. M. B. MEAKIN

[Tx/1] 115A Harley Street, / W.   6th. June, 1932.
[Annette M. B. Meakin (d. 1959) was a writer; her *Goethe and Schiller,
1785–1805: The Story of a Friendship* was published in 1932.]

Dear Miss Meakin,

I return you the third volume of *Goethe and Schiller*. Forgive
the delay, caused in great part by my desire to read your book with the
utmost care.

If your first and second volumes are on a level with your third
I should have no hesitation in pronouncing the whole to be a fine
work. It is true that certain chapters in this third volume have a
particular interest for me; but apart from that, I am deeply impressed
by the ease and clarity of your style, the skilful way in which you
marshal your facts, and the wide range of your knowledge. To my
regret, I am not a German scholar, but, in my opinion, no special
scholarship is needed to enable one to appreciate your work, so far
as I have read it, and to derive from it a considerable education in
the subject you deal with.

Pray accept my warm congratulations. Very heartily I hope that
the publication of *Goethe and Schiller* will amply reward you for
your labours. / Yours faithfully / Arthur Pinero.

333. TO JOHN DRINKWATER

[Tx/19(i)] 115A Harley Street, / W.   15th. October, 1932.
[Louis Napoleon Parker (1852–1944) was the author of over 100 plays,
and also produced civic and patriotic pageants. Pinero sent similar
letters to Shaw, St. John Ervine, Max Beerbohm, and Granville-Barker.]

My dear Drinkwater,

Mr. Louis N. Parker—who is staying at the Basil Street Hotel Knightsbridge—will be eighty years of age on the 21st. of this month. You will remember the fine work he did for the theatre in his active days. If you were to send him a note or telegram of congratulation on his birthday I am sure it would make him very happy.

Forgive me for troubling you. / Yours ever / Arthur Pinero.

334. TO JOHN DRINKWATER

[Tx/19(i)] 115A Harley Street, / W.   21st. October, 1932.
[Drinkwater's two books were (vol. I) *Inheritance* (London, 1931) and *Discovery* (London, 1932).]

My dear Drinkwater,

I should very much like to go with you to the United States on Saturday week, but I fear my frequent appearances on that continent would give rise to a feeling among the natives of satiety and boredom. You see, I was last in America as recently as the autumn of 1885.

While you are on the high seas I shall be deep in the second volume of your reminiscences, with, I am sure, a pleasure equal to that given me by Vol: I.

All good luck to you on your voyage and thereafter. / Yours ever / Arthur Pinero.

335. TO MRS. L. E. SHIPMAN

[Ax/11(iii)] 115A Harley Street, / W.   4th. July, 1933.
[Mrs. Shipman wrote to tell Pinero that Shipman was very ill at this time.]

My dear Mrs. Shipman,

The contents of your letter disturb me very much. Thank you for letting me hear from you, bad as your news is. I am sending the dear fellow a line by this post. I am deeply attached to him, as you know, and shall be uneasy till I receive better tidings.

Should he be unable to write, may I rely on you to keep me informed of his condition? / Yours most truly / Arthur Pinero.

336. TO MRS. L. E. SHIPMAN

[Ax/11(iii)] The Norfolk Hotel, / Brighton   4th. Aug: 1933.
[Shipman died on 2 August 1933.]

My dear Mrs. Shipman,
    Your telegram, addressed to the Garrick Club, reached me here
last night. The sad news was not unexpected, but none the less the
blow is a severe one. I feel it very deeply.
    My tender sympathy is with you. I hope we shall meet some day,
when I can give you a warm and understanding grip of the hand. /
Believe me / Always yours most truly / Arthur Pinero.

337. TO W. D. DUNKEL

[Pp/25] 115A Harley Street, / W.   21st. November, 1933.
[Wilbur Dwight Dunkel (b. 1901), an American professor emeritus
of English at the University of Rochester where he spent most of his
academic career, is the author of *Sir Arthur Pinero: A Critical Biography with Letters*. Pinero sent Dunkel *Two Plays*, which contains *Dr.
Harmer's Holidays* and the unperformed *Child Man*.]

My dear Sir,
    Thank you for your kind letter. I cannot tell you anything about
myself beyond what appears in the books of reference. Self-advertising
in any form is not to my taste.
    I am sending you a book published in 1930, of which I beg your
acceptance. The Foreword may be of some little use to you. / Believe
me / Yours most truly / ARTHUR PINERO.

[Pinero died on 23 November 1934 following an emergency operation
at the Marylebone Nursing Home, London. A memorial service for
him was held at St. Marylebone Parish Church on 28 November 1934.
When his will was proved, Pinero left an estate valued at £63,310.16.10
(gross), the principal beneficiary of which was his stepdaughter, Myra.
Upon her death, the residue of the estate and income from such matters as copyright royalties passed to the Garrick Club, the Royal Literary Fund, and the Middlesex Hospital.]

INDEX

Index